Reforming Community Penalties

To J.C. and J.C.

Reforming Community Penalties

Sue Rex

WILLAN
PUBLISHING

Published by

Willan Publishing
Culmcott House
Mill Street, Uffculme
Cullompton, Devon
EX15 3AT, UK
Tel: +44(0)1884 840337
Fax: +44(0)1884 840251
e-mail: info@willanpublishing.co.uk
Website: www.willanpublishing.co.uk

Published simultaneously in the USA and Canada by

Willan Publishing
c/o ISBS, 920 NE 58th Ave, Suite 300
Portland, Oregon 97213-3786, USA
Tel: +001(0)503 287 3093
Fax: +001(0)503 280 8832
e-mail: info@isbs.com
Website: www.isbs.com

First published 2005

ISBN 1-84392-114-6

British Library Cataloguing-in-Publication Data

A catalogue record for this book is available from the British Library

Project managed by Deer Park Productions, Tavistock, Devon
Typeset by TW Typesetting, Plymouth, Devon
Printed and bound by TJ International Ltd, Trecerus Industrial Estate, Padstow, Cornwall

Contents

List of tables   *vii*

Acknowledgements   *viii*

1 Introduction: researching communicative penal theory   1
   Why penal communication?   1
   Insights from stakeholders   2
   Outline of book   4
   Conclusions   6

2 Communicative theory – origins, evolution and application to
   communicative penalties   7
   Introduction   7
   A recent history of community penalties   8
   Blurred boundaries: a 'customised' community order or custody
      plus/minus   12
   Re-framing punishment as communication   15
   Applying a communicative perspective to community penalties   19
   Restorative justice   20
   Replacing or reforming criminal justice?   24
   Moving from theory to communication on the ground   26
   Conclusions   27
   Notes   28

3 Seeking stakeholders' views of punishment   31
   Introduction   31
   I. Assessing public views   31
   II. Collecting stakeholders' views   41
   Conclusions   51
   Notes   51

4 Prioritising penal aims   55
   Introduction   55
   I. Reconciling proportionality and crime prevention in theory   55
   II. Understandings of proportionality on the ground   64
   Conclusions   75
   Notes   77

5 **Penal messages**   **80**
  Introduction   80
  I. Overall aims of punishment   80
  II. Sentencing as communication   94
  Conclusions   106
  Notes   107

6 **Responding to punishment**   **109**
  Introduction   109
  I. Responding to the penal message   109
  II. Leniency for the remorseful offender?   123
  III. The efficacy of the message   125
  Conclusions   129
  Notes   132

7 **Towards a framework for community penalties**   **133**
  Introduction   133
  Punishment as a communicative enterprise   135
  Balancing retribution with crime prevention: what weight
    proportionality?   140
  Using community penalties to communicate   143
  A communicative framework for community penalties?   147
  Conclusions   151
  Notes   152

8 **Conclusions**   **154**
  Introduction   154
  Communicative penalties – a summary   154
  Obstacles and opportunities   158
  Using community penalties to restore   161
  New forms of custodial and community provision   162
  Conclusions   164
  Notes   164

Appendix: The questionnaire   **165**

References   *172*
Index   *181*

List of tables

3.1 Characteristics of questionnaire respondents   47
4.1 Prioritising punishment: views from questionnaire respondents 64
4.2 Views of proportionality   69
4.3 Views of offender-related factors   70
4.4 Other factors   72
4.5 Offender-related mitigation   74
5.1 Moralising   81
5.2 Exacting recompense   82
5.3 Normative aims: mean scores   84
5.4 Stopping further offending   85
5.5 Variations on reform   86
5.6 Instrumental aims: mean scores   88
5.7 Purposes of different orders   90
5.8 Normative messages   96
5.9 Normative messages: mean scores   97
5.10 Instrumental messages I   99
5.11 Instrumental messages II   99
5.12 Instrumental aims: mean scores   100
5.13 Messages conveyed by different orders   104
6.1 Accepting behaviour was wrong   116
6.2 Taking disapproval on board   116
6.3 Avoiding future offending   120
6.4 Offering recompense   121
6.5 Responses: mean scores   122
6.6 Response justifies reduced sentence   124
6.7 How many offenders 'respond' to penal message   125
7.1 Levels of confidence in different sanctions   146

Acknowledgements

First of all, thanks must go to the Economic and Social Research Council whose funding of my research fellowship made this project possible. Nor would the work have been viable without the contribution of a considerable number of people in the magistracy, Magistrates' Courts Service, Magistrates' Association, Probation Service and Victims' Support who commented on draft interview schedules and questionnaires and helped to arrange interviews and distribute questionnaires. Staff at the Institute of Criminology, particularly in the Library and General Office, also helped with the piloting of questionnaires and gave me a great deal of support during my fellowship.

I am most grateful to those people – magistrates, those working in probation and community service and those under their supervision, and victims – who willingly gave me their time and insights in interview and by completing questionnaires. I am also indebted to Loraine Gelsthorpe, both for her considerable support during the project and for commenting on draft interview schedules and questionnaires, and on a number of versions of draft chapters. Antony Duff was immensely helpful in offering detailed comments on draft chapters, as were Anthony Bottoms and Andrew von Hirsch – both in commenting on chapters and through more general discussions that helped formulate my ideas and analysis.

Chapter 1

Introduction: researching communicative penal theory

The core subject matter of this book concerns community penalties (non-custodial options that restrict the offender's liberty in some way). It arises from a conviction that instability, if not confusion, about the purposes of community orders and their place in the sentencing framework has been partly responsible for enabling custody to flourish during the last decade as the only punishment with real public credibility. In undertaking the research reported in the book, in which I sought the views of people with a particular interest in criminal justice about the role of community penalties, my aim was therefore to consider how the theoretical underpinnings for community penalties might be strengthened. I hope that, in turn, this will aid their development in policy and practice so enabling them to command greater support as punishments in their own right. In the book, I consider the implications of my findings for the kind of role that community penalties might be expected to play and how they might best be developed to perform that role, taking account of recent research and policy and practice initiatives relating to community-based disposals.

Why penal communication?

In reviewing the theoretical framework for community penalties, I turn to the ideas put forward by von Hirsch (1993) and Duff (2001) in which punishment as communication is a central feature. My interest in the theories of these two writers has been prompted by their attempt to reconcile at the theoretical level two functions that undoubtedly coexist in community penalties, but coexist in considerable tension. One function is for the sanction to act as a retributive punishment 'deserved' by the offence; the other is for it to reduce the likelihood that the particular individual will reoffend in the future. I believe that any account of community penalties that fails to accommodate either component is incomplete. What has bedevilled efforts to develop community penalties in the UK over the last three decades has been a failure to integrate the two elements and find an appropriate balance between them.

The communicative theories put forward by von Hirsch (1993) and Duff (2001) have been highly influential in working out what justifies the practice of punishment. In a review of Duff's book, Gardner (2002) commented that his writings in the 1980s and early 1990s did much to revive scholarly interest in the moral philosophy of criminal law and criminal justice. For his part, von Hirsch (mostly fully in 1993) has been responsible for developing and articulating a highly influential version of desert theory of punishment, shaping both legislative provisions and much of the academic debate about the proper role of punishment and the limitations upon its use.

In addition to their search for a balance between the blaming and the crime preventive elements in punishment, what also attracted me to the work of these two writers is the centrality of communication in their accounts and their emphasis on offenders as self-determining agents capable of a normative outlook. This fits in with my own experience of how offenders portray themselves when interviewed: as knowledgeable, self-aware individuals who are responsible for making the decision to stop offending and implementing the necessary steps (see, for example, Rex 1999). It has important implications for how we should deal with offenders in sentencing them and carrying out those sentences. Not only do offenders need to be addressed as active participants rather than as the passive recipients of punishment or treatment, but they also need to be positively motivated to engage in the processes of change to law-abiding lives.

Unusually, both writers have devoted some effort to considering how his ideas might apply to community penalties, von Hirsch as proportionate punishments that adequately reflect the seriousness of many offences and Duff as intrinsically apt communicative punishments. Community-based sanctions is an area to which relatively little attention has been paid in writings on penal theory, and so it is valuable to have the opportunity to examine two accounts in which there has been a real attempt to accommodate them. This is especially the case given the lack of a strong intellectual framework to guide their development in policy and practice.

Insights from stakeholders

What is perhaps unusual about the book is that I have used empirical findings – the views of lay magistrates, probation staff, offenders and victims – to try to shed light on normative questions raised by these two writers (and, where relevant, other penal theorists). Those views have been collected by interview and survey research funded through a post-doctoral fellowship with the Economic and Social Research Council. In carrying out the research, I have sought to bring together the insights that might be gained from in-depth qualitative interviews with what can be learnt from quantitative analysis about the relative weight that different groups attributed to various ideas and considerations. This was not 'public opinion' research as such, in the sense that I was focusing on people's understandings of particular concepts as they apply to punishment rather than their knowledge and views of, or levels of confidence in, how criminal justice actually operates. However, it clearly bears some similarities to that strand of research, which I have drawn on in exploring the context for my own work and in interpreting its findings.

My purpose in conducting this research has been to consider how the insights of people with a stake in criminal justice might take forward what has been primarily a theoretical debate. I do not believe that this kind of empirical work can prove or disprove a particular theory, an exercise that I would argue is in any case futile in the case of normative theory (you cannot prove an 'ought'). However, I do believe that both the theory and practice of punishment will benefit from a closer relationship between what Raynor (1997) calls high-level normative thinking and ground-level practical decision-making. The ideas and views of those making decisions, or affected by decision-making, in criminal justice seem likely to tell us something useful about the relevant theories: whether certain aspects might require development or adjustment, or whether they might require certain changes to criminal justice practices, in order to work. I also hope that strengthening its intellectual foundations will enable policy and practice relating to community penalties to become more robust and less susceptible to the kind of turbulence that has been a feature of their recent past.

The specific normative questions on which I have explored people's understandings are these: the aims of sentencing; how different sanctions fit in; and what should guide courts in deciding how much punishment to impose. Here, I found that research participants explained punishment in terms of a mixed or hybrid rationale, in which backward-looking (retributive) and forward-looking (consequentialist) goals were combined. Within that model, crime prevention was prioritised in that people seemed unable to perceive the point of punishment if not to serve a purpose that they regarded as socially useful. This did not mean that people expected sentencing to contribute to a reduction in overall crime rates; they seemed to see turning the individual concerned away from offending as a valuable enough exercise in its own right without more general benefits. They also expected sentencing to be fair, and showed a commitment to proportionality in how amounts of punishment should be decided.

Exploring the role and nature of penal communication, I asked research participants what sentencing communicates to offenders (and to others), how they see community sentences contributing to those processes of communication, and how offenders are expected to respond to the penal messages communicated to them. The first point to make is that people readily understood punishment in terms of the messages that it conveyed. In interview, the terminology of what punishment 'said' to various audiences was often used to express its meaning even before the topic of communication was raised. In line with their understanding of punishment as serving both retributive and crime preventive goals, research participants detected both normative (censuring) messages and instrumental ones in which the intention was to bring about change. Indeed, it seemed central to people's accounts that some sort of response was expected from the offender, chiefly in the form of efforts at self-restraint in the future. Community penalties were seen to have rich communicative potential, and figured prominently in descriptions of how particular disposals might be used to reinforce sentencing messages and to encourage offenders to respond appropriately. The ideas expressed by the people who participated in my research also suggested that there might be scope to develop community penalties to maximise their contribution to penal communication.

During the course of the book, I will enlarge on these findings, looking, for example, at how the elements of retribution and crime prevention were balanced in accounts of sentencing and which it was thought courts should prioritise in deciding the quantum of punishment. I will also relate my findings to the theories put forward by von Hirsch (1993) and Duff (2001), discussing the extent to which penal communication as understood on the ground reflects their conceptualisations or indicates that some adjustments or developments to those ideas should be considered. In view of my particular interests in conducting this research, an important question will be the extent to which perceptions of community penalties fit in with the communicative potential that Duff ascribes to them. Given Duff's (2003) view that restoration is best pursued through retributive punishment, restorative justice is another important area of investigation, and I will be looking at the implications of my findings for the kind of role that restorative processes might play in community penalties.

Outline of book

In the next two chapters, I set out the theoretical and research context for the substantive empirical findings reported in the following part of the book. *Chapter 2* looks into communicative penal theory in some detail, examining its theoretical origins and recent development. Having discussed the (recent) history of non-custodial penalties and considered the possible impact of recent legislation, it concludes that a stronger conceptual framework is needed for what have been known since 1992 as community penalties. It then explains why one might look to communicative theory to provide a possible framework, and explores the connections with restorative justice (a number of restorative theorists sharing Duff's view that it is desirable to pursue reintegrative and restorative outcomes). Towards the end of the chapter, I turn to the questions that I addressed in attempting to take the relevant debates forward, and to explore the application of these ideas to community penalties.

In *Chapter 3*, I explain how I set about seeking the views of 'stakeholders', first drawing insights from the parallel strand of research into public opinion and victims' views of punishment. Having considered the possible value of this kind of research in taking forward theory as well as policy and practice, I set out the research questions addressed and methodology used, acknowledging the limitations of the research. In particular, I explain how I sought to take advantage of both the insights that might be gained from a qualitative approach and the systematic comparison that might be achieved through quantitative analysis, by using material generated from in-depth interviews to design questionnaires administered to larger samples whose views could be quantified.

The next three chapters form the core of the book, as they report my empirical findings (the views of the groups I interviewed and surveyed). In *Chapter 4*, I explore the balance between retribution and crime prevention by examining the role played by proportionality, first according to the theories of Duff (2001) and von Hirsch (1993). I then look at an attempt to implement proportionate community penalties in practice, the English Criminal Justice Act 1991 and its impact on subsequent thinking, noting the increased emphasis that recent sentencing policy has placed on prior criminal record. The second part of the chapter reports how my research participants balanced – or prioritised – the aims of punishment, and how much weight they gave proportionality as against the other factors that might be seen as relevant to sentence lengths or amounts. *Chapters 5* and *6* then focus on the question of penal communication, reporting understandings of the messages communicated to offenders in the court room, how these messages are reinforced through particular disposals (especially community penalties) and how offenders are expected to respond. An important question addressed in *Chapter 6* is why penal communication might not be seen to work as intended.

In the final part of the book, I seek to draw out the main implications of these findings, starting (in *Chapter 7*) with a discussion of how this kind of empirical work might help to take forward normative theory. I then look at whether communicative penal theory offers a promising approach for community penalties, and how the processes and material forms of these punishments would need to be developed to maximise its effectiveness. *Chapter 8* concludes my discussion by asking how we might be able to use 'communication' to make punishment more constructive, exploring the possible role of restorative processes and considering the implications of the custody-community provisions in the Criminal Justice Act 2003.

Conclusions

In this book, my aim is to examine the role of community penalties in sentencing, arguing that they have been under-theorised and that the absence of a strong intellectual framework has hampered their development in policy and practice. In an attempt to redress that deficiency I go back to fundamentals, asking people with a particular stake in criminal justice what the whole point of punishment is and what courts are seeking to achieve in sentencing offenders. My enquiry is informed by two particular theories of punishment in which communication is a key feature, which seek a balance between the blaming and the crime preventive elements in punishment. This is the kind of blend that I would argue we should be looking for if we are to produce a robust and durable framework for community penalties.

Chapter 2

Communicative theory – origins, evolution and application to community penalties

Introduction

This chapter sets much of the theoretical framework for the questions addressed through the empirical work reported in Chapters 4–6 of this book (further theoretical questions concerning the role of proportionality are considered in Chapter 4). Two theories of punishment in which communication performs a central role form the main subject matter of the present chapter: the theories put forward by von Hirsch (1993) and Duff (2001). Before discussing these theories and their possible application to community penalties, the chapter first considers the contemporary context against which community penalties are delivered. In doing so, I make the case for a stronger conceptual framework for sanctions that are non-custodial but still personally restrictive. My central argument is that community-based interventions have fared badly in a comparison with custody and that the provisions for mixed custody-community disposals in the recently enacted Criminal Justice Act 2003 do not improve their future prospects.

A problem discussed in the chapter is conceptual confusion: the failure to identify a clear rationale for community penalties that gives them a firm position within the sentencing framework. One challenge that has yet to be met is to mediate the tension between two functions that undoubtedly coexist in community penalties but which do so uneasily. One is to act as retributive punishments 'deserved' by the offence; the other is to reduce offending in the future. The tension arises because the

respective penal aims – retribution and consequentialism – are traditionally opposed to each other. In order to reconcile and therefore to achieve
a balance between the two aims in community sentences, we might turn
to writers that have tried to reconcile retribution and crime prevention
at a theoretical level. This is what von Hirsch and Duff have sought to
do, although each has found a different balance between backwards-
looking retribution and forwards-looking crime prevention. There are
links between the inclusive communicative form of punishment envisaged by Duff and restorative justice theories, to which I turn towards
the end of the chapter.

A recent history of community penalties

Community penalties as we see them now have emerged from a
turbulent recent history. In their various permutations since the collapse
of the rehabilitative ideal in the 1970s (Allen 1981), community orders
(so-called since the Criminal Justice Act 1991) have gone through the
successive phases of 'alternatives to custody' to 'punishment' in the
community to 'public protectionism'. What has accompanied these
transitions, and perhaps added to the consequent confusion, is a
proliferation of new orders whose varying aims have depended upon the
phase during which they were introduced.[1]

During the period of 'penal-welfarism' that started in the early
twentieth century and prevailed until the 1960s (investigated by Garland
1985), the main options were to sentence an adult offender to custody, to
discharge or fine him or her, or to order the person to be supervised
under a probation order as a welfare-oriented alternative to a sentence.
Following the decline of the 'rehabilitative ideal' (Allen 1981), the key
aim during the era of 'alternatives to custody' in the 1970s and 1980s was
to offer judges and magistrates options that might avoid the costs
(personal and economic) of a custodial sentence. This produced the
power to order the person to undertake compulsory work for the benefit
of the community under a Community Service Order as well as the
power to suspend a prison term in the Criminal Justice Act 1967.

In the event, 'alternatives' failed to offset a rising prison population
(Bottoms 1987), quite possibly because they replaced terms of imprisonment in just half the cases in which they were imposed.[2] Confronting
expanding prison numbers, the government turned to the 'justice model'
to provide a positive rationale for community-based sanctions in an era
of 'punishment in the community'. With the Criminal Justice Act 1991
came the Combination Order and the Curfew Order, intended to
persuade sentencers that community orders imposed sufficient restrictions to count as 'punishments' in their own right. The Combination

Order allows probation supervision to be combined in a single sentence with a requirement to perform compulsory work. A Curfew Order requires the offender to stay in one place (typically his or her home) during a specified period of the day, with provision for electronic monitoring (or tagging) to ensure that the person is indeed at the specified address during the relevant period (for example, 7 p.m. to 7 a.m. the next day). I will be discussing the attempt to apply desert principles to community penalties under the Criminal Justice Act 1991 in Chapter 4.

Since the mid-1990s, there has been a growing emphasis on 'public protectionism' in a 'new generation' of community orders in which technology and effectiveness have been added to the 'punishment' theme (see Bottoms et al. 2004). This has seen the introduction of the Drug Treatment and Testing Order in the Crime and Disorder Act 1998 and the Exclusion Order and Drug Abstinence Order in the Criminal Justice and Court Services Act 2000 as well as powers to combine curfews and testing with other interventions. These developments mark a shift towards more intensive orders, or combinations of orders, in which sentencers can 'creatively mix' surveillance or testing with interventions designed to change offenders' behaviour through drugs treatment or offending behaviour programmes.

The rapid and significant shifts in thinking evident from the above account have left considerable instability and uncertainty about the purpose and status of community orders. It is hardly surprising then that, despite the expansion in the range of community-based orders, the use of custody has not diminished, nor is it expected to do so. The unprecedented rise in the prison population over the last decade has been the topic of much discussion and debate. Projections according to a variety of models predict further rises by 2009 to well over 90,000 and perhaps as high as 109,600 (see Home Office Statistical Bulletin 14/02 at http://www.homeoffice.gov.uk/rds). An important reason for these trends is an undeniably more punitive climate in England and Wales, as discussed by commentators such as Nellis (2001) and Garland (2001). It is almost certainly *not* explained by a more serious mix of offences coming before the courts (Hough et al. 2003). However, I would contend that a contributory factor has been confusion about the purposes of the various community penalties and their position in the sentencing framework, which has enabled custody to flourish during these punitive times.

Numerically, community penalties have been on an upward trend as well as custody; 187,000 offenders were sentenced to community orders in 2002 compared with 102,000 in 1992. Yet, a closer examination of probation statistics for England and Wales reveals a use of these orders for less serious offences and offenders than before. The proportion sentenced to a community order for summary only as opposed to indictable offences has grown from 28 per cent in 1992 to 41 per cent in 2002 (Home Office 2003). Furthermore, those sentenced to community orders are less likely than before to have prior records: 27 per cent of those sentenced to probation in 2001 had no previous convictions compared with 11 per cent in 1991; the equivalent proportions for CS were 51 per cent compared with 14 per cent (Home Office 2002; corresponding figures are not available for 2002). According to the most recent available figures, nearly half the offenders sentenced to CS are convicted of the least serious type of offences, over half of them upon their first conviction. It is a relief that these trends are beginning to be brought to the attention of the policy and practice worlds (Morgan 2003). As the then Chief Inspector of Probation, Professor Rod Morgan, recently pointed out (HMIP 2003a), they raise questions over whether the probation service should continue to supervise its caseload of low-risk offenders.

Predicting the consignment of community penalties to a criminal justice backwater, Mair (1997) saw their best hope in a reversion to their recent task of providing alternatives to custody (the rising prison population being the one bright light on the horizon for community orders). However, it is perhaps an indication of the extent to which community options have failed to prove themselves as 'punishments' that they are still commonly referred to as 'alternatives to custody' (by people participating in the research for this book as well as in other research projects). Reflecting their perception of public opinion, recent Home Secretaries – both Conservative and Labour – have not shied away from a rising prison population, and there seems little debate let alone consensus on the point at which the custodial population might become intolerable. It no longer appears credible or feasible to rely on the argument that the use of custody is inherently undesirable in order to promote non-custodial alternatives. Accordingly, commentators have recognised the need for a long-term strategy to develop demonstrably constructive and effective methods of dealing with offenders in the community, which earn public support in their own right.[3]

One abiding theme in the recent history of community penalties has been what Worrall (1997) described as their subordinate relationship with custody. The relationship between custody and community senten-ces in fact featured in speeches made on the same day by the then Home Secretary and the Lord Chief Justice, Lord Woolf – see Straw (2001) and Woolf (2001). However, whereas the Home Secretary saw little promise in community penalties for persistent offenders who have 'almost without exception been through the mill of community penalties and still reoffended', Lord Woolf described a short custodial sentence as 'a very poor alternative to a sentence to be served in the community'. To shift public perceptions from the view of community penalties outlined by Straw to that depicted by Woolf seems a challenging – even a daunting – task.

With an eye to improving public – and sentencers' – confidence in community penalties, the Home Office has taken steps to tighten up the arrangements by which they are enforced. National Standards governing how offenders should be supervised on community sentences were first introduced in 1992, specifying how often they should be seen and what should happen if they missed appointments. The most recent version (Home Office 2000) introduced stricter rules, so that proceedings to take an offender back to court for breach of the order must now follow a second unacceptable absence, whereas before breach proceedings became obligatory upon the third unacceptable absence. There have been three 'audits' of probation enforcement to compare practice on the ground with the requirements laid down in National Standards.[4]

Recent times have been active for community penalties in the UK. There has been the establishment of the National Probation Service for England and Wales with a new Integrated Strategy (National Probation Service 2001), recently brought within the command of a new Commissioner for the Correctional Services and shortly to be subsumed within the new National Offender Management Service. We are in the heyday of the 'What Works' movement, the aim of which is to build up a core curriculum of offender programmes, approved by the Correctional Services Accreditation Panel (CSAP), whose success in reducing recidivism is measured against targets set by the Home Office.[5] What have received comparatively little publicity are the 'Pathfinder' projects sponsored by the Home Office under its Crime Reduction Programme. The aim of the Pathfinders is to enable practitioners to develop independently evaluated programmes for accreditation against a set of criteria based on 'What Works' principles covering how and with whom such programmes should be run (see Raynor 2004 for a full account). This initiative has enabled interventions to be developed in the areas of offending behaviour, drugs treatment, resettlement from prison, basic skills and community service.[6] The latter has led to a scheme for Enhanced Community Punishment (ECP), which was awarded 'Recognised' status by CSAP in September 2002.[7]

This brings my account to another recent change, apparently more 'surface' than substance: the change in name of the three main community orders – from probation to Community Rehabilitation Order; community service to Community Punishment Order; and combination to Community Punishment and Rehabilitation Order (or combined order).[8] The new nomenclature will inevitably have had consequences for how these orders are perceived, strengthening the impression that probation is all about rehabilitation (even welfare) and community service all about punishment. The coincidence in its timing with a Pathfinder project developing the reintegrative, and crime reductive, aspects of community service seems unfortunate (see Johnson and Rex 2002).

The 'What Works' initiative has undoubtedly given fresh impetus to probation work. However, its exclusively rehabilitationist focus may have eclipsed the other important aim of community-based options with which I started this chapter: to restrict someone's liberty because of the offence that she or he has committed (an aim enshrined in the Criminal Justice Act 2003, as in earlier legislation). Heralding the era of 'punishment in the community', the Criminal Justice Act 1991 applied desert-based sentencing principles to community orders, but exposed tensions between what might avert an offender's further offending and what is deserved for his or her offence, tensions that I will examine in Chapter 4 below. Recent trends in the use of community sentences point to a danger that a focus on reducing offending will ironically draw in offenders the nature of whose crimes, and the likelihood of whose offending, does not justify – or require – the use of probation resources (as argued by HMIP 2003a). What does seem certain is that the period of change for community penalties is set to continue with the implementation of the Criminal Justice Act 2003. This legislation will have major implications for all criminal justice agencies, including the probation service. It is to the provisions impinging on community penalties that I turn next.

Blurred boundaries: a 'customised' community order or custody plus/minus

The new Criminal Justice Act is a radical measure. It covers a host of pre-trial and trial practices and introduces a sentencing framework intended to be clearer and more flexible than the current one, based on the purposes of punishment, crime reduction, public protection and reparation. Originating from proposals in the Home Office Consultation Paper widely known as the Halliday Report (Home Office 2001) and implementing policy set out in *Justice for All* (Home Office and Lord Chancellor's Department 2002), the Act introduces major changes to the sentences available to the courts. The various kinds of community orders mentioned above will be replaced by a single community sentence including any or a combination of the requirements currently available.[9]

Other measures in the Act that impinge on the use of community orders are custody plus, a new form of suspended sentence (originally 'custody minus') and intermittent custody. The first replaces prison sentences below 12 months with a short period in custody (up to three months) followed by supervision and requirements in the community. The second allows a short custodial sentence to be suspended on condition that the offender complies with requirements identical to those that can be included in a community sentence; breach will result in the activation of the term of imprisonment. Intermittent custody enables a prison sentence to be served at night or at the weekend, combined with a community programme during the day or through the week. These new custodial provisions follow concerns that many persistent offenders are sentenced to a short custodial sentence with no provision afterwards for supervision or intervention to tackle their offending. The old-style suspended sentence was widely seen as a 'let off' that allowed an offender convicted of a serious offence to remain at liberty in the community provided he or she was not convicted again during its term and did nothing to address his or her offending.[10]

According to the government, the aim of these reforms is to 'ensure [short prison sentences] support our overall aim of reducing offending' following widespread recognition in the consultation on sentencing reform that short sentences needed to be more effective (Home Office and Lord Chancellor's Department 2002: 92). In compensating for the perceived inadequacies of the current arrangements, however, the new custodial powers seem likely to blur the boundaries between custody and community penalties. Fine judgements will be required of sentencers as to whether to impose an intensive community order, to reinforce community requirements with the threat of conditional (or suspended) custody, or to give an offender a short taste of custody combined with or followed by community requirements. It may prove only too easy for sentencers to yield to the temptation to use custody plus/intermittent custody as a 'short sharp shock' or a suspended sentence as a threat to prompt compliance. Based on earlier experience of the suspended sentence (Bottoms 1981), the consequence could be a greater use of custody for those who might previously have received a community-based disposal or who have breached community requirements, with a net overall increase in the use of short custodial sentences. The government believes that short prison sentences will continue to be appropriate for some offenders, but fails to explain for whom – and why – custody might be required and for whom the 'customised' community sentence will be suitable.

Proposals for a 'generic' community order have been considered twice before (Home Office 1988; Home Office 1995), latterly to give sentencers greater flexibility to impose more appropriate community orders and because a single 'community sentence' might command greater public confidence. In the event these proposals were not pursued, the government having been apparently persuaded by some respondents to the consultation process that the current range of community penalties already provided a sufficient range of options (Home Office 1996). Instead, 'demonstration' projects explored what could be achieved to promote judicial and public confidence in community options within the current legal framework. Reporting the results of those projects, researchers found that sentencers were more satisfied with the information they received and felt more informed about probation programmes following the projects (Hedderman et al. 1999). The most marked impact on sentencing, in both higher and lower courts, was not on the use of custody but an increase in the use of probation orders with additional requirements, largely at the expense of other community penalties, and especially relating to summary cases (in other words, 'net-widening'). Significantly, in view of the provisions in the 2003 Act for custody plus, sentencers expressed an interest in being able to fuse a community sanction with a short spell of custody (Roberts 2002a).

So why introduce provision for a generic or 'customised' community order now? The context has certainly changed since 1996, partly because of extensions to the range and combinations of community penalties available to the courts. As the National Probation Directorate commented in its response to the Halliday Report, the relevant legislation has become highly complex and we have moved some way towards a single sentence through the Criminal Justice and Court Services Act 2000 (National Probation Directorate 2001). But what of the objection raised to the 1995 proposal by Ashworth et al. (1995): that a 'pick 'n' mix' generic order would threaten a reasonable relationship between the gravity of the offence and the overall severity of the order (an issue considered in detail in Chapter 4 below)? Alive to this concern, the Halliday Report offered proposals aimed at preserving proportionality, which went some way towards the agreed understanding of the comparable restrictiveness of different community orders advocated by Ashworth et al. For example, the idea was for the 'punitive weight' of the sentence to be proportionate to the current offences (and any additional severity for previous convictions). Halliday offered an 'outline tariff' with three tiers to illustrate how the ingredients in the sentence might be compared, which was 'not intended to be prescriptive in illustrating possible combinations' (Home Office 2001: 41). He also envisaged that requirements to give reasons for the sentence and to justify its punitive weight would inject greater 'rationality' in sentencing and reduce the risk of 'condition creep' (Home Office 2001: 43). The Sentencing Guidelines Council established under the 2003 Act will have the opportunity to address these matters.

The proposals in the Halliday Report were intended to address the need for urgent clarification of the purposes of the various community orders. In this regard, one welcome difference between the Halliday Report and the 2003 Act is for the government to have moved away from the terminology 'community *punishment* order', which seemed likely to obscure the constructive aspects of community sanctions that might attract public support. That aside, it is difficult to see how the use of the term 'community' sentence will enhance public understanding of what happens when an offender is sentenced to perform certain requirements in the community. The public, and offenders, seem more likely to understand what an order involves when its name describes the relevant activity or restriction, such as a *curfew* order, a *drug treatment* and *testing* order or a *compulsory work* order.

Irrespective of whether we have a range of different orders that may be combined or a single community sentence allowing different requirements to be combined, what we still lack is a developed understanding of what community-based sanctions have to offer, and therefore their position in the sentencing framework. This problem is not confined to England and Wales. Internationally, a clear consensus is lacking about the rationales underlying community sanctions and this undermines their credibility and application (Roberts 2002, citing Kalmthout 2002). Without that understanding, the Criminal Justice Act 2003 may well cause community penalties to become even more subordinate to custody. The danger will then be that a sanction is only seen as a credible 'punishment' if it contains an element of custody so that community requirements on their own come to be used for progressively less serious offences and offenders. It seems to me, however, that we cannot develop a more rounded understanding of community sanctions without paying attention to their theoretical underpinnings. Their underlying rationale is what I therefore now seek to address in looking at communicative penal theory.

Re-framing punishment as communication

The tensions between reducing recidivism and desert that became apparent following the Criminal Justice Act 1991 mirror the polarisation between the consequentialist and retributive penal theories to which the respective approaches owe their origins. Indeed, until recently, debate in penal theory centred on the competing claims of consequentialism (an approach that looks forward to the crime reductive consequences secured through deterrence, incapacitation and rehabilitation), and retributivism (an approach that looks backwards to the offence for which it exacts retribution). However, contemporary debate has largely focused on approaches that combine elements of both consequentialism and retribution (the latter recently developed as desert theory, most fully by von Hirsch 1976, 1985 and 1993). As Bottoms points out, for example, 'no modern version of desert theory completely excludes instrumental considerations in sentencing' (1995: 22), and this allows for considerable variation in interpretation. It is to these hybrid theories that we might look in order to develop a framework for community penalties which accommodates the need for them to be both just (deserved) and socially useful (in preventing crime).

In relation to that objective, what is promising about von Hirsch's (1993) desert theory and the communicative penal theory put forward by Duff (1996, 1999 and especially 2001) is that they have both made a serious attempt to reconcile theoretically retribution with crime prevention.[11] The idea of communication is central to both theories, as is the requirement to treat offenders in line with a Kantian account as moral agents – as ends in themselves, autonomous and capable of choice. Furthermore, each writer has considered how his theory might be applied to non-custodial options or community penalties – von Hirsch in Chapter 7 of *Censure and Sanctions* (1993) and Duff in Chapter 3 of *Punishment, Communication, and Community* (2001). In short, theirs might both be said to be hybrid theories of punishment. However, as well as these similarities, there are important differences in how von Hirsch and Duff approach the balance between retribution and crime prevention, as I hope to show in the following discussion.

In a desert model in which von Hirsch (1993) interlocks both 'censure' and 'crime prevention' in the general justification for punishment, censure is plainly paramount. For him, punishment's central feature is its role in conveying censure or blame. This is as part of a morality that holds people accountable for their conduct, an important function of which is to communicate certain messages. These are addressed to the offender, victim and to other people: punishment acknowledges that the victim has been wronged; it conveys disapproval to the offender; and it appeals to other people's sense of the conduct's wrongfulness as a reason for refraining from the proscribed behaviour. Moreover, 'some kind of moral response is expected on [the offender's] part – an expression of concern, an acknowledgement of wrongdoing, or an effort at better self-restraint. A reaction of indifference would, if the censure is justified, itself be grounds for criticising [the offender]' (von Hirsch, 1993: 10).

For von Hirsch, however, the primary aim of punishment is not to induce actual changes in the offender's moral attitudes. This is an important point of departure from the rationale put forward by Duff (2001). Another major difference between the two writers is how they conceptualise the preventive function of the sanction. For von Hirsch, the hard treatment element in punishment 'supplies a prudential reason that is tied to, and supplements, the normative reason [for desisting from offending] conveyed by penal censure' (1993: 13). This 'supplementary prudential disincentive' – in effect a deterrent – operates only *within* a censuring framework; otherwise the actor is being treated as a creature to be controlled rather than as a person with normative reasons for acting. Thus, when it comes to sentencing decisions, von Hirsch argues that proportionality should determine the severity of the sentence, with the effect that offences are punished according to their relative blame-worthiness, or seriousness. Motivated by a wish to restrict the power that the state takes over offenders' lives, von Hirsch also hopes to use proportionality to set absolute as well as relative constraints on senten-ces, and he proposes a decremental strategy for the penalty scale (von Hirsch 1993: 45–6).

In developing what he calls a *communicative* theory of punishment, Anthony Duff (2001) is more ambitious, claiming to move beyond a compromise between retribution and consequentialism to a unitary justification. He sees the central aim of punishment as a communicative enterprise. This is both forward-looking – the reform of the offender through what Duff calls 'moral persuasion' – and backward-looking (or retributive) in the sense that the communication condemns or censures the crime. The fact that punishment is retributive requires a reasonable relationship between the severity of the punishment and the relative gravity of the offence. However, Duff puts less emphasis than von Hirsch on proportionality. As this is not a purely expressive condemnatory communication, Duff argues that the seriousness–severity relationship is only one dimension of the relationship between a crime and its communicatively apt punishment. I explore the positions of the respect-ive writers on the role of proportionality further in Chapter 4.

Duff argues that the material form the punishment takes (for example, supervision, treatment programme or compulsory work) should be intrinsically appropriate to the aim of bringing offenders to recognise the wrongfulness of their crimes and the need for them to reform (an aim that may not necessarily be achieved). Crime reduction benefits are not merely contingent as in consequentialist accounts, but must arise from the offender's own moral understanding; he or she is addressed as an autonomous agent who may accept or reject the message conveyed in punishment. Thus the hard treatment element in punishment is not a 'prudential supplement', as for von Hirsch, but part of the moral communication. Crime prevention plays a prominent role, pursued through moral persuasion.[12]

Duff's definition of punishment, then, can be summarised as a secular penance, justified as part of a morally communicative process that aims to persuade offenders to repent of their crimes, to communicate their reparative apology to others, and to undertake to reform their future conduct. This definition contains a number of interesting features, raising questions that I will explore later in this book in looking at views expressed in interview and survey. One is the 'religious' language in which the definition is couched, and whether this is applicable to processes within our criminal justice system (even if Duff does emphasise the 'secular' nature of the exchange that he envisages). Another is the internal, somewhat intimate, character of the communication and response (such as repentance, remorse and apology), and whether this describes processes that offenders (and other relevant actors) recognise. There is also the extent to which the state is even entitled in principle to seek to extract any particular response when punishing an offender, a point contested by Andrew von Hirsch.

Von Hirsch (1999) has acknowledged that, as developed most recently in *Censure and Sanctions*, his desert theory shares with Duff's 'a *communicative* perspective'. However, the key differences between von Hirsch's and Duff's accounts bear on the nature of the communication. For von Hirsch, penal censure 'gives an individual an opportunity to respond in ways that are typically those of an agent capable of moral deliberation' (1999: 69). However, whether and how to respond to the punishment is a matter for the offender: 'censure is not a technique for evoking specified sentiments' (von Hirsch 1993: 10).[13] Accordingly, von Hirsch doubts whether the State is authorised or required to impose the secular penance envisaged by Duff, seeing it 'at best debatable whether the State should seek an abbot-like role [. . .], and that it is very unlikely to be able to perform such a role effectively (1993: 77). While efforts might be made to 'reform' offenders, these are *additional permissible activities* rather than a justification for punishment (von Hirsch, 1999: 78, my emphasis).

In an extended review of von Hirsch's desert theory, Bottoms (1998) sees the fundamental distinction between these two writers as lying in how they conceptualise dealings with offenders. According to Bottoms, von Hirsch approaches this 'externally', whereas Duff is concerned with the individualised internal states that punishment induces (and by the material forms that punishment therefore takes). Bottoms offers a third possibility of dialectically defensible censure, taking place in the context of an individualised moral dialogue with the offender. In effect, Bottoms (drawing on Lucas 1980) sees a conversation taking place, in which the offender's point of view is fully considered and where a decision adverse to the offender is reached for reasons that he or she ought to be able to acknowledge as cogent. The approach outlined by Bottoms is intended to imply a more future-oriented and more individualised view of the offender than in von Hirsch's account without involving the direct attempt to induce penitence envisaged by Duff. While a response from the offender – in the form of a change in attitude or reformed behaviour – might be encouraged, it is not formally part of the point or process of punishment.

Applying a communicative perspective to community penalties

Having compared and contrasted their respective theoretical frameworks, we are now in a position to consider how von Hirsch (1993) and Duff (2001) apply their ideas to community penalties. In line with the overall thrust of his theory, von Hirsch concentrates on how non-custodial sanctions might be accommodated within a framework of proportionality. He is not greatly interested in the particular forms that community penalties might take, although his insistence on proportionality would set limits on what forms he would accept. By contrast, Duff's position that the material form of the punishment should be intrinsically appropriate to the aim of moral persuasion obliges him to take an interest in how particular sanctions might be developed in line with a communicative account. Duff therefore has more to say on the actual content of community-based interventions.

Von Hirsch's (1993) main concern with intermediate sanctions (i.e. community penalties) is how desert principles might be used to determine their size. As long as the gravity of the offence dictates how severely the offender is punished, so the argument goes, the sentencer is free to base the choice between two or more equally 'deserved' sanctions on other grounds, such as crime prevention (Wasik and von Hirsch 1988). Thus rehabilitative or reparative goals may be pursued within a framework provided by desert. This was in fact the model implemented in the Criminal Justice Act 1991, as discussed in Chapter 4. According to von Hirsch, the aim of a desert-based scheme is to address three problems that have detracted from the ability of community penalties to lessen our reliance on custody: recruitment from the shallow end (i.e. bringing in less serious offenders); sanction stacking (i.e. a proliferation of requirements that increase the risk of breach); and the use of imprisonment as a breach sanction. Desirable as these objectives are, von Hirsch has little to say about the positive rationale for community penalties: how they might be socially useful as well as just, and therefore how they might be developed so as to earn public confidence and support.

Duff's (2001) interest in community penalties arises from his argument that sanctions that allow an offender to remain in the community are more fitting as inclusive communicative punishments than imprisonment, which excludes the offender from the normal life of the community for a period. It also arises from his interest in the reparative – and restorative – aspects of punishments, as discussed in the next section. He therefore discusses the communicative potential of various community orders and what they have to offer in bringing offenders to face up to and recognise the wrongs that they have done, to perform apologetic reparation and to recognise the need to avoid such wrong doing in the future.

For Duff, the central aims of probation – as understood by many probation officers – cohere with the communicative aims of transparent persuasion: 'to confront offenders with the effects of their offending and thus to help them to face up to the need for changes in their attitudes and behaviour' (2001: 101). Thus the requirement for supervision reminds the offender that his/her offence cast doubt on his/her commitment to the community's public values and threatened to undermine the mutual trust on which the community depends. The conditions attached to a probation order aim to bring home to the offender the character and implication of the offences as public wrongs, and to persuade the offender that he or she must (and can) modify his/her future behaviour. Accordingly, offending behaviour pro-grammes should not be seen as therapeutic, but as communicative punishments in which recognition of the wrongfulness of past conduct helps offenders to bring about a change in their behaviour.

According to Duff, community service orders (now community punishment orders) are undeniably punishments, but should be seen as public forms of the kind of reparation to which victim–offender mediation can lead. As a sentence, community service offers rich and substantial censure that aims to bring home to the offender the nature and implications of the offence. Performing work for the community further enables the offender to express his or her understanding of what he or she has done and his or her renewed commitment to the community. It also requires him or her to perform apologetic reparation to the community; even if the offender him or herself does not come to recognise it as such, other citizens should accept that in completing community service the offender has sufficiently apologised for the crime. The restorative nature of this portrayal of community service will be apparent to the reader, bringing the discussion to a consideration of restorative justice initiatives.

Restorative justice

The current influence of restorative justice undoubtedly stems from growing dissatisfaction with traditional criminal justice systems as neglecting victims and failing to address the damage to victims and communities wreaked by crimes. Accordingly, restorative justice advo-cates have sought to develop approaches in which the emphasis is on repairing the harm caused by crime and promoting reconciliation through a process involving the victim, offender and the community (Zehr 1990). It will already be obvious that there are parallels here with the inclusive communication proposed by Duff (2001). On the other hand, proponents of restorative justice are often keen to distance themselves from retributive theories of the kind propounded by von Hirsch, of which there are elements in Duff's ideas. There is by now a vast literature on restorative justice, a wide range of advocates and an extensive debate about the exact nature of its underlying principles, enabling detractors to claim that it lacks a sound theoretical basis or set of unifying concepts. It is impossible for me to do justice to the entire literature here. I have been necessarily selective in drawing on writings relevant to the questions I am seeking to address, but see Braithwaite (1999) and Ashworth and von Hirsch (1998) for useful summaries of why restorative justice is advocated and why critiqued. I will be returning to the literature discussed below as relevant in presenting and discussing the implications of my findings during the remainder of this book.

An important respect in which restorative justice is said to differ from the theories offered by Duff as well as by von Hirsch is that 'censure' or 'blame' does not play a role in restorative processes, which are presented as 'repairing harms' and promoting 'healing'. However, as with many of the supposed differences between restorative theorists and more traditional theorists, this distinction begins to fade under close analysis as shall be seen below. For example, shaming is a crucial element in Braithwaite's (1989) model of reintegrative shaming and Dignan (2003) sees restorative justice as dealing with 'wrongs' that require a proportionate response. Partly the problem lies in the sheer range of theories and interventions that have been bundled together under the term restorative justice. This makes generalisation virtually impossible.

The classic – if somewhat disputed – definition of restorative justice has come from Marshall: 'a process whereby parties with a stake in a specific offence collectively resolve how to deal with the aftermath of the offence and its implications for the future' (Marshall 1996: 37). As Dignan (2003) points out, this approach has been criticised for neglecting the expected outcomes of a restorative process, although for many advocates it is the dialogue process itself that constitutes the essential meaning of restorative justice. However, Walgrave (2003) clearly sees restoration in terms of an outcome, and argues that it is one that is not best pursued through the dispensation of criminal justice.

When it comes to measures intended to meet the perceived needs of victims, an important development influenced by restorative justice has been that of models for conflict resolution in which the outcome is negotiated between victim, offender and others (victim–offender mediation, conferencing).[14] For desert theorists, for the victim to have a say in the outcome conflicts with notions of justice, since the level of disposition might well depend on the preferences of the victim rather than the gravity of the offence (Ashworth 1998). Other reservations concern the possibilities that a victim might be brought in, not so much for his or her benefit, but as a 'pawn' in the offender's rehabilitation or therapy, or might not be contacted at all because it is demanding and difficult to do so (see Shapland 2003).

A fundamental debate concerns the nature of the relationship between restorative justice and traditional criminal justice, on which some advocates set restorative approaches in opposition to retributive justice (Christie 1982; Zehr 1990; Braithwaite 2003). What is at stake here is a philosophical question about the public or private nature of the proceedings, with some restorative theorists seeing 'conflicts' as essentially private matters between the offender, victim and others with an interest in the matter. By contrast, the criminal process rests on a view of crimes as public wrongs that concern the state and all its citizens, so that victims cannot claim the final word on what restoration requires. Some commentators suggest, however, that restorative processes and sanctions could develop or improve or supplement more traditional 'public' approaches to punishment (Duff 2001; Daly 2002; Dignan 2003). One problem for those who would advocate restorative initiatives in England is the low rates of victim participation recorded in the youth offender panels (Holdaway et al. 2001) and the Thames Valley restorative cautioning project (Young and Hoyle 2003). This cast doubts on the potential for a fully participatory restorative process as a viable alternative to the regular criminal justice system (Dignan 2003).

Duff's position on the relationship between restorative justice and retributive justice is to argue that 'restoration' is entirely compatible with retribution. In fact, Duff goes so far as to suggest that it *requires* retribution, in that the kind of restoration that crimes make necessary can (given certain deep features of our social lives) be brought about only through retributive punishments' (2003: 44). In common with other critics and commentators, including advocates such as Dignan (2003), he sees some restorative theorists as mistaken in describing crimes as 'harms' rather than 'wrongs' that victims suffer at the hands of culpable offenders. As 'wrongs', they require a response that involves the offenders' punishment. Thus he presents victim–offender mediation as a punishment: as a communicative enterprise in which censure plays a central role and which is deliberately burdensome to the offender, who is required to listen to the victim's point of view and undertake reparation to give real weight to his or her apology. Because he acknowledges that this model of criminal mediation is a far cry from criminal punishment as normally understood, Duff's (2001) argument is that more orthodox paradigms of criminal punishment should be shifted in the restorative direction.

Turning to the use and development of restorative processes in community penalties, recent theoretical work has produced a variety of ideas. Duff (2001) takes community-based sanctions as his model for exploring how a restorative approach might be developed within more traditional criminal punishments (as summarised in the previous section). Other commentators, too, have noted the reparative potential of community service, or the opportunity in cognitive behavioural programmes to make offenders more aware of victims' perspectives or even to have contact with victims of offences similar to those they have committed (Raynor 2001; Johnson and Rex 2002).

Efforts have also been made to identify the scope to introduce reforms to move community penalties even further towards a restorative paradigm. Duff, for example, foresees that victim–offender mediation could be routinely built into probation orders, organised and conducted by the supervising probation officer, so that 'the offender communicates to the wider community, as well as to the victim, his apologetic recognition of the wrong he has done' (2001: 104). Raynor argues for the incorporation of a reparative element in every community sentence, perhaps by involving victims in the choice of rehabilitative work to be carried out by offenders, to 'demonstrate that rehabilitation is itself fundamentally restorative and benefits the community as well as the offender' (Raynor 2001: 197). Against the reality of criminal justice as currently delivered, and the lack of victim involvement even in restorative schemes, such proposals seem ambitious. I return to them in Chapter 8 in the light of my research findings.

Starting from a fundamentally different position, John Braithwaite (1989) is well known for developing reintegrative shaming as a more effective 'social control' model than the traditional pain infliction involved in formal criminal justice and punishment. In essence, his is a consequentialist theory: shaming (social processes expressing disapproval with the intention or effect of invoking remorse in the transgressor and condemnation by others) followed by reintegration (of the offender into the law-abiding community through ceremonies to decertify the offender as deviant) will produce low crime rates.[15] Stigmatisation, on the other hand (where no effort is made to reconcile the offender with the community so deviance is allowed to become a master status), produces high crime rates and fosters criminal subcultures. Discussing the implications of this hypothesis for criminal justice, Braithwaite argues that if formal punishments must continue, they should be visible and nurture the social integration of the offender (citing community service and restitution as sanctions that allow the offender to be redeemed by 'paying his debt').[16]

Recently, Braithwaite and Braithwaite (2001) have offered revisions to the theory of reintegrative shaming to refine the foundational concepts and to accommodate procedural justice as supportive of reintegration, following Tyler (1990) and Sherman (1993).[17] In the light of analysis of drink-driving cases from the Reintegrative Shaming Experiment (RISE) in Canberra reported by Harris (2001), Braithwaite and Braithwaite conclude that reintegration and procedural justice work through generating shame-guilt (feelings of shame accompanied by feelings of remorse). As self-shaming of the act, an apology can be the most powerful and symbolically meaningful form of shaming. However, unresolved shame can block these processes because the offender is left uncertain as to how wrong the offence was or bothered by thoughts of being unfairly treated. Unresolved shame can be reduced by reintegration and the offender's being convinced that the offence was wrong (perhaps in dialogue with friends and family), but it will be intensified by stigmatisation.[18]

Replacing or reforming criminal justice?

In common with Duff (2001) in relation to moral persuasion, Braithwaite argues that the current conditions of traditional criminal justice are hardly conducive to reintegrative shaming: 'offenders are on an assembly line populated by lawyers who are anything but moralising about what the offender has done' (1989: 181). Braithwaite's proposals for reintegrative social control are in fact remarkably similar to Duff's ideas of censure leading to remorse, reparation and reconciliation. However, the implications each draws are radically different. Whereas Duff sees a prior need to reform existing criminal justice practices and the wider political context in which they are delivered, Braithwaite would establish an alternative system, for which he has been an ardent advocate in the shape of restorative justice.

Whether to establish a separate system of restorative justice or to subsume it within criminal justice is itself a hotly debated topic largely beyond the scope of a book in which my aim is to elucidate certain processes within criminal justice rather than to contemplate an alternative model. As Shapland (2003) notes, it has become difficult to form clear boundaries around 'restorative justice' and 'criminal justice', to decide, for example, whether to classify a reparative disposal such as community service as a criminal or a restorative sanction. Rather than pursue that debate, I prefer to concentrate on developing the constructive aspects of community sanctions within criminal justice on the basis that these still form the largest group of disposals for offenders convicted of indictable offences (around 100,000 in 2001, as recorded in Home Office 2002b).

In practice, it is rarely proposed that restorative justice should largely replace criminal justice as the main disposal for offenders, usually because of the recognition that retributive justice is required as a back-up sanction where cooperation is not forthcoming (but see Walgrave 2003 for a different view).[19] Even Braithwaite's (1999) 'enforcement pyramid' for integrating restorative processes within criminal justice reserves restorative justice for 'virtuous' actors. He envisages that the threat will escalate in response to a failure to cooperate, culminating in custodial incapacitation for recalcitrant offenders, a strategy criticised as having the possible effect of encouraging more punitive responses for repeat offenders. Dignan (2003) seeks to mitigate such effects in proposing an alternative enforcement pyramid in which restoration would be more fully integrated with criminal justice, so that court-imposed restoration orders would be used for recalcitrant offenders or unwilling victims and restorative punishment applied to serious or persistent offenders. In Dignan's scheme, incapacitation would be reserved for offenders likely to inflict serious physical harm on others. In other cases, a range of non-custodial measures could be adapted to promote restorative out-comes, for example the development of more restorative elements in community service (reparation) and probation (conferencing and medi-ation). Here, his proposals begin to merge with those suggested by Raynor (2001) and Duff (2001) and considered above.

Finally, in a somewhat different approach again, von Hirsch et al. present an ideal 'making amends' model of restorative justice as a means of suggesting 'how RJ's aims and limits might be specified more clearly' (2003: 21). Resembling, so the authors state, criminal mediation as sketched by Duff, the 'making amends' model would comprise a response negotiated between offender and victim involving the implicit or explicit acknowledgement of fault and an apology by the offender conveyed through undertaking a reparative task. Posing their model as a 'thought-experiment' rather than a serious proposition, the authors hypothesise that a modest 'making amends' scheme might apply within a proportionalist sentencing system to property offences. Following a determination of guilt, the court might refer a property offender to a victim–offender conference for a negotiated disposition, which would still count as a 'punishment' subject to proportionality requirements.

Reflecting on the above, it occurs to me that a number of recent theorists coming from very different perspectives have produced some very similar arguments:

- crimes are wrongs for which it is right and crime-reducing to express disapproval (whether through censure or shaming);

- victims' interests and needs should be accorded greater recognition (whether through conferencing or more modest forms of restitution or mediation);

- disposals should pursue reintegrative and restorative outcomes (whether we integrate these in 'punishments' or call them something else).

25

Given such similarities, it is interesting – and I hope useful – to explore whether these goals are seen as desirable by people with on-the-ground experience of crime and criminal justice.

Moving from theory to communication on the ground

Most of the debate outlined above has been conducted at a theoretical level. Indeed, Duff (2001) is careful to offer his account as an ideal and to argue that it does not describe or justify criminal justice processes as they operate in practice. He is aware, for example, that a communicative system of punishments could become humiliating, excluding and intrusive. However, he raises more serious questions about the social context from which the penal system derives its legitimacy. Are offenders morally bound to the law? Has that law the authority to call offenders to answer for their crimes? Does the language of the law express public values that offenders can be expected to share?[20] In the light of these, Duff concludes that justifying the institution of punishment requires a 'serious collective commitment to begin to remedy the kinds of exclusion that undermine the preconditions of criminal liability and punishment' (2001: 200).

Despite Duff's caution, my aim in this book is in fact to start exploring the possible application of the ideas discussed above to how state punishment is actually delivered, or could be delivered, in the form of community penalties. This is partly because I agree that effective thinking about punishment requires a closer relationship between high-level normative thinking and ground-level practical decision-making (Raynor 1997). As Duff himself argues, 'until it starts to show how sentences are to be determined [. . .], [normative theorising] has not yet provided a theory of punishment as a possible human practice' (2001: 131).

In short, I embarked on the research that forms the subject matter of the rest of this book in the hope that the insights of those making decisions, or are affected by decision-making, in criminal justice might inject some fresh thinking into the normative debates. They might suggest possible ways to take forward the ideas and the debates outlined above. Ultimately, my aim is to contribute to normative theorising, and in particular the development of a stronger conceptual framework for community penalties. In turn, I hope that this might provide a firmer and more enduring foundation for policy and practice relating to non-custodial sanctions that restrict offenders' liberty.

These, then, were my aims in conducting interviews and surveys to explore the above ideas with four groups who might be seen to have a practical stake in the criminal justice and penal systems: lay magistrates, probation and CS staff, offenders and victims. In the next chapter, I explain how I set about eliciting and analysing the views of people in these groups. I also set my research within the context of other research on public opinion and victims' views of punishment. In the three chapters that follow the next, I discuss my findings in relation to the questions posed by the theoretical debates.

My underlying concerns are these: the aims of sentencing and what it communicates; how offenders respond to that communication; and how the material forms that community orders do and could take contribute to the communication. The first question I am interested in is whether people see punishment as serving primarily retributive or consequential-ist goals, or a mixture of the two. In other words, is punishment seen as both backwards- and forwards-looking? If so, how do people balance the two elements (for example in questions about the quantum of punish-ment)? I then look at the extent to which understandings of the messages conveyed to and responses expected from offenders fit Duff's account or von Hirsch's, or lie somewhere in between. What do people make of the normative aspects of punishment and what do they see as its instrumen-tal goals? How much weight do they place on offenders' responding to the penal messages and what sort of responses would they look for? Specifically, I explore the communicative potential that Duff ascribes to community penalties, and the extent to which this resonates with the perceptions and experiences of the people I interviewed and surveyed. Can the processes of moral persuasion, repentance and apologetic reparation described by Duff be recognised in on-the-ground accounts? Or are people aware of different processes, and how might these be seen to fit a communicative – and/or a restorative – conceptualisation of punishment?

As explained in Chapter 1, the idea is not to 'test' the relevant theories, but to explore how the ideas fit in with everyday understandings, and to assess the extent to which they already inform practice or could be put into practice with what implications and under what conditions. These are the questions to which I will turn in the final two chapters of the book, after I have presented and discussed my findings.

Conclusions

In this Chapter, I started by reviewing contemporary arrangements relating to community penalties. I argued that what they lacked was an adequate conceptual framework in which a balance can be found between the retributive and crime preventive elements that undoubtedly coexist in community penalties. The need to seek such a balance took me to the theories put forward by von Hirsch (1993) and Duff (2001), both of whom seek to reconcile theoretically retribution (in the form of censure for the offence) with crime prevention. Communication is central to both theories and each treats the offender as a rational moral agent capable of responding to the experience of being punished. However, while censure is paramount in von Hirsch's conceptualisation of punishment, Duff puts the emphasis on looking for a communicatively apt punishment through which to seek the offender's reform by moral persuasion. Bottoms (1998) explores the middle ground between the two theories in putting forward dialectically defensible censure.

Duff (2001) has developed his ideas specifically in relation to community penalties, which – along with criminal mediation – he sees as inclusive communicative punishments that enable offenders to face up to the wrongs they have done, to perform apologetic reparation and to recognise the need to avoid future wrong doing. As explicitly recognised by Duff, there are links here with proposals by restorative theorists, and he suggests ways in which restorative processes might be developed within community penalties. In the following chapters I shall be looking at the communicative and restorative potential of community penalties as understood by the groups I have interviewed and surveyed, placing that within their broader understanding of the aims of punishment and the role played by communication. In the next chapter, I start by setting out how I sought views from people with a practical stake in criminal justice, placing that within the context of research into public opinion and victims' views. Chapter 4 then explores theoretical and practical aspects of reconciling proportionality with crime prevention before reporting how my respondents prioritised the aims of punishment and what role they attributed to proportionality.

Notes

1 There have been important developments too for young offenders, (see Bottoms and Dignan 2004). However, my focus here is on the sentencing of adult offenders and I have therefore confined my analysis to the disposals to which adults may be sentenced (many of which apply also to young offenders).

2 See Bottoms (1981) on the suspended sentence and Pease (1985) on the Community Service Order.

3 As stated at Key Conclusion A4, Appendix to Bottoms et al. (2001).

4 The third audit of probation enforcement practice suggested that National Standards had not yet produced tighter procedures although there were signs that compliance with requirements has increased (see Hedderman and Hearden 2001).

5 The target being to achieve actual reconviction rates 5 per cent below predicted rates for general offending behaviour programmes, 25 per cent

below in the case of drugs programmes – see National Probation Service (2001).

6   See Probation Circular 35/1999 for the selection of Community Service, Resettlement and Basic Skills Pathfinder projects.

7   See Rex et al. (2004) for the evaluation of the CS Pathfinder project.

8   Under the Criminal Justice and Courts Services Act 2000.

9   These include: compulsory work; activities or prohibited activities; offending behaviour programmes; treatment for substance misuse or mental illness; residence requirements; curfews and exclusions; supervision; and attendance centres for offenders aged under 25.

10 Because the suspended sentence was not seen to fit within the framework of sentences commensurate with the seriousness of the offence, its use was confined in the Criminal Justice Act 1991 to 'exceptional circumstances' (see Home Office 1990). The effect was a dramatic fall in the use of the suspended sentence – from over 20,000 in 1991 to less than 3,000 after the 1991 Act was implemented in October 1992 (see *Criminal Statistics for England and Wales 2001* (Home Office 2002b)).

11 Although Hart (1968) and Rawls (1999) both seek to combine utilitarian general justifications for punishment with proportionality in how punishment is distributed, I am persuaded by Lacey's (1988) objection that the general justification for the institution of punishment should include a justification for its use in individual cases. Matravers (2000) has much in common with Duff in seeing punishment as both expressive and educative; however, he is primarily concerned with the relationship, at a philosophical level, between justice and morality and not with the practical questions that I seek to address.

12 Duff (2001) distinguishes moral persuasion from 'moral education', which might be justified because it benefits the offender. He rejects an interpretation of punishment as education on the grounds that it is objectionable and paternalistic to impose punishment for the offender's own good – following Mill's famous dictum that the only purpose for which coercive power can be rightfully exercised over a citizen is to prevent harm to others. Moreover, it is unclear why punishment should be the preferred method of moral education – even if this form of intervention is what most offenders need. 'Education' implies that offenders are rather like children who have yet to receive the education they need rather than responsible moral agents who need to be persuaded to attend to the wrongfulness of their behaviour.

13 Although von Hirsch's (1993) observation that indifference from the offender would be grounds for criticism implies a less 'liberal' approach.

14 In New Zealand and Australia, and latterly in England and Wales, conferencing has been implemented as an alternative to court proceedings, especially suitable for juvenile offenders, involving the victim and his/her significant other(s), the offender and his/her significant other(s), community representatives, police, social or youth services, and the facilitator or coordinator (see Dignan 1999; Morris and Gelsthorpe 2000).

15 Von Hirsch dismisses Braithwaite's model as 'a quasi-rehabilitative strategy: a therapy for reducing the offender's inclination to offend again' (1993: 71). However, this perhaps underplays the role of disapproval in the form of shaming.

16 Maruna (2001) provides some empirical support for the significance of rituals of redemption for promoting desistance. Offenders who persist, he argues, remain locked in 'condemnation scripts'.

17 This is reminiscent of Bottoms' (2001) work in incorporating procedural justice within a theoretical model for compliance both with the immediate requirements of an order and with the requirements of the law.

18 These findings have important theoretical and practical implications, discussed in some detail by Harris (2001). At one level, they may help to explain why in the RISE evaluation drink-driving was one of the four major offence categories in which those offenders assigned to a conference did *not* have significantly reduced rates of reoffending compared with those assigned to court proceedings (Sherman et al. 2000). Harris also makes the point that 'shame' is not necessarily destructive of one's self respect if one is ashamed as a result of a criminal offence rather than as a result of a generalised sense of being a bad person. On this point, he distinguishes his findings from those of Morris and Maxwell (2003) in the New Zealand conferencing experiments, where a significant relationship was found between not being reconvicted and, among other factors, *not* being made to feel a bad person (shamed) and feeling remorse (sorry for what one has done and feeling that one has made good the damage done).

19 In a recent collection edited by Walgrave looking at various models for how restorative justice might be placed within an adequate legal framework, Bazemore and O'Brien (2003) suggest that rehabilitation is entirely compatible with a restorative focus on repairing harm and that there is great untapped potential for applying core restorative values to treatment and rehabilitation. However, they argue that the prevention of recidivism, an offender outcome, should not be presented as the primary goal of restorative justice, which should be focused on victims of crime.

20 On this point, Matravers argues that where a group are disadvantaged to the extent that they form an 'underclass', 'they do not reject morality and the moral standards of the community that surrounds them. Rather they react to the rejection of morality by that community' (2000: 266). In such as case, there is no morality and there can be no (justifiable) punishment.

Chapter 3

Seeking stakeholders' views of punishment

Introduction

In this chapter, I first look at what we know about what members of the public – as consumers – think about crime and sentencing and why their views might matter. This sets the context for the second section of the chapter, in which I describe how I used a mixed, primarily exploratory, research design to collect the views of people who I call 'stakeholders' because they might be seen as having a particular interest in sentencing and its outcomes.

I. Assessing public views

As Hough and Roberts (2002) note, the limitations of survey research on public opinions about criminal justice and sentencing are well known. When answering general questions, people usually have the worst kinds of cases and offenders in mind and often think about atypical (i.e. lenient) sentences when asked about sentence severity, relying on impressions gained from the news media. People also fail to consider the wide range of alternative punishments to prison. More can be learnt by asking people about their sentencing preferences in relation to specific scenarios or vignettes.

Stalans asserts that, by focusing on what the public wants, 'studies on attitudes to punishment have barely scratched the surface of the public's real attitudes' (2002: 20). A somewhat different view is expressed by Cullen et al. (2000) following a review of research conducted in the US: that more research is unlikely substantially to revise our view of the basic parameters of public opinion. So what do we know of public views of criminal justice and sentencing?

English research: The British Crime Survey

Until very recently, much of our knowledge about public attitudes in the UK derived from British Crime Surveys (BCS) (Hough and Roberts 2002; Hough and Roberts 1998; Mattinson and Mirrlees-Black 2000).[1] Data from two sweeps of the BCS (1996 and 1998) in particular have shown that the public are poorly informed about the operation of the criminal justice system and sentencing, and that as a result they have little confidence in judges or magistrates. For example, widespread ignorance of the sentences available to the courts and substantial underestimates of the courts' use of imprisonment were revealed. It tended to be older people, tabloid newspaper readers and those with lower educational qualification who displayed least knowledge and the most negative views of the criminal justice system.[2]

When people were asked to sentence a real case of an adult burglar with previous convictions who took a television set from the home of an elderly man during the day, their preferences were actually close to, or even slightly more lenient than, current sentencing practice. Around half wanted a prison sentence, but a quarter suggested community service and financial compensation was popular (Hough and Roberts 1998; Mattinson and Mirrlees-Black 2000).[3] There was no evidence in either survey that having been a recent victim of crime increased the punitiveness of preferred sentences. Similar findings emerged in research commissioned by the Sentencing Advisory Panel (Russell and Morgan 2001): three-quarters of participants believed that the courts are too lenient in sentencing for burglary, yet the majority favoured a less severe sentence than generally passed by the court when asked about specific cases.

Such findings are consistent with earlier research, both the BCS of 1982 and 1984 (Hough and Moxon 1985) and Maguire's (1982) study of dwelling house burglary in which the researchers were surprised at the lack of vindictiveness displayed by victims in relation to 'their' offenders. One interesting finding, common to both Maguire's research and the BCS, is the support shown by victims for reparative or restorative disposals. In 1998, around two-thirds of victims in the BCS were prepared to consider a mediation meeting with their offender or receiving reparative compensation from them.

Deliberative polls – informed views

These findings raise the possibility of seeking to raise public awareness about criminal justice. This approach has been incorporated in a research technique, the deliberative poll, in which a general public sample completes a questionnaire, of whom a subsample is provided with information. The 'informed' sample's responses to the same question-naire are then compared with those given by the general sample in order to assess the impact of the information on people's views (see Roberts and Stalans 1997). Such a research strategy carries methodological difficulties: response rates to the second part of the exercise can be low or biased in favour of certain groups, producing an unrepresentative 'informed' sample, and it may be unclear whether 'changed' responses are attributable to the information provided. The costs of mounting this kind of exercise are also prohibitive and they have been used more often in the US than in the UK (see Hough and Park 2002 for the only UK example of a deliberative poll).[4] A comparatively practical and economi-cal approach to the provision of information was adopted in a recent Home Office study (Chapman et al. 2002, also reported at Appendix V, Home Office 2001). Given its contemporaneity and use in the Halliday Report, a consultative document on sentencing reform leading to provisions in the Criminal Justice Act 2003, it is worth considering how that research was carried out and what it found.

The Home Office study surveyed a nationally representative sample of 1,022 people about their knowledge of crime, sentencing and the criminal justice system, attitudes to sentencing and confidence in the criminal justice system. A subsample of 220 then participated in an experiment to test the impact of providing information, in which 109 were given a booklet designed to be attractive and accessible, 37 attended presenta-tions by experts and 74 watched a video (some response rates at this stage were low). From a poor starting point,[5] their level of knowledge of criminal justice processes was found to increase significantly as a result of information, whatever its source, and the study supported findings from other research that surprising or repeated facts were more likely to be recalled. Importantly, however, it seemed difficult to get ethnic minority respondents to participate in any of the three information groups.

There was, however, less change in beliefs about the aims and efficacy of sentencing as a result of receiving information. There were few changes in preferences for the main aim of sentencing, with 'changing behaviour to prevent reoffending' being chosen by the largest number of people in the general public sample (47 per cent). Comparatively few selected 'deterring others' (6 per cent), 'making amends to the victim' (5 per cent) or 'expressing society's disapproval' (2 per cent), this being a question to which only one answer was invited. Although there was some increase in support for disposals other than prison, the already high ratings for imprisonment as effective in reducing crime increased by a larger margin.[6] When asked to sentence a typical case, respondents used considerably less custody than the rates given by the courts for both burglary and robbery; sentencing changed little as a result of being given information, but people were less likely to think that judicial sentencing was too lenient.

A finding relevant to the next chapter which examines proportionality and related questions concerns the factors that the general public sample thought should have a great deal of influence on sentence. Here, previous convictions and the likelihood of reoffending were seen as very important; 86 per cent believed that a great deal of notice should be taken of the former, 72 per cent the latter. Factors related to the seriousness of the offence were also seen to warrant a great deal of notice: whether the crime was planned (68 per cent), the effect on the victim (54 per cent) and whether the offender was mentally ill (52 per cent). Comparatively few respondents saw personal circumstances as worthy of a great deal of notice: domestic responsibilities (20 per cent), the age of an adult offender (17 per cent) and whether the offender was employed (11 per cent). The same was true of victim-related issues: whether the offender has made amends to the victim (28 per cent) and the wishes of the victim (25 per cent). However, the questionnaire did not ask specifically about the seriousness of the offence nor did it ask whether the stated factors should influence the mode or the amount of punishment. These considerations were all seen as important by participants in my research, as will be seen in Chapter 4.

The Halliday Report (Home Office 2001) reported findings from a survey of ten practitioner groups: judges, district judges, magistrates and justices' clerks; police officers and crown prosecutors; defence solicitors and barristers; and probation and prison officers. Those surveyed expressed considerable concern about the perceived weaknesses of the criminal justice system. Of particular relevance here was the inflexibility of the current framework to: combine custody and community disposals; vary implementation (such as weekend imprisonment); combine punishment and rehabilitation; or to match offenders' needs (for example, by using community penalties rather than fines). There was thought to be insufficient attention to rehabilitation and a failure to take account of previous offending or risk of reoffending. The public was seen to think of community penalties as 'soft options', because of a combination of: insufficient resources, insufficient restrictiveness and inadequacy as a deterrent, lack of monitoring of offenders, levels of breach and limited options for enforcement, and limited options for the mentally ill and drug users.

Practitioners' views on the main aims of sentencing were comparable to those expressed by the general public, with rehabilitation ranked first by five groups (justices' clerks, crown prosecutors, probation officers, solicitors and barristers). Punishment was ranked first by the three groups of sentencers and incapacitation by police and prison officers (these options had been ranked second and third respectively by the general public). There was less support for expressing disapproval or for deterring others or the offender (though there was more support among the public for the last aim). Practitioners seemed to put more emphasis than the general public on making amends to the victim, and expressed concerns that the criminal justice system failed to give sufficient attention to the needs and rights of victims. There was a fair amount of support for restorative justice schemes, especially from probation officers, 73 per cent of whom supported such schemes. Around half of most other groups were in support, the main dissenters being the judiciary – of whom a quarter expressed opposition and a third indifference to the idea.

On influences on sentencing, views were again similar to those expressed by the general public. The majority view was that the seriousness of the offence and the risk of reoffending should be given equal weight in sentencing (the public survey did not include this question). Frequency and seriousness of offending and risk of reoffending were ranked highly, as were factors related to the gravity of the offence. However, in line with public views, less emphasis was given to the victim's wishes or to the age, employment status and domestic responsibilities of the offender.

All practitioner groups supported the idea that recent and relevant convictions should result in a more severe sentence than warranted by the offence (ranging from 94 per cent of police officers to 51 per cent of probation officers), but many found it difficult to articulate the reasons why. A wide variety of reasons were put forward: protecting the public from the hard core of offenders; meeting public expectations; deterrence; the expression of intolerance and just deserts; and rehabilitation. Community penalties were considered to be less likely to be used for offenders with previous convictions. This is in line with previous research summarised by Roberts and Stalans (1997) to the effect that the prior record of an offender influences perceived seriousness ratings either through perceptions of intent or the likelihood of recidivism. Reflecting on their finding that a greater interval between offences actually *increases* the severity of the proposed response, Robinson and Darley (1995) suggest that this results from a process of personal attribution in which information about a person's actions is treated as providing information about his or her underlying disposition. Thus if essentially the same act is committed in different situations, people are likely to conclude that the act is dispositional or habitual, reflecting the true underlying personality of the person.

Cross-national studies

The International Crime Victimisation Survey (ICVS) shows that many of the views discussed above are replicated across Western Europe

(Roberts 2002b; Mayhew and van Kesteren 2002).[7] Respondents were asked what sentence they saw as most appropriate in the case of a 21-year-old burglar who has stolen a colour TV and is found guilty of burglary for the second time: fine, prison, community service, suspended sentence or another sentence. Taking Western Europe as a whole, 46 per cent of the sample selected community service and 29 per cent prison.[8] Along with Malta, Scotland and Northern Ireland, England and Wales was among the most punitive jurisdictions in the region, with 51 per cent favouring prison. These were in fact the only Western European countries in which the majority of respondents (i.e. over 50 per cent) selected prison. Incidentally, this was the case in none of the Eastern and Central European countries, and in the USA alone from the New World (see also Kury and Ferdinand 1999 for a comparison of attitudes in West Germany and East Germany since reunification).

Fascinatingly, Mayhew and van Kesteren (2002) are able to present trends over time, revealing that there has been a 13 per cent increase in the proportion of the sample in England and Wales selecting prison between 1989 and 2000.[9] In the light of the discussion in the previous chapter, one can speculate as to what might have caused this. Reflecting on similar trends across Eastern and Central Europe and Western Europe, Kury et al. (2002) suggest that a loss of faith in the criminal justice system – and in the wider political system – can foster more punitive attitudes amongst the general public. This produces a climate in which it becomes difficult to promote rehabilitative sanctions or restorative schemes.

Roberts addresses the implications of international public opinion research for the future development of community penalties, arguing that 'politicians are reluctant to create and judges slow to impose community punishments if the general public is perceived to be hostile' (2002b: 34). One difficulty identified by Roberts is the lack of public knowledge of community-based sanctions, as revealed by studies in England and Wales (Hough and Roberts 1998) and Canada (Stalans and Roberts 1997; Sanders and Roberts 2000).[10] However, there is considerable evidence from representative surveys conducted in a variety of countries that the public supports these sanctions when it is told about them. For example, Hough and Roberts (1998) found that when they divided the BCS sample into half and provided a list of all sentencing options to one group, that group made less use of custody than the other group not given the full list of possible sanctions. Sanders and Roberts (2000) found much greater support for the conditional sentence among Canadians when the nature of the conditions was spelled out.[11]

Preference for alternative measures such as community service over sending offenders to prison has been found in Canada, England and Wales (Shaw 1982) and the USA (Doble 2002), as well as Europe.

According to Roberts (2002a), the few studies that have explored support for specific community sanctions have found that it is highest for those with a restitutive element or those that respond to victims' needs. Thus compulsory work or compensation receives more support than electronic monitoring or probation supervision, partly because compensatory sanctions are seen as being effective in reducing crime. In particular, Roberts concludes that the public image of probation (minimal conditions coupled with minimal supervision) undermines public support; if it is to support community sanctions for more serious or repeat offenders, the public needs to know that these offenders are incurring serious consequences for their offending.

US research – a 'get tough' public?

Given frequent portrayals of the American public as punitive, pressurising politicians to lock offenders up for lengthy periods, it is interesting to consider the findings of research on public opinion in the US (where research seems somewhat more advanced than in England and Wales or other jurisdictions). It may also be instructive in the light of the view sometimes expressed that the UK is adopting a milder form of the US model in its crime control policies, for example by introducing a mandatory 'three strikes' style sentencing provision for recidivist burglars (see Garland 2001). Reviewing the literature from the past decade, Cullen et al. conclude that 'the [US] public shows a tendency to be punitive and progressive, wishing the correctional system to achieve the diverse missions of doing justice, protecting public safety, and reforming the wayward' (2000: 1). Similarly, Cullen et al. (2002) report that support for rehabilitative goals from a utilitarian US public who wants 'to do something' about crime has persisted over two decades of research despite shifts in correctional policy over the same period. Doble draws from surveys since the late 1980s in Alabama, Delaware, Pennsylvania, North Carolina, Oregon, Oklahoma and Vermont the lesson that the American people favour efforts to 'rehabilitate those offenders the public believes can be turned around without serious risk to the community' (2002: 161). According to Roberts and Stalans (1997), the preponderance of evidence from survey research is that the American public is *less* punitive than the courts when it comes to sentencing comparable cases, and more supportive of community corrections.

Specifically, Cullen et al. (2000) reach the conclusion that the American public is punitive towards crime but will moderate its punitiveness in relation to non-violent offenders when less stringent interventions have utility for victims, the community and offenders; hence, there is emerging support for restorative sanctions. When tolerance rather than preference is analysed, although wary of regular probation – a sanction that in the US involves minimal contact with the offender – citizens will accept alternatives to incarceration if community sanctions involve meaningful intervention. Nor do they support 'three strikes' laws: the seriousness of the offence has been found to outweigh the impact of prior record on sentencing preferences in factorial surveys.[12] Making sense of varied findings on the aims of sentencing and the role of prior record, Roberts and Stalans (1997) offer the interpretation that the public sees general deterrence as an important sentencing purpose, but pursues a just deserts model in expressing their sentencing preferences when confronted with particular scenarios. Thus in a number of studies the principle of proportionality seemed to be strongly endorsed in that a high degree of association was found between the seriousness of a particular crime and the severity of the assigned penalty. Respondents to one factorial survey were also influenced by characteristics of the offenders and victims and the consequences of the offence; yet public support for sentencing on record does not seem to extend to very harsh penalties for recidivists regardless of the gravity of the latest offence.

The studies suggest that, although there is some evidence that support for rehabilitation has waned since the 1960s, it continues to be widely endorsed by US citizens as an important function of the correctional system (although retribution or just deserts seems more influential at the sentencing phase). Indeed, data from a recent survey reported by Cullen et al. (2002) point to a more recent revival in support for rehabilitation, perhaps inspired by the development of intermediate sanctions in the US.[13] Importantly, Cullen et al. (2000) suggest that the public does not perceive the philosophical and pragmatic conflicts between punishment and treatment discussed by scholars and is reluctant to see the two goals as mutually exclusive.[14] Finally, it is possible to 'draw one broad policy implication from the existing survey research: lack of political will – not public opinion – is the main barrier to developing a more balanced approach to sentencing and correctional policy' (Cullen et al. 2000: 57).

Is public opinion research useful?

Summarising the above, it seems fairly clear that, despite a general perception that courts are over-lenient, the public are in fact no more severe and quite possibly more lenient than courts when asked to sentence particular cases. There is a fair degree of support for community penalties once the public is made aware of them (and what they involve), and support for rehabilitative or restorative disposals – but less so for recidivist offenders. Even so, although the public in the UK and US appear less tolerant than their counterparts in Europe and the New World, they are still prepared to contemplate sanctions other than custody for burglars with prior convictions. Surveys in the US show endorsement of the principle of proportionality and restraint in the sentencing of recidivist offenders, although prior record has been shown to inflate ratings of the seriousness of the offence. The evidence in England and Wales indicates that persistence is seen to warrant a more severe sentence, but it is arguable that the relative importance of the seriousness of the offence and the offender's prior record has yet to be tested more sensitively through factorial surveys.

Needless to say surveys of public opinion should be accompanied by strong health warnings. How the research is approached and the way questions are phrased can shape responses. Roberts and Stalans (1997) sometimes found it difficult to make sense of apparently discrepant findings from different polls and surveys in the US, and argue that self-reports of the factors influencing people's decisions can be quite inaccurate. Cullen et al. (2000) suggest that the charisma of the presenters may be telling in deliberative polls; different presenters providing different criminological 'facts' may well have a different impact on the audience. Moreover, informing the public may have potentially uncomfortable consequences for those wanting to reduce reliance on custodial sentencing. There is evidence that this kind of work may prompt a wish to 'net widen' probation or intermediate sanctions because they will benefit offenders currently given less severe penalties. It may also stimulate support for the efficacy of prison as 'rehabilitative' or for 'tough' community sentences for which imprisonment is the only realistic enforcement option.

Another question is whether the research so far has succeeded in penetrating authentic public attitudes. Stalans (2002) believes not, identifying a need to understand what underlies people's sentencing preferences and how people process information before placing much reliance on attempts to assess the impact of information on people's views. Being pragmatic social thinkers who conserve energy for the most important tasks, people may change their 'surface' attitudes because someone is an 'expert' rather than because they have processed the information presented in the systematic way required to bring about enduring attitude change. One way in which to explore 'the public's kaleidoscope of sentencing preferences' (Stalans 2002: 16) is by measuring 'inner attitudes', for example through the use of detailed descriptions of criminal cases (perhaps of the kind deployed in factorial surveys used in the US). There seems scope to develop more sophisticated research methodologies in the UK in order to gain a better understanding of people's views on punishment.

Given that public attitudes have been described as 'mushy' (Cullen et al. 2000: 8), easily susceptible to change in the light of minimal new information, is there any point in seeking to find out what people think about criminal justice and sentencing? Can one even gauge public opinion reliably? Mushiness aside, Cullen et al. imply that it is worth assessing what citizens think should be done with those who have broken the law, the full body of survey data indicating that the public is more rational than irrational in the penal and correctional policy agenda it embraces. Similarly, Stalans argues that humans are socialised to think about what is just or unjust punishment for violating rules; therefore, 'people hold general attitudes towards sentencing and are appropriately motivated and able to make sentencing preferences in specific cases' (2002: 25). Roberts and Stalans (1997) suggest that people who embrace conflicting values deserve particular attention because criminal justice policies are often based on a choice between conflicting values. Indeed, such views may be less susceptible to manipulation than more polarised attitudes because the person has thought more about the issue in order to reconcile the relevant values (for example, in the punishment context, whether to punish or rehabilitate offenders).

Assuming that it is possible to research public attitudes, what relationship should we pursue between public views and sentencing policies? Why should policy-makers or theorists pay any attention to public opinion? Part of the answer at least lies in the fact that penal policy rests on determinations of values on which ordinary citizens might be considered to have a legitimate voice. Robinson and Darley (1995) argue that the moral credibility of the criminal law is its single most important asset. Investigating ordinary people's moral intuitions about liability and blameworthiness and the possible discrepancies between community standards and outcomes dictated by criminal codes,[15] they suggest that such a discrepancy at the very least points to a tension that requires analysis. From a utilitarian perspective, they argue that it will reduce the effectiveness of judicial condemnation as a deterrent and weaken the force of the law as an arbiter of proper conduct. For Morgan (2002), there is an additional obligation to inform the public about criminal justice in order to address a lack of confidence based on ignorance and misperception (though he adds the caveat that more knowledge may not necessarily increase confidence in all sections of the population). Hough (2003) expresses a similar view, lamenting the lack of progress in improving public satisfaction despite the government's modernisation agenda. According to the official view, too, improving public confidence in sentencing is an important goal (Carter 2003; Home Office 2001).

Maruna and King (2004) perceive a recent substantial shift away from the expert-driven bureaucratic model of penal policy to a system driven more explicitly by symbolic and expressive concerns in which public sentiments play a significant role. This may explain why a poorly informed public is seen as having the potential to drive policy towards ineffective or unfair responses to crime, sometimes through exploitation by politicians seeking electoral advantage (Indermaur and Hough 2002). Hough (2003) discerns an interaction effect as politicians' demands for tougher sentences feed the public belief that sentencing is indeed far too lenient, a dynamic observable in Canada, Australasia, Europe and the USA as well as the UK (Roberts et al. 2003). As Freiberg (2001) argues, given the symbolic role of punishment in reasserting the social order, public clamour for punitive responses to crime will take precedence in the absence of more convincing or reassuring alternatives for offering security.

II. Collecting stakeholders' views

Research questions and research design

I had somewhat different aims from the research discussed above, in that I wanted to know what people with a particular interest in criminal justice and sentencing (lay magistrates, victims, offenders and probation staff[16]) thought about certain normative questions concerning punishment as an institution. My purpose was to use respondents' views to explore the issues introduced in Chapter 2. In pursuing this investigation, my starting point was how retributive and consequential goals featured in people's understandings of the purposes of sentencing. Related to this was how people balanced the two elements in decisions about how much punishment should be given an individual offender and what factors should be taken into account (such as prior record, offenders' backgrounds and domestic circumstances, and demonstrations of remorse or attempts to put things right).

Beyond the aims of sentencing, I wanted to explore the role played by communication in punishment – an area not previously examined in looking at on-the-ground understandings of punishment and sentencing. Thus another of my research questions was what people thought punishment should be communicating to offenders, particularly when courts were using community penalties. Here, again, I was interested in the balance between normative (or moralising) and instrumental messages: the extent to which it was thought that courts should be conveying disapproval and how far conveying an expectation that the offender should refrain from offending in the future. Finally, there was the response expected from the offender: how important it was for the offender to show some response and what sort of response was desirable. Did people perceive the processes of remorse, repentance and apologetic reparation identified by Duff (2001), and what other responses did they think punishment should be prompting?

I did not see this as 'public opinion' research as such, although there were a number of parallels with that body of research. My chief concern was with normative questions rather than how criminal justice and courts were seen to operate in practice. However, it was relevant to consider whether sentencing was seen as achieving what people thought it should and, if not, why not.[17] Nor was I soliciting views from the general population; I deliberately sought views that might be seen as 'informed' or shaped by a particular interest in what happens to lawbreakers. However, in selecting lay magistrates rather than professional sentencers (district and circuit judges) I was hoping to get closer to what Robinson and Darley (1995) might call 'community standards'. Victims, too, represent one community view that has been explored in previous research (see Maguire 1982; Hough and Roberts 1998; Mattinson and Mirrlees-Black 2000). Offenders are members of the public with a particular experience of criminal justice, to whose views of sentencing virtually no attention has been paid.[18] I sought the views of probation staff because of their role in administering community penalties. It would have been useful, too, to explore the views of other criminal justice agencies such as police officers, crown prosecutors, defence solicitors and prison service staff, and to compare the findings with those reported by Halliday (Home Office 2001). Unfortunately, time and resources did not permit me to expand my research in this way.

In examining the questions outlined above, there were good reasons to use a mixed research design combining both qualitative and quantitative elements. However, the underlying perspective would be seen as predominantly qualitative (see, for example, Bryman 2001 for a comparison of the two approaches and discussion of how they might be combined). I was not setting out to test the theories discussed in Chapter 2, but to explore them and to add to them in the light of people's everyday understandings. Indeed, I would argue that these normative theories do not lend themselves to being 'tested' since they do not offer 'true' explanations of social phenomena but principled answers to 'ought' questions (Bottoms 2000). The question I was interested in is whether those answers 'work' for the people involved.

Although coming from the theoretical starting point set out in Chapter 2, I wanted to avoid restricting my enquiry to that theoretical framework or imposing it upon research participants. As far as possible, I wished to encourage people to describe in their words how they made sense of the purposes and processes of sentencing, so that the research remained open to ideas other than those put forward in the theoretical literature reviewed in the previous chapter. I also wanted my fieldwork to produce findings that could be quantified to enable me to analyse the relative weight that different groups ascribed to the various factors and systematically to compare the views expressed by different groups. But the overall approach remained exploratory and interpretative rather than theory testing.

I settled on a three-stage strategy as the best way in which to achieve these aims: stage 1 comprised in-depth exploratory interviews (referred to henceforth as 'first-round interviews'); stage 2 utilised questionnaires that were predominantly pre-coded; and in stage 3 I interviewed selected questionnaire respondents ('follow-up interviews'). The idea was for first-round interviews to generate themes (and phrases) that could be incorporated in questionnaires to collect the views of sufficiently large samples to produce data for systematic comparative analysis. Follow-up interviews would then be used to explore patterns revealed in the questionnaire analysis, so enriching the qualitative insights gained from first-round interviews. Below, I consider each stage of the research in some detail.

In choosing the sites for my research, my aim was to combine fieldwork efficiency with a geographically mixed sample. For the first-round interviews with magistrates, probation staff and offenders, I approached courts and probation offices in Bedfordshire, Cambridgeshire and Hertfordshire to provide a mix of comparatively urban sites, smaller towns and rural locations. Victims were the most difficult group to reach, and interviews followed a letter sent on my behalf by a victims organisation to 100 victims of 'middle-range' crimes – theft, motor crime and less serious burglaries – two of whom actually admitted to being ex-offenders.[19] The victims contacted were unknown to me unless they came forward for interview. For the questionnaires, I was able in addition to pursue contacts made during the first stage of the research to negotiate a postal administration to probation staff, offenders and victims (again of middle-range crimes) in London. Regional events in the East of England enabled me to administer questionnaires to a wider group of CS staff and probation trainees. The Magistrates' Association also offered to send questionnaires via e-mail to its members with internet access.

Exploring punishment as communication: first-round interviews

I interviewed 63 individuals in total.[20] Interviews were mostly conducted in the office where probation staff worked and offenders were supervised, or court where magistrates were sitting, although some interviews with magistrates were conducted at their homes. I interviewed victims either at the Institute of Criminology or at their places of work. In interviewing offenders, I sought to dispel any impression they might have that what they said would assist them – perhaps because they imagined I would put in a good word for them with probation staff who made decisions impinging on their life and liberty.

In order to gauge how much thought victims had previously given to the question of punishment, I asked them how important this was to them.[21] They all said that the issue was very or pretty important – no doubt this had prompted these victims to come forward for interview in response to my invitation. In any event, their comments showed that they had given the matter considerable attention; they displayed a great deal of thoughtfulness and in some cases an impressive amount of knowledge. In common with other groups, victims were aware of tensions between the various aims of punishment and had ideas about how these might be resolved. Furthermore, as found in previous research, these victims did not appear particularly vindictive in their views about what society should do with lawbreakers (I made it clear that I was asking these questions at a general level rather than about 'their' offenders, although discussion of the latter inevitably occurred). These matters will emerge in subsequent chapters as I report my findings.

All interviews followed the same broad guide but were otherwise unstructured so that they followed the person's train of thought and enabled me to probe ideas as they came up. Having made assurances about maintaining participants' anonymity, I started the interviews by exploring what they thought a court was attempting to achieve in sentencing an offender and how community penalties fitted in. Drawing on the lessons of previous public opinion research, I asked what type of offender the interviewee had in mind and whether he or she might have answered differently, as the case might be, for a recidivist or a first-time offender, or a violent or property offender. I then sought to prompt as many ideas as possible about the kinds of messages that courts might be seeking to transmit in sentencing and the kinds of responses that might be expected from offenders. I also asked how the court should decide how much punishment to give an offender and whether there were any situations in which punishment should be reduced or where there should be no punishment. Finally, I asked whether interview participants saw any messages as being sent out while the person was actually serving the sentence, and whether the relevant processes or penalties might be developed to send out clearer or more appropriate messages.

Often exceeding an hour in length, the interviews produced an enormous amount of complex material, which I analysed using NUD.IST (all interviews were tape recorded, with participants' consent, and fully transcribed).[22] 'Communication' emerged as a theme right at the start of the interviews, even before I specifically raised the topic of the messages transmitted through the act of sentencing. The interviews generated the themes that – together with specific ideas from the theoretical literature – I drew upon in formulating the questionnaires for the next phase of my research. They were also the source of a number of phrases that I adopted in the questionnaires as the best way in which to convey particular sentencing purposes or messages in ordinary language. In addition, they produced a great deal of explanatory material that helped to make sense of questionnaire findings from which it was possible to conclude that a particular principle or idea was seen as important but not necessarily *why*.

Adding quantitative weight: questionnaires

The draft questionnaire was piloted with at least half a dozen individuals in each group before being administered, enabling me to refine it considerably to ensure that instructions were clear and phrases interpreted as I intended.[23] During these pilots, I actually went through the questionnaire with the person completing it, so that they could point out phrases that were unclear or misleading and I could check that they had read the questionnaire as intended. Although it is not possible to be entirely sure that respondents have interpreted a questionnaire uniformly, the piloting process together with the detailed exploration of the relevant ideas in interviews gave me considerable confidence that this was the case, as did the consistency of responses as they emerged in analysis.

The final version of the questionnaire appears in the Appendix; questionnaires administered to each group of respondents were identical except for the final question asking for background information, which was tailored for each group. I introduced the questionnaire by reminding people that their answers would be handled confidentially and giving them an indication of how long it would take them to complete the questions (about 20 minutes). I left the request for some background information about respondents until the end of the questionnaire. Mindful of the finding from public opinion research that people tend to think about serious crimes and not about non-custodial options, I reminded respondents at the top of each page to think about offenders sentenced for crimes such as theft, car crime, break-ins and minor assaults or fights. I also asked them not to think only of a prison sentence.

In constructing the questionnaire, I made every effort to ensure that different ideas were presented as neutrally as possible and given equal status, so as to avoid leading respondents towards or against one idea or another. The questionnaire began by asking people about the purposes of sentencing and about the purposes of specific orders. It also asked them whether they saw the most important aim in sentencing an offender as retributive or consequentialist. It then moved on to the question of 'how much' punishment a court should impose, and the circumstances in which offenders should receive a reduced sentence. The second part of the questionnaire dealt with the role of communication within punishment: what the court should be saying in sentencing and in using particular orders, and how offenders should respond. Mostly, respondents were invited to select or to indicate how far they agreed with given statements. This was unavoidably a relatively complex and quite demanding questionnaire. I was aware that I would need to work hard to achieve my target of 600 completed questionnaires (150 from each of the four groups).

In the event, I received 771 completed questionnaires: well over twice my target for magistrates (385), but considerably below it for victims (111). I achieved close to my target for probation staff (132) and offenders (143). Administering questionnaires through similar routes as I had secured access to interview participants, my strategy varied slightly for different groups according to what I was able to negotiate and what seemed most likely to generate the highest response rate (response rates varied widely). To some extent, then, my sampling was opportunistic. E-mail administration proved the least successful, and face-to-face administration the most (people rarely rejected a direct appeal). Postal administration (or via pigeon holes), where the questionnaires had to be returned in a stamped addressed envelope, yielded response rates varying between 30 and 50 per cent. Victims receiving questionnaires at their home addresses did not return them in great numbers (even with the inducement of a Boots voucher), but for an unknown proportion this may have been because addresses had changed (some letters were returned through the post office).[24] The following summarises how I administered questionnaires to each group, and the response rates secured:

- *Magistrates.* Questionnaires were deposited in the pigeon holes of all magistrates sitting on two benches in Hertfordshire and two benches in Bedfordshire (Cambridgeshire declined to take part in this stage of the research). Of 285 questionnaires administered in Bedfordshire, 88 were completed (a response rate of 31 per cent). In Hertfordshire, 209 were administered and 78 completed (a response rate of 37 per cent). In addition, 271 questionnaires were returned by magistrates from across the country who had received them by e-mail from the Magistrates' Association (around 3,000 were administered in this way, a response rate of 9 per cent). Unfortunately, 52 of these were lost in onwards transmission while still in electronic form, leaving 219 usable questionnaires.

- *Probation and CS staff.* Of 100 questionnaires administered to CS and probation staff at a regional CS conference, 40 were completed (a response rate of 40 per cent). A further 29 questionnaires were administered face to face to CS staff on visits to CS offices and sites (none refused). Questionnaires were generally administered to probation officers by being deposited in their pigeon holes; response rates in different offices varied between 30 and 48 per cent and a total of 35 questionnaires were completed out of 95 administered in this way (an overall response rate of 37 per cent). A further 20 questionnaires (out of 24) were completed by probation trainees at a regional training event, and the remaining 7 questionnaires were administered face to face on visits to probation offices.

• *Offenders.* Of 143 questionnaires completed by offenders, most were as a result of face-to-face administration on my visits to CS work sites or probation offices (very few refused). They were serving community rehabilitation, community punishment or combined orders. Question-naires were administered by post via probation officers to London-based offenders but very few completed (3 out of a batch of 40 questionnaires).

• *Victims.* Questionnaires were administered by victims organisations to victims of 'middle-range' crimes who were unknown to me. Of 500 victims contacted (200 in London, 300 locally, in batches of 100), 111 completed questionnaires. This amounted to a response rate of 22 per cent, which was slightly higher for second and third batches of questionnaires where there was an offer of a Boots voucher to compensate people for their time in completing a questionnaire.

Table 3.1 shows the characteristics of the different groups of respondents. It will be seen that magistrates were considerable older than other groups and offenders considerable younger. Offenders, as one might expect, were overwhelmingly male, while victims comprised a higher proportion of women than any other group. In analysis, it was difficult to establish whether a particular view expressed by women, for example, reflected male–female differences or the fact that women were more likely to be victims and less likely to be offenders. When it came to prior experiences, 39 (27 per cent) of the offenders had previously served a

Table 3.1 Characteristics of questionnaire respondents

Group	Number (% total)	Male (%)	Female (%)	Average age
Magistrates	385 (50%)	216 (57%)	164 (43%)	49
Probation staff	76 (10%)	38 (50%)	38 (50%)	36
CS staff	56 (7%)	31 (55%)	25 (45%)	42
Victims	111 (14%)	43 (40%)	65 (60%)	39
Offenders	143 (16%)	126 (90%)	14 (10%)	25
Overall	*771*	*454 (60%)*	*306 (40%)*	*41*

custodial sentence (the method of administration ensured that all had some experience of community disposals). Around a quarter (33) of the probation staff described themselves as managers, and just over 40 per cent (158) of the magistrates were bench chairs as opposed to wingers. As the overall sample was so heavily weighted towards magistrates, in presenting my findings I have treated the different groups as individual samples rather than as subgroups of one overall sample. Approaching the analysis in this way has provided plenty of scope to compare the views of magistrates with those of offenders or victims, with some revealing results.

Questionnaire analysis was conducted in SPSS (Statistical Package for the Social Sciences), giving me maximum flexibility to compare the views of different groups of respondent, according both to whether they were magistrates, staff, victims or offenders and to characteristics such as age or sex. Where appropriate, tests of statistical significance were conducted to assess whether different patterns in responses represented real or chance differences.[25]

Follow-up interviews

The questionnaire package included a slip inviting respondents to indicate whether they were prepared to participate in a follow-up interview to explore their questionnaire responses, to which a relatively large proportion responded positively (ranging between about 30 per cent of probation staff and 50 per cent of victims). For a variety of reasons, this element of the fieldwork was delayed so that it was no longer feasible to conduct the number of follow-up interviews I had originally planned (10 from each of my groups of respondents, or 40 in total). I therefore arranged interviews with 12 individuals (three from each group) whose views reflected the range emerging from question- naire analysis. One of the victims failed to keep our appointment, so I completed 11 interviews (most of these were by telephone, with two people taking up the option of coming to the Institute for an interview). These follow-up interviews (again, tape recorded and fully transcribed) yielded fascinating insights which feature significantly in the analysis reported in subsequent chapters. I was able to ask respondents to discuss very specific questions raised in my analysis of first-round interviews and questionnaires, using hypothetical examples to probe an issue in greater depth. They also enabled me to investigate apparent tensions revealed by questionnaire responses, for example how an individual would see the balance between crime reduction and retribution on certain questions where both appeared to have been rated equally on the questionnaire. Unfortunately, their importance is limited by my conduc- ting fewer follow-up interviews than I had wished.

It is necessary to acknowledge the limitations to the research reported in this book. First of all, I cannot claim that the findings can be generalised: that I have 'proved' that magistrates, probation staff, victims or offenders hold certain views. To the extent that individuals were selected, or self-selected, to participate in the research, these were not randomly selected representative samples.[26] Response rates were low, especially for victims, and I had no way of checking whether the people who chose to put themselves forward for interview or to complete questionnaires had similar characteristics to those who did not. However, I believe that the findings are useful as an exploration of how particular groups of people with an interest in criminal justice made sense of the role of sentencing and how they dealt with some of the normative questions debated in the literature. In deploying a quantitative analysis through the questionnaires, my chief concern was not with 'proof' but to clarify how people weighed up various considerations, for example what priority they gave to proportionality and the relative importance ascribed to deterrence or to more constructive methods of inducing law-abiding behaviour. Given the assumptions often made about what people think, it seems useful to give individuals an opportunity to speak for themselves (and it was certainly very interesting to do so). Readers will be able to judge, on the basis of the literature and their own knowledge and experience, whether the views reported below might plausibly be held by other magistrates, victims and so on. It could be argued that my interviews and surveys captured views that, albeit not representative, might be typical of those groups of people. My respondents did not seem unusual in terms of their age, gender or mix of experience; as will be seen, their views seemed cogent and well-reasoned.

Another limitation was that I used questionnaires and interviews with different respondents (although a number of first-round interviewees were given the opportunity to and did complete questionnaires). It is questionable to say the least whether discussions in first-round interviews bore any relation to questionnaire responses given by different participants. Connections between the two are therefore necessarily tentative, but it was often the case that views expressed in first-round interviews were consistent with the patterns of responses to questionnaires. Explanations in follow-up interviews often fitted in with what had been said (albeit by different individuals) in first-round interviews, and they added analytical depth by allowing me to probe very specific questions in the light of questionnaire responses. In presenting findings in the following chapters, I will discuss the interplay – and the tensions – between data yielded in the respective phases of my fieldwork.

I was taking on a challenging task in seeking stakeholders' normative views on what the aims of punishment ought to be in principle, and what messages it ought to be used to convey. It was difficult to ensure that people addressed those 'ideal' questions rather than what penal practices actually achieve or mean or what those who are using those practices might be seeking to achieve (or even what might be achievable in the current system). Although I used my best endeavours in constructing and piloting the questionnaire and in bringing people back to the questions I was seeking to address in interview, it would have been unrealistic for me to expect people always to deal with these questions at the idealised conceptual level. Nonetheless, the research has generated much interesting material about the 'ought' questions. I would not see it as providing definitive answers to those questions, but as opening up some fresh lines of enquiry that might advance the theoretical debates.

Do stakeholders' views matter?

An important question raised by research of the kind I was pursuing into people's views of normative questions is 'why bother?' Views on these sorts of issues are often seen as predictable, subjective, prejudiced or informed by ignorance of the relevant considerations. This is a viewpoint with which I strongly disagree. Like Stalans (2002), I believe that human beings are socialised to think about questions of fairness and justice from a very early age and have vast personal experiences on which to draw. With Robinson and Darley (1995), I would urge us to care about the moral credibility of the criminal and penal code. From a normative perspective, a discrepancy with thinking on the ground, requires a penal theorist to re-examine his or her position – or at least so it seems to me. Moreover, the theoretical debates have opened up questions on which it seems useful to introduce some fresh, practically minded thinking, especially from people who have to make – or who are affected by – the practical decision-making in which such questions have necessarily to be resolved. As Bottoms (2000) argues, empirical work can advance normative analysis.

From a utilitarian perspective, criminal justice requires a certain level of consensus – and compliance – if it is to secure cooperation and prove effective. Without that, people might, depending on their positions, fail to report crimes, take the law into their own hands, ignore its strictures or subvert its purpose. If we want those who implement the law, whether they are sentencers, probation staff or other criminal justice agents, to comply with it in spirit as well as letter, it seems important to investigate whether it accords with their understanding of how things should be. To take a particular theoretical position set out in Chapter 2, if the aim of punishment is morally to persuade offenders to desist, is this sort of moralising comprehensible to those who are supposed to be doing it or those who are at the receiving end? If not, why might that be the case? Does it mean that the theory is 'wrong', or that the conditions for its implementation have yet to be satisfied?

Conclusions

This chapter started by reviewing the research on public opinion, mainly in the UK and the US, in order to provide a context for my own – albeit somewhat different – empirical study. One common finding to emerge from that body of research that is directly relevant to my enquiry is that victims are no more 'punitive' than the general population, that they are not especially vindictive and that they show a considerable level of support for reparative or restorative disposals. Despite the complexities of undertaking this kind of research, the literature indicates that it is possible to find out what members of the public think about sentencing and that their views are worth investigating and relevant to sentencing policies. A slightly different question is whether it is possible, and desirable, to inform the public about criminal justice and sentencing. My concerns lay in a different direction again: in what 'informed' (or at least, in the case of victims, 'interested') groups thought about certain normative questions about punishment as an institution. The research methodology I used to address these matters was primarily qualitative and exploratory in focus, albeit with a strong quantitative component, the aim being to take forward normative analysis rather than to test explanatory theory. In all, I conducted 74 interviews and received 771 completed questionnaires; both presented analytical challenges and yielded fascinating insights, as the next three chapters reveal.

Notes

1   The BCS was set up in 1982 by the Home Office as a national survey of a representative sample of people aged 16 or over, asking about their experiences of victimisation and their views of various aspects of crime and criminal justice, and is now conducted annually. In 1996, there were 16,348 respondents, a response rate of 83 and in 1998, 14,947, a response rate of 79 per cent.
2   In both 1996 and 1998, over half the respondents made large underestimates of the use of custody for burglary and rape.
3   There was evidence that persistence was seen to warrant a more severe sentence, and that it was a more important factor than age.
4   Hough and Park (2002) reanalysed data from a deliberative TV poll conducted in 1994 in which a nationally representative sample of 869 respondents were asked about their views about crime and punishment, of

whom 297 subsequently attended a televised weekend event. Those attending the event were sent briefing materials and given presentations by criminal justice practitioners, academics and politicians, and were able to question the speakers and participate in discussions. They completed the questionnaire again immediately after the weekend and were reinterviewed ten months later to assess the durability of any changes in their views. Significant and enduring changes were found that could be attributed with some confidence to the deliberative poll event: reduced support for imprisonment and punitive options; increased support for rehabilitation and prevention aimed at 'root causes'.

5 In line with the BCS, knowledge of current sentencing practice was particularly poor, with the use of custody for burglary being considerably underestimated.

6 Those who thought prison was very or fairly effective at reducing crime increased from 83 per cent before receiving information to 91 per cent afterwards. There was also a considerable, and increased, level of support for prison + supervision (87 per cent very or fairly effective before receiving information and 93 per cent afterwards). Support for probation also increased, from 44 per cent before receiving information to 61 per cent afterwards, as did that for community service (from 37 per cent to 46 per cent) and drug treatment schemes (from 67 per cent to 77 per cent). In the case of prison and prison + supervision, most of the change occurred in the proportions seeing the disposal as 'very effective'; in the case of drug treatment, probation and community service, it was in the proportions seeing the disposal as 'fairly effective'. Support for electronic tagging actually fell following information (from 55 per cent to 51 per cent). Looking at an 'informed' subsample of all groups, the Halliday Report (Home Office 2001) reported higher levels of support for probation (69 per cent) and community service (54 per cent).

7 The ICVS has covered 60 countries across the world in sweeps conducted in 1989, 1993, 1996 and 2000, achieving samples of 2,000 people aged 16 or over in most industrialised countries.

8 A majority (40 per cent versus 34 per cent) was also in favour of community service in Eastern and Central Europe. Elsewhere, in the New World, Latin America, Asia and Africa, a higher proportion was in favour of prison.

9 There was an upwards trend over time across Western Europe and the New World as a whole, but the rise was largest in England and Wales. Canada and the Netherlands both showed a 12 per cent increase.

10 In Canada, there was widespread confusion and ignorance about the 'conditional sentence' despite widespread media coverage in the five years since its creation. In the BCS, only a third of the sample named probation when asked to identify community sentences.

11 When the conditions were not specified, 72 per cent of the sample opted for custody for a recidivist offender convicted of breaking into a shop and stealing $1,500, and 28 per cent for the conditional sentence. However, the sample told that the conditional sentence required the offender to remain at home after 7 p.m. every night, pay the money back, perform community service and report to authorities twice a week for six months expressed

greater support for the conditional sentence (65 per cent as opposed to 35 per cent who would send the offender to prison for six months).

12 According to Cullen et al., the factorial survey approach allows respondents to rate fairly detailed scenarios reflecting the features of real-life criminal cases. The researcher selects the information to be included (type of crime, offender and victim characteristics) and uses a computer to randomly combine these variables to create a pool of unique vignettes. The impact of the different variables can then be distinguished in analysis. By providing a considerable level of detail, this kind of survey avoids the possible bias of punishment scores being inflated because respondents assume that the offence is the most serious of its kind.

13 In the polls presented by Cullen et al. (2000), the proportions agreeing that the main emphasis of prison should be rehabilitation declined from 73 per cent in 1968 to 59 per cent in 1982 and well below 50 per cent in the mid-1990s, but the corresponding proportion was 55 per cent in the study reported in Cullen et al. (2002).

14 Likewise, Stalans and Roberts (1997) interpret research from the US, Canada and Australia as showing that the public endorses several aims simultaneously depending upon the nature of the crime and the offender (thus rehabilitation was seen as the main purpose of prison for first time offenders but not for recidivists).

15 The authors concede that they did not use large randomly selected samples that would provide an entirely convincing mapping of community standards, but argue that their research subjects (at least 30 for each set of cases) were sufficiently broad in their demographic distribution to reflect the views of typical US citizens.

16 I made efforts to include staff working in both probation and community service. Where there are interesting differences, I have distinguished between the two staff groups in presenting findings.

17 Here, I supplemented my data collection with a certain amount of courtroom observation on my visits to magistrates' courts to interview and administer questionnaires to lay magistrates. Although not a systematic aspect of my research, as my opportunities to observe 'sentencing in action' were limited, this observation helped me make sense of the views expressed.

18 One exception is a New Zealand survey of people sentenced to periodic detention (Searle et al. 2003). However, its scope was somewhat restricted: offenders were asked to rank sanctions in terms of severity and which were most likely to serve the purposes of deterrence and rehabilitation. They were also asked about the fairness of their sentence. When asked general questions about crime rates and sentencing practice, they revealed similar misconceptions to the public samples discussed earlier: crime rates were thought to be increasing and sentence lengths were underestimated. Sentencing scenarios revealed a high level of support for custody for assault on a female and aggravated burglary, and support for a community-based sentence and reparation for theft through fraudulent use.

19 Here, I was motivated by the wish both to research the views of victims of the kinds of offences that might well result in a community penalty and to avoid recreating traumatic experiences for people who had experienced very

serious crimes. I therefore agreed with the victims organisation that an approach would be made to people who had been referred to them having experienced a theft, theft from a vehicle or minor break-in within the previous year. Needless to say, this strategy was not foolproof; in one case, the burglars had returned to commit a far more serious burglary shortly before my interview with the victim.

20 My aim was to interview 60 people, 15 from each of the four groups listed above. In the event, I interviewed 29 women and 34 men – fewer victims than I had hoped (just 10, compared with 22 magistrates). There were 18 probation staff and 13 offenders; perhaps inevitably, the latter had a younger profile than the other groups and only three of them were female (other groups were fairly equally composed of men and women).

21 It seemed reasonable to assume that magistrates, probation staff and offenders had all given the issue considerable thought given their involvement with sentencing and its consequences.

22 NUD.IST (Non-numerical Unstructured Data Indexing Searching and Theorising) is a software package for the analysis of unstructured data of the type generated in exploratory interviews (see: http://www.sagepub.co.uk). It enables data to be coded in an index system so that text or patterns of coding can be searched to develop and explore theories about the data; codes can be created as one goes through the interviews, so that they emerge directly from the data. It is particularly beneficial in enabling large quantities of unstructured text to be handled with relative ease, coded systematically and coded material retrieved (see Richards and Richards 1998).

23 Because of the difficulties of gaining access to 'real' victims, I piloted the questionnaire with volunteers among the Institute's library and administrative staff who had experienced crime.

24 Postal administration relying on names and addresses held by another body, which I had no way of checking, is hardly likely to yield high response rates, but was the only available method that guaranteed the complete anonymity properly required by the victims organisation.

25 Using chi-square tests, T-tests and one-way analysis of variance as appropriate. These tests in SPSS enabled me to test significance at both the 99 per cent level of confidence ($p < 0.01$) and at the 95 per cent level ($p < 0.05$) – see Bryman and Cramer (2001).

26 However, in some cases, invitations to participate in the research went to the whole of the relevant population, for example to all magistrates sitting on a particular bench, to all victims who fitted the criteria, etc.

Chapter 4

Prioritising penal aims

Introduction

This chapter addresses one particular debate in the penal theory literature: whether it is possible to reconcile proportionality with crime prevention and how a proper balance might be achieved between them. It is in two sections. The first looks at the theoretical questions and examines what might be learnt from the implementation of a supposedly deserts-based model in the Criminal Justice Act 1991. The second then draws on my own empirical work to explore the views expressed by magistrates, probation staff, offenders and victims on the underlying issues. A question that is pertinent in the UK context is how courts deal with prior record. Is taking an offender's history into account consistent with a principle of proportionality or does it amount to covert incapacitative sentencing?

I. Reconciling proportionality and crime prevention in theory

Most penal theories incorporate some notion of proportionality. Even where the emphasis is on crime prevention, a relationship between the sentence and the gravity of the offence is often envisaged. For utilitarians, the seriousness of the harm is indeed relevant to the amount of punishment that may be justified to restrain it, to guard against the relevant mischief at as cheap a rate as possible (Jeremy Bentham, 1789, extract in von Hirsch and Ashworth 1998). Similarly, Braithwaite (2003) argues that it is possible to develop a consequentialist justification against breaching upper constraints on punishment.[1] In contrast with these consequentialist positions, Andrew von Hirsch and Andrew Duff both give the gravity of the offence a central role in the penal theories explained in Chapter 2. However, they do so with very different emphases, as will become clear in the following discussion.

For von Hirsch, because the primary function of a sanction is to express disapproval or blame, its severity must reflect the comparative blameworthiness of the conduct in order to sustain the normative message. If the preventive message is allowed to become too prominent, it would amount to treating offenders, not as moral agents, but as 'tigers in a circus' capable of responding only to threats (1993: 11). This means that when one moves from 'why punish' to decisions about 'how much' in von Hirsch's desert theory, the severity of the sentence is determined by the requirements of proportionality. This dictates that offences should be punished according to their rank ordering in terms of seriousness (ordinal proportionality) and offenders who are similarly culpable should receive punishments that are similarly severe. When it comes to sentencing decisions, then, von Hirsch's scheme is not so much a hybrid as an accommodation of crime preventive *content* within desert-based *amounts* of punishment. Von Hirch is clear that 'making prevention part of the justification for punishment's existence, in the manner that I have, does not permit it to operate independently as a basis for deciding comparative punishments' (1993: 17).

By contrast, Duff argues that 'a communicative system of . . . punishment . . . should be structured by a negative . . . principle of proportionality' (2001: 139), such as that espoused by Morris and Tonry (1990). This proscribes disproportionate sentences but does not require sentencers to impose sanctions that are proportionate in a positive (or defining) sense. The position of 'limiting retributivists' such as Morris (1998) is that, within the upper and lower limits set by the injunction against disproportionately harsh or disproportionately lenient sentences, other considerations (such as crime prevention or penal parsimony) will determine the actual size of the punishment. However, Duff distinguishes himself from limiting retributivists by asserting that he is not advocating that proportionality 'merely sets side constraints on our pursuit of penal aims in which proportionality plays no part' (2001: 142). His aim is to set strong constraints on sentencing, while leaving sentencers with a range of possible sentences from which to select the one that is substantively apt 'to communicate an appropriate understanding of the particular crime and its implications' (2001: 143). That understanding is, according to Duff, hindered by the requirements to rank all crimes on a single scale of seriousness, and to set strict limits on the range of available modes of punishment that would be imposed by a defining principle of proportionality as propounded by von Hirsch.[2]

Unfortunately, to reiterate a point Bottoms (1995) makes about varied interpretations, without specific attention to how proportionality constrains sentencing in practice, the effect may well be that it becomes secondary to consequentialist considerations. I shall illustrate this point below by discussing the English experience of applying desert principles to community penalties. It means that, although Duff (2001) may intend proportionality to be intrinsic to his scheme, it may easily come to assume a minor role if not pursued positively. A similar difficulty is encountered by Bottoms's (1998) argument that it makes little sense to describe censure or prevention as primary; they should be seen as co-equal and interactive. For Bottoms, the important point is to seek the right balance between allowing a wide range of non-custodial measures to swamp the principle of proportionality and allowing that principle to swamp other justifiable grounds of punishment. However desirable in theory, the question raised by the English experience is whether it is possible in practice to achieve this kind of equality between the two sentencing goals. As von Hirsch (1993) points out, a hybrid strategy confronts a fairness–effectiveness dilemma, in which there is little to gain in terms of incapacitation or rehabilitation if one is to preserve a reasonable relationship between the gravity of the offence and the severity of the sentence. On the other hand, if large departures from proportionality are allowed, as seems to have been the case under the English model, the scheme can no longer be said to have a basis in desert.

An English case study

An attempt was indeed made in the English Criminal Justice Act 1991 (the 1991 Act) to adopt a hybrid model in relation to community penalties which accorded proportionality (or censure) and prevention apparently co-equal status. At the time of writing, the statutory provisions relating to community sentences remain in force, as does the desert-based sentencing framework in the 1991 Act, and the Criminal Justice Act 2003 largely preserves the main principles. It is useful to examine experience under the 1991 Act, as it illustrates some of the complexities of combining proportionality with crime-preventive goals.

The first legislative restriction that the 1991 Act placed upon the sentencer was a negative principle of proportionality, in that the sanction imposed for a given offence should not be undeserved. The use of community sentences was confined to offences falling within an intermediate band of seriousness contained by the requirements for the offence to be 'serious enough' to warrant a community sentence (section 6(1)), but not 'so serious' that only custody can be justified (section 1(2)). But the legislation did not merely proscribe an 'undeserved' community order. Having decided that an offence fell within the community sentence band, the sentencer applied the criteria in section 6(2). These required the judge or magistrate to select the community order that was *most suitable* for the offender and imposed restrictions on liberty *commensurate with* the seriousness of the offence. The intention seemed to be that desert will actually determine the size of the penalty and suitability its form. For example, where the sentencer(s) were of the view that it was appropriate to rehabilitate the offender, they might use a probation order (consistent with the rehabilitative criteria under section 8 of the 1991 Act).

As discussed in Rex [1998], a model proposed by Wasik and von Hirsch (1988) seemed to have been the inspiration for the provisions in section 6 of the 1991 Act. Wasik and von Hirsch would allow an equally 'deserved' sanction within each sentencing band to be substituted for a standard penalty – usually a financial one – on the grounds that it might be more effective in preventing the offender from offending again in the future. Bottoms (1989) suggested that there was no need to prescribe a penalty as standard within each band, and queried the prominence given to the fine. His modifications appear to have been adopted in the legislation, which placed fines beneath community orders in the overall hierarchy of sentences (Ashworth 2000). Unfortunately, whether or not it was the statutory intention to introduce strong desert constraints, sentencing trends immediately following the Act suggest a different outcome, attributable largely to a failure adequately to define the all-important phrases 'so serious' or 'serious enough' either in statute or in judicial guidance (see Rex [1998]). The lack of guidance on seriousness was compounded by the absence of legislative assistance on when a court should prioritise proportionality and when suitability. For individual offenders, and those making sentencing decisions in relation to them, this is hardly an academic – or formal – matter. In one case, a court may want to give an offender an order requiring him or her to attend a lengthy programme that might tackle the behaviour underlying his or her offending but 'justice' might demand a short period of community service. In another case, a court may be compelled to give an offender a 'deserved' 12-month prison sentence that will deny access to a rehabilitative programme.

Despite his scepticism about the feasibility of true hybrid models, von Hirsch (1993) supports the application of a limited 'range' model to non-custodial options, which allows substitutions between sanctions to be made more easily and slightly more severe sanctions to be imposed for breach of a community order. This is the kind of pragmatic compromise apparently sought in section 6 of the 1991 Act; unfortunately, it is unclear whether the product is a workable scheme. In practice, tensions between the aims of rehabilitation and desert – between what might avert future offending and what might be warranted by the gravity of the offence – were revealed by experience following the implementation of the 1991 Act. The consequence has been that one consideration has overshadowed the other, so that a balance between the two has remained elusive. Initially, when the legislation was introduced in October 1992, the focus was on desert (and punishment), and rehabilitative sanctions, such as probation, suffered. Since the emphasis on public protectionism began in the mid-1990s, the focus has shifted to preventing further offending, to the detriment of proportionality. Not only has community service (traditionally a retributive sanction) declined in fortunes as a result, but there are also signs that community-based penalties have been used for less serious offences and offenders, as discussed in Chapter 2. It is entirely arguable that the 1991 Act was not really given an opportunity to work (Rex [1998]; Nellis 2001), and that it is still worth seeking a balance between proportionality and crime prevention.

Reconciling proportionality and crime prevention in practice

The specific question that arises in the light of the experience of the 1991 Act is whether it is possible to pursue crime reduction within a framework of proportionality, a question to which there are several parts. A practical consideration is whether principles of proportionality can be applied meaningfully to community-based options. Another consideration is more philosophical in nature, arising from the possibility that rehabilitation and retribution are at some fundamental level irreconcilable, but has important practical implications.

Dealing first with the practicalities, the question in effect is whether it is possible to translate the different community orders into 'restrictions on liberty' (to use the 1991 Act terminology) that can be measured and compared. There is a prior question: whether 'severity' can ever be objectively measured, a point on which there is considerable disagreement.[3] The futility of attempting to achieve objective measurement is often put forward as an argument against the positive principle of proportionality adopted by von Hirsch. Morris and Tonry, for example, argue that 'in sentencing, . . . no generic man stands before the court, but countless individuals' (1990: 94). The most one can feasibly aim for is therefore the not undeserved, and least intrusive, sanction likely to have the desired effect (whether deterrent, rehabilitative or incapacitative).

One aspect of the problem, as Tonry (1998a) has pointed out in relation to US sentencing guidelines, is the tendency for the proportionality principle to be interpreted as meaning that punishments must be tied predominantly to offenders' crimes and criminal records, thereby ignoring important social considerations. This is not an inevitable consequence of a desert-based approach to sentencing – see discussions on social deprivation in von Hirsch (1993: epilogue), Hudson (1998), von

Hirsch (2002a). Drawing on research on pre-sentence reports, Raynor points to 'strong indications that even under the 1991 Act sentencers believe that a just sentence must take into account the social context of the offender and the offence and the prospects for future behaviour under different sentences' (1997: 256).

Walker (1992) specifically challenges a genuinely desert-oriented approach to achieve true 'equality of impact': to ensure that similarly culpable offenders personally suffer the same amount of hardship, given the differences in people's sensibilities (or perceptions of painfulness). Von Hirsch's (1993) response is that objective values can be placed upon the freedoms of which punishments deprive offenders; severity is not simply a matter of variable subjective unpleasantness. Drawing upon ideas developed with Nils Jareborg (von Hirsch and Jareborg 1991) as a starting point for gauging the comparative seriousness of different crimes, he suggests that a living standards analysis can be used to gauge the comparative severity of different penalties. This would take certain 'interests' (such as freedom of movement and privacy) as the basis for analysing the impact of different penalties on the quality of persons' lives. In Bottoms's (1998) judgement, von Hirsch has the better of the argument. For Bottoms, the inevitable – and unjustifiable – consequence of the 'sensibility' approach is that individuals of a higher status will benefit because a given penalty will be seen to hit them harder than individuals of a lower rank.

It has proved difficult to compare community service (compulsory work) with the kinds of restrictions imposed by probation (community supervision) where it is the person themselves rather than their performance of a task that is being supervised. Measured in terms of 'contact hours' (attendance at appointments), a one-year standard probation order would involve approximately 21 hours of formal 'restrictions on liberty', as actually calculated by one English probation service following the implementation of the 1991 Act (Rex 1997). This does not even equate with the minimum length of a community service order (40 hours, normally completed within just six weeks). As I have argued elsewhere (Rex 1997, cited in Bottoms 1998), a focus on *physical* restrictions such as the number of actual contact hours fails to do justice to the demands of a probation order. Probationers may often be attempting lifestyle changes such as refraining from alcohol or drugs or restraining aggressive reactions to particular situations. But can such activities actually be *measured*?

Schiff (1998) has in fact developed an interests-based approach to the assessment of different intermediate sanctions (those between prison and probation) in the United States, to which Rex and von Hirsch (1998) have proposed modifications to accommodate the psychological restrictions and loss of privacy entailed in probation supervision.[4] This might provide a practical starting point for the development of a standard scale for assessing the severity of different community orders, a possible task for the Sentencing Guidelines Council established under the Criminal Justice Act 2003. Modified by Rex and von Hirsch, the scale proposed by Schiff would look as follows (different 'values' could be assigned to the various parameters to reflect their relative weight):

1. Restriction to prescribed space (such as the home under a curfew order).

2. Prolonged period of supervision (under a probation order, for example).

3. Directly supervised compulsory activities (such as CS work, drug treatment).

4. Restrictions on normal activities and constraints on choice (such as refraining from consuming alcohol).

5. Loss of privacy.

Whether, to what extent and in what circumstances proportionality *should* prevail over crime prevention in sentencing decisions involves normative as well as practical considerations. Even as interactive co-equals (Bottoms 1998), there will be occasions when desert will have to be prioritised over crime preventive goals and vice versa. As a proponent of 'new rehabilitationism', inspired by a wish to distinguish it from the 'treatment' model so thoroughly discredited in the 1970s, Raynor (1997) is looking for synthesis between effective rehabilitation and justice, though he is aware of the tensions between backwards-looking retributivism and forwards-looking consequentialism. For him and others, the appropriate compromise is to pursue rehabilitative goals within a framework of sentences proportionate to the gravity of the offence (Raynor 1997; Hudson 1995).

This is a point on which some degree of consensus is emerging. More recently, Tonry too appears to have been prepared to contemplate relatively stringent proportionality constraints, proposing 'sentencing ranges in which the upper bounds are set in accordance with the proportionality principle and the lower bounds are sufficiently flexible to honour the parsimony principle' (1998b: 201).[5] Reviewing US sentencing guidelines, Tonry (1998c) suggests that the most promising approach might be to introduce four to six 'zones of discretion' with provision for roughly equivalent community (or intermediate) sanctions to be interchanged. This proposal seems to be bear some resemblance to the model developed by Wasik and von Hirsch (1988). It is similar to Raynor's

(1997) suggestion that it is possible to rank community sanctions in broadly comparable levels of seriousness, citing the five bands introduced by some probation services under the 1991 Act. The Halliday Report came up with the same sort of idea in proposing an outline tariff arranging community sentences into three tiers (Home Office 2001: 41)

Looking at the content of interventions as opposed to their size, Raynor and Vanstone (1994) have attempted to illustrate how rehabilitative programmes with the specific object of preventing further offending can respect people's moral agency, as demanded by desert theorists. In the light of new evidence about programme efficacy, the authors suggest modifications to the contractual 'non-treatment' paradigm put forward by Bottoms and McWilliams (1979), in which the principles of negotiation and informed consent were embedded. Provided the emphasis on collaboration is retained, Raynor and Vanstone argue, the tasks negotiated between probation officer and offender can be directed at reducing the latter's likelihood of offending without necessarily slipping into the model of offender pathology associated with 'treatment'. As reviewed by Rex (2001), offending behaviour programmes developed since Raynor and Vanstone were writing in the early 1990s do indeed rely heavily on teaching offenders cognitive skills to help them think about the consequences of their actions and find other ways of responding to situations (clearly based on an assumption that offenders are at least capable of reasoning and self-determination). However, as discussed in Chapter 2, these developments have come at a time when public protectionism has eclipsed proportionality in sentencing decisions. One consequence has been a growing reliance on 'risk of reconviction' to guide decision-making in criminal justice such as the assessment of offenders for suitable interventions, with implications for justice (Raynor 2001).

Accommodating prior record

A related question is how to accommodate an offender's prior criminal record in the sentencing decision. There is considerable theoretical unease as to whether prior record has any place in a deserts-based framework in which the gravity of the offence is what determines sentence. Fletcher (1978) argues that it should be ignored. Not only should offenders not be punished again for crimes for which they have already served sentence, but taking record into account amounts to covert incapacitative sentencing (previous convictions being the most useful tool for predicting future criminality – see Philpotts and Lancucki 1979). However, the prevailing view among desert theorists is that record does have a legitimate role in sentencing. The principle of progressive loss of mitigation, in which previous convictions count less than the gravity of the offence, has been justified by Wasik and von Hirsch (1994) on the basis that a sentence discount reflects the fact that a first offence represents an uncharacteristic lapse.[6]

As Duff (2001) acknowledges in supporting this theoretical justification, it is intuitively plausible. Understanding human frailty, we are prepared to tolerate momentary lapses from acceptable standards of behaviour. The difficulty lies in ensuring that, in responding to prior criminal record, sentencers are indeed excusing an uncharacteristic lapse rather than increasing sentence in response to the accumulation of past convictions. As von Hirsch has himself acknowledged, it is not necessarily easy to distinguish a discount for the first offender from a premium for the recidivist. His proposed approach is to prescribe a narrow range of deserved punishments for a given offence in excess of which recidivists should not be punished (see Wasik and von Hirsch 1994). That this does not appear to have been achieved in the case of the 1991 Act begs the question how narrative sentencing guidelines can be formulated to provide a sufficiently narrow range of deserved punishments to preserve desert as the primary consideration in sentencing.[7]

More recent sentencing policy has placed an increased emphasis on the criminal record, on the basis that 'persistent offending should justify a more severe view and more intensive efforts at preventing reoffending' (Home Office and Lord Chancellor's Department 2002: 88). These are rationales that von Hirsch (2002b) has comprehensively dismissed in examining the reasoning in the Halliday Report (Home Office 2001) for according a greater role to prior record, making points on which Duff (2001) takes similar positions – see also Roberts (2002a). On the first, taking a more severe view, von Hirsch argues that defiance of the law does not in itself warrant substantially increased penal censure. As Duff puts it, we cannot 'punish "disrespect" [for the law] as a wrong distinct from or additional to the particular substantive crimes in which it may be manifested' (2001: 168). Nor, Duff believes, can we assume that a repeat offender has shown him or herself to be determinedly committed to wrongdoing without an improper intrusion into his or her general moral character. On the 'more time for treatment' point, Halliday having rejected incapacitation and deterrence as justifications for sentencing, von Hirsch doubts that the kind of premiums envisaged by Halliday would yield the desired rehabilitative benefits. Nor would they square with proportionality constraints – whether determining or limiting. Duff perhaps offers the more principled objection that a failure to respond to moral persuasion does not justify increasing sentence until the offender is persuaded. An offender retains an essential freedom to remain unpersuaded; as punishment is not 'moral education', it can not be increased until it has the desired effect.

II. Understandings of proportionality on the ground

In this section, I turn to the empirical findings from my interviews and surveys with magistrates, staff, offenders and victims that impinge on questions of proportionality. Since a greater emphasis on the relationship between the offence and sentence is traditionally associated with retributive as opposed to consequentialist penal theory, I start with whether respondents saw retribution or consequentialism as paramount in sentencing. This might be thought to provide an indication of the extent to which they might regard proportionality as at all relevant in the first place. I then look at views concerning how decisions are made about the quantum of punishment: how respondents understood the balance between proportionality and prevention and how they weighed factors relating to the offender, his or her social circumstances and the impact of the punishment on him or her.

Prioritising penal aims

The questionnaire asked people to select what they saw as the most important aim when the court was sentencing an offender: to make the offender pay for the crime (retributivists); to stop the offender committing another crime (consequentialists); or whether they were 'not sure'. The proportions selecting each response are given in Table 4.1. Not only was this question useful in quantifying how people prioritised punishment overall, but I was also able to examine how retributivists and consequentialists reacted to other questions. I will be returning to this analysis both in this chapter and in Chapters 5 and 6 where I look at how people saw retributive and consequentialist ends being pursued.

A number of points emerge from Table 4.1.

Table 4.1 Prioritising punishment: views from questionnaire respondents

Groups*	N	Retributivists %	Consequentialists %	Not sure %
Magistrates	383	21.4	60.1	18.5
Probation/CS staff	132	11.3	84.8	3.8
Offenders	137	13.1	67.2	19.7
Victims	109	19.3	71.6	9.2
Men**	447	19.5	64.0	16.6
Women**	303	15.2	72.6	12.2

*Excludes non-respondents to this question.
**Excludes cases where sex is unknown.

- A clear majority of all groups were consequentialists, particularly staff and victims.

- Magistrates and victims were most likely be retributivists.

- Offenders are alone in selecting 'not sure' more often than retribution, but there are also a high proportion of 'not sures' among magistrates.

- Females were statistically significantly more in favour of consequentialism than were males ($p < 0.05$); this difference seems likely to be a function of being a victim or a member of staff, both groups comprising a comparatively high proportion of women.[8].

No clear age-related pattern emerged in analysis. Looking at the experience of different groups, chairs of the magistrates' bench were only slightly more in favour of consequentialism (64.3 per cent) than magistrates as a whole, and slightly less inclined towards retribution (20.4 per cent). Offenders with prior experience of custody were slightly less in favour of retribution than those without that experience. Managers in probation and CS were more willing than any other group to prioritise one option or the other (just 3 per cent said they were 'not sure'). They were more retributive than main grade staff (18.2 per cent choosing 'to make the offender pay' as the most important aim in sentencing). However, the difference fell short of statistical significance.

The priority accorded to preventing further offending by probation staff and offenders might well be a product of the current policy emphasis on crime reduction, much promoted within the Probation Service and likely to have made an impression on offenders. However, victims were also strongly in favour of sentencing being used to stop the person offending in the future, and it was a clear priority for magistrates. It is, incidentally, a common finding of public opinion research, as reported in Chapter 3. The relatively high proportion of magistrates who were apparently unclear about their priority in sentencing may seem surprising. However, comments on questionnaires suggested that this was often indicative of a wish to choose both options as 'a priority' rather than arising from indecision. In other words, those selecting 'not sure' were not necessarily dismissing retribution, but were unable to accord it (or consequentialism) the greater priority. Support for a blend of these two aims in sentencing, albeit with some emphasis on the prevention of further offending, is apparent in responses to other questions, as we shall see below and in later chapters. It was also apparent in interviews, both during the first round and the follow-up case studies, and I now turn to these interview discussions for further elucidation.

When interview participants were asked to prioritise penal aims, the need for the punishment to prevent further offending was clearly paramount. First-round interviewees expressed a belief that punishment should be serving a socially useful purpose over and above marking the offence as a wrong. However, this cannot be equated with a purely 'consequentialist' position. Strong elements of retributive thinking were evident: a sense of fairness and endorsement of proportionality, and an almost universal perception of punishment as an expression of censure. These are all ideas that I shall explore further below and in Chapters 5 and 6. Very similar themes emerged in follow-up interviews when I asked participants to place the priority they had identified in the questionnaire within the context of their overall understanding of the main purposes of sentencing – what was the whole point of the exercise. Although none had answered 'not sure' to the priority question in responding to the survey (four had prioritised retribution), retributive blended with consequentialist thinking in their views of punishment.

Interviewed probation staff often saw sentencing as serving retributive, rehabilitative and reparative aims. Within these, the prevention of further offending was prioritised, sometimes over and above the punitive element (though more usually both were recognised). Generally, retribution was rarely prioritised, and none saw punishment solely in these terms. In one follow-up interview, a female probation officer who had prioritised consequentialism in her questionnaire identified three elements. These were: punishment as the 'very first reason for sentencing' ('to represent the public in dealing with an incident of lawbreaking'); compensation for the victim (by showing that 'something has been done about the crime'); and rehabilitation ('teaching offenders a new way of behaving'). A male CS manager described himself in follow-up interview as having shifted from 'hardline retribution' in his questionnaire towards a consequentialist position as a result of 'being educated' in the course of his experience of working with offenders on CS. In the following quote from a first-round interview, a sense of reintegration and 'making amends' is expressed:

> There has to be seen to be some punishment, but I think it's also about trying to integrate people back into society and getting people to make up for what they've done wrong. (Probation officer – first-round interview)

Magistrates too saw penal purposes as mixed, placing a great deal of emphasis on preventing further offending to protect future victims. Retribution was rarely emphasised, though there was an acknowledgement that 'society as a whole expects it to be a punishment'. One female magistrate who had prioritised consequentialism in her questionnaire and in her follow-up interview disclosed a certain amount of discomfort with her retributive reactions in admitting 'sometimes, deep down, I do want them to be punished'.

One male offender who had prioritised retribution on the questionnaire saw the overriding consideration as to 'dissuade them from repeating [the offence]' when asked in follow-up interview. However, he went on to talk about 'paying for unlawful behaviour', and confirmed that punishment offered a mixture of disapproval and deterrence (an interpretation reminiscent of von Hirsch 1993). A female offender had prioritised consequentialism on her questionnaire, but portrayed punishment somewhat cynically in follow-up interview as discharging a formal duty to show that the court had done something about someone crossing the boundary of acceptable behaviour. In her view, the proper aim should be to help offenders 'sort things out themselves', but she doubted this was achieved in practice.

Similarly, the prevention of further offending seemed uppermost in victims' minds. One male victim prioritised retribution on his questionnaire and in interview described the sentence as a lesson and a reprisal, a 'measure of justice' for the victim, but was shocked at the level of punitiveness in the UK. This first-round interview with a victim conveyed particularly positive ambitions – though others shared the underlying sentiments:

> Once they have become an offender a lot of people would say that's too late. I don't. I say, well, now is our opportunity. They've got to this point in their lives where they've offended, let's look at what we can do to stop them offending again. Rather than saying 'well, OK, we'll give them a punishment, once they've done their punishment they can go on their way, that's the end of the matter.' Let's follow it through. (Victim – first-round interview)

It was already emerging in interviews that securing a response from the offender was often seen as central to the court's aim in sentencing. How and of what kind I shall be examining in more detail in Chapters 5 and 6. In expressing their sense of priorities in sentencing, the people I interviewed seemed unlikely to support an argument that seeking a response is secondary to the aim of expressing censure for the offence. In von Hirsch's terms, they do not seem to be portraying efforts at reform as merely 'additional permissible activities' rather than forming part of the justification for punishment. An element of deterrence was also evident in some thinking; whether as a prudential disincentive supplementary to penal censure (von Hirsch 1993) is a question to which we will return later. Overall, however, respondents described a 'mixed' model for sentencing, serving retributive as well as consequentialist aims. Within that model, what role was accorded to proportionality?

Deciding amounts of punishment

The complex – sometimes apparently contradictory – views expressed on proportionality in first-round interviews reflected the difficulties of the academic debate in settling the question of how strictly sentencing should be constrained by the seriousness of the offence. Despite cautious endorsement of this approach, participants saw real practical difficulties in ensuring correspondence between severity and gravity. A desire was also expressed for the punishment to fit the individual – their circumstances and the impact the punishment was likely to have on them – as well as the crime. Not only were people sceptical of the practicality of aiming for precision in matching the severity of the punishment to the gravity of the offence, but they also expressed a somewhat individualised approach to sentencing. For some, 'justice' required an understanding of the offender and the circumstances surrounding his or her offending – just as Raynor (1997) reports of magistrates working under the Criminal Justice Act 1991.

Of the theoretical positions discussed above, views conveyed in interview might be interpreted as closest to 'limiting retributivism' (Morris and Tonry 1990), allowing sufficient flexibility to enable the sentence to accommodate differing individual circumstances as well as offenders' sensibilities (Walker 1991). There was both a recognition that community service and probation might have a harsher impact on people in employment, and a feeling that some individuals might suffer more, emotionally and psychologically, than others as a result of a particular punishment. In addition, in wishing to avoid 'setting offenders up to fail', and to ensure that the sentence should consist of what was required to turn that individual away from offending, interviewees also seemed to be aware of other (crime preventive) considerations that needed to be accommodated alongside proportionality. Provisionally, it might be seen that they were looking for a disposal that was more 'substantially apt' (Duff 2001: 143) than might be achieved by strict adherence to the formal requirements of proportionality. However, it was not entirely clear how strong a role was envisaged for proportionality, and whether it was seen as acting as a real constraint in sentencing.

More detailed and specific exploration was clearly required of how proportionality figured in people's thinking and how it interacted with other considerations. Accordingly, in the questionnaire I asked the extent to which respondents agreed with ten statements concerning how the court should decide how much punishment to give an offender (5 being 'strongly agree' and 1 'not at all'). One group of statements was intended to explore the importance of proportionality; ratings are provided in Table 4.2. There is clear endorsement here of 'proportionality', particularly from magistrates, victims and staff, and relatively little support

Table 4.2 Views of proportionality: percentage agree* (and ranking in list of all statements)

Groups	N**	Proportionality 'The court should aim to match the punishment to how serious the crime was'	Fairness 'It is unfair for, say, a small theft to get more punishment than a large theft'	Crimes differ 'All crimes are different and we can't compare how serious they are'
Magistrates	378	97% (1st)	24% (9th)	27% (8th)
Staff	129	83% (1st)	36% (7th)	29% (8th)
Offenders	106	65% (4th)	62% (5th)	59% (7th)
Victims	134	85% (2nd)	38% (7th)	29% (9th)

*By selecting '4' or '5'.
**N sizes differed slightly; in this and all subsequent tables I have provided those for the statement with the highest number of responses.

beyond offenders for the view that 'crimes differ', findings that fit in with what we know from the public opinion research discussed in Chapter 3. On the other hand, support was low for 'fairness', with the exception of offenders who ranked this statement very close to 'proportionality'. Generally, this may reflect a recognition that 'crimes that share a label can be very different [. . . and] offenders committing the same crime can be very different' (Tonry 1998a: 702). It certainly does not imply an over-rigid focus on the offence to the exclusion of other factors, some of which are reviewed below, although people clearly did not find comparisons between offences impossible.

The difference in view between magistrates and offenders in relation to 'proportionality' and 'fairness' is highlighted by the fact that differences between the mean scores given by each group were statistically significant ($p < 0.01$) in both cases. However, whereas magistrates gave 'proportionality' a mean score of 4.76 and 'fairness' 2.90, offenders gave both statements a mean score of 3.86.

Some follow-up interviewees expressed strong views about the need for the sentence to match the gravity of the offence. An offender and a probation officer both thought there should be some kind of ranking of the relative gravity of different offences (although the offender had rated 'crimes differ' at 5 in her questionnaire). In the view of the probation officer, this provided some sense of justice; sentencing was a 'punishment event', so that sentence length – whether prison or probation – should reflect the gravity of the offence. A CS manager recounted the strong sense of unfairness than an offender felt at being given 180 hours CS whereas another – very similar offence under very similar circumstances – had received 40 hours. A victim thought that to base sentence length on crime preventive grounds would carry a risk of going over the top:

> If someone keeps doing petty crimes, what are you going to do to stop them? Manacle them to a railing? There has to be a line, and you have to consider what they've done, and not think too far ahead about what they're going to do in the future. You just have to say, well that's what you've done, so we'll punish you for that. And stopping you from doing things in the future is another job. (Victim – follow-up interview)

Another set of statements addressed the extent to which factors related to the offender should be taken into account. Ratings, provided in Table 4.3, show that offenders most strongly favoured an approach that acknowledged their differences, and took account of their background and the impact of the punishment on them. The view that 'offenders differ' received moderate support from all groups but comparatively strong support from offenders. Similarly, support for 'background' was moderate from magistrates and staff, with offenders giving it most support and victims being least convinced; the difference in mean scores given by victims (3.53) and offenders (4.32) was statistically significant (p <0.01). The same pattern emerged for 'impact', although differences between the respective groups were less marked. When it came to 'history', however, the reverse was the case, with offenders giving the statement less support than other groups and victims ranking it first. Here, there was a statistically significant difference (p <0.01) between the mean scores given by magistrates (4.70) and offenders (3.84).

Table 4.3 Views of offender-related factors: percentage agree (and ranking in list of all statements)

Groups	N	*Offenders differ* 'All offenders are different and they should get different punishments'	*Background* 'The court should take account of the offender's background'	*Impact* 'The court should take account of the impact of the punishment on that person'	*History* 'The court should take account of the offender's previous convictions'
Magistrates	379	61% (6th)	66% (4th)	68% (3rd)	94% (2nd)
Staff	131	49% (6th)	68% (4th)	73% (3rd)	83% (2nd)
Offenders	135	71% (3rd)	78% (1st)	74% (2nd)	61% (6th)
Victims	109	45% (6th)	56% (5th)	59% (4th)	87% (1st)

Looking at how these factors interacted with how people prioritised the overall purpose of punishment, 'history' gained higher mean scores from retributivists than from consequentialists (p < 0.05). This may indicate that the accumulation of previous convictions was seen to warrant a greater level of disapproval rather than being related to preventive considerations, according to which theoretical model is a question to which I return in the conclusions. By contrast, consequentialists gave 'impact' higher mean scores than did retributivists (p < 0.05). There was also a significant (p < 0.01) but very low correlation (0.111) between 'impact' and 'prevent' – see Table 4.4 below. Together, these perhaps indicate that people meant 'impact' in the sense of stopping that person from offending or bringing about positive change rather than the physical or psychological effect of the punishment on him or her (i.e. sensibility). However, the fact that there was a significant (p < 0.01) but low correlation (0.224) between 'impact' and 'proportionality' in the case of offenders (but not others) might suggest that offenders associated impact with whether the sentence was proportionate and just for that particular offender.

Explanations in follow-up interviews supported a crime preventive interpretation of 'impact'. An offender argued that it was important to take the possible impact on that person into account in that someone might come out of prison worse than they went in. A magistrate described sentencing as a balancing act to fit the crime and the individual, in which one question was: 'are we doing this bloke any good by sending him to prison?' A probation officer showed awareness both of the possibility that the sentence might impose undue hardship and that it might reduce the likelihood of offending, talking about the sentence as 'almost a new beginning'. Another view to emerge was that 'background' might provide an insight into how 'bad' or serious an offender was, for example whether they were offending out of need, to feed a drug habit or as a result of disregard for others. I shall return to these points below in looking at offender-related mitigation.

Finally, a group of statements asked people to rate other relevant factors. What is striking from the ratings given in Table 4.4 is that offenders favoured 'certainty' to a considerably greater extent than other groups – this fits in with their support for 'fairness' but is difficult to reconcile with their claims for particularity (as shown in Table 4.3). It is less surprising that offenders gave comparatively little support for 'prevent', while victims favoured this option (public protection being quite clearly of concern to victims in interview). There was very little support for 'victim say', even from victims, with offenders actually expressing less opposition to this idea than other groups.

Follow-up interviews suggested that the unpopularity of the victim having a say arose from fears of undue vengefulness and doubts as to

Table 4.4 Other factors: percentage agree (and ranking in list of all statements)

Groups	N	Prevent 'The court should give enough punishment to stop that person offending'	Certainty 'People should know exactly how much punishment they will get for an offence'	Victim say 'The victim should have some say in the choice of punishment'
Magistrates	377	65% (5th)	28% (7th)	16% (10th)
Staff	128	59% (5th)	27% (9th)	20% (10th)
Offenders	134	50% (9th)	53% (8th)	43% (10th)
Victims	107	71% (3rd)	36% (8th)	27% (10th)

whether a particular individual was qualified to speak for other victims or should be given that responsibility. One victim thought that such technical issues should be entrusted to the professionals: 'you would not give the passengers a say about flying an aircraft'. I asked another victim about a suggestion that had been made in a first-round interview that victims might be given a list of appropriate punishments from which to chose, but she questioned how it would benefit the victim to have a say in punishment. Asked about the same proposal, a probation officer was wary of tokenism in giving victims something that was not a real say in punishment. These views should not be taken as indicative of a lack of interest in the victim's point of view. A number of respondents had added comments to the questionnaire to the effect that the crucial factor in measuring a crime's gravity was its impact on the victim, and support emerged in interviews for versions of victim impact statements to enable the victim to explain the impact of the crime. There was also some awareness of – and support for – victim–offender mediation and other restorative processes. However, these findings suggest that we may be some way from proposals such as Raynor's (2001) to involve victims in the choice of rehabilitative work to be carried out by offenders (Chapter 2).

That no greater agreement with 'proportionality', 'fair' or 'prevent' was found according to how respondents prioritised the aims of punishment argues against a false dichotomy: for the sentence to match the seriousness of the offence was supported equally by Consequentialist and Retributivist. Nonetheless, I explored possible tensions between 'proportionality' and 'prevent' in follow-up interviews, by asking respondents who had scored each equally (usually 4 or 5) whether they would be able to compromise one for the other. Overall, crime preventive considerations were seen ultimately as more important than adherence to proportionality, but it is interesting that respondents illustrated their views with examples in which departures from desert were downwards rather than upwards. The implication was that crime prevention was seen to justify leniency rather than extending the sentence.[9]

A victim saw proportionality as the starting point, so that the more serious the offence, the less prevention formed a separate consideration. A tension between the two would be resolved according to the record of the person; society should start with a milder punishment and address preventing reoffending with a young (implicitly a less experienced) person. But a repeat record might indicate that society was unable to cope with that individual; incapacitation might then become desirable to limit pain for others. An offender seemed influenced by his own experiences on probation in saying that it was easier to balance in your own mind that the punishment might not match gravity but might stop the person doing the same thing again (i.e. implying a reduction of sentence to accommodate prevention). A magistrate was clear in interview that prevention would be uppermost (and had prioritised prevention as an aim of punishment in her questionnaire).

To complete the analysis of questionnaire respondents' views on how courts should make decisions about the amount of punishment, I examined male/female and age-related differences. With the exception of 'crimes differ', those that attained statistical significance appeared to follow offenders' and victims' preferences, as shown below (offenders being younger than other groups and comprising 90 per cent males, while victims comprised 60 per cent females):

- Males selected high scores more often than females: victim say and fair ($p < 0.01$); offenders differ ($p < 0.05$).

- Females selected high scores more often than males: history and proportionality ($p < 0.01$); crimes differ ($p < 0.05$).

- Means decreased with age: fair, victim say and crimes differ ($p < 0.01$); certain ($p < 0.05$).

- Means increased with age: proportionality, history and prevent ($p < 0.01$).

Offender-related mitigation

Another part of the questionnaire took factors related to the offender further by asking people the extent to which they agreed that offenders should receive less punishment than they otherwise would in certain circumstances. What is immediately apparent – and not surprising – from the ratings given in Table 4.5 is that offenders are far more strongly in favour of offender-related mitigation than other groups.

Table 4.5 Offender-related mitigation: percentage agree

Groups	N*	First time 'It is their first time in court'	Character 'The crime is out of character for them'	Sensibility 'The punishment will hit them very hard'
Magistrates	379	65%	50%	24%
Staff	130	52%	52%	29%
Offenders	135	75%	68%	64%
Victims	108	40%	45%	29%

Looking at respondents' characteristics, the only statistically significant differences in means were for males and the youngest age group to favour 'sensibility' ($p < 0.01$), a pattern that follows offenders' preferences. Nor were there any statistically significant differences between the mean scores given by retributivists and consequentialists. There was a significant ($p < 0.01$) but very low negative correlation (-0.153) between 'proportionality' (see Table 4.2) and 'sensibility', suggesting that if there is any association between the two it is between a greater inclination towards proportionality in determining the amount of punishment and *less* sympathy for the offender who would be hit particularly hard. This hardly supports Walker's (1992) argument that offenders' individual perceptions of painfulness need to be taken into account in passing proportionate sentences.

This lack of endorsement for 'sensibility' was confirmed in follow-up interviews, where I asked participants about two types of cases in which the penalty might be seen to impose particular hardship. The first was where a parent would be separated from children by virtue of a prison sentence, the second where an employed offender might have less 'spare time' and therefore community service might hit him or her harder than someone who was unemployed. Overall, there was little support for mitigation in either case, and views were surprisingly adamant on this point. There was some concern about the harm that separation from its mother might inflict on a child, and a victim was in favour of a prolonged non-custodial sentence for a parent to take advantage of the restraining influence of family responsibilities. However, a magistrate and a victim both pointed out that a mother might not necessarily be a positive figure in the child's life. An offender who herself had been in prison with a young child commented 'we all have choices and chose to offend even though we have children' – a view shared by magistrates. The 'choices' argument was applied too to the employed person on community service, and it was pointed out that employment was not necessarily a fixed category. One probation officer recalled cases where employed offenders with a reasonable income had received stringent financial penalties rather than community service. His comment alluded to a reservation expressed by Bottoms (1998) – that taking 'sensibility' into account benefited offenders who were already socially advantaged:

> It's the people that had less money and more time that were definitely given community punishment [. . .]. I don't necessarily think it's wrong, but of course, somebody who's unemployed is given the sentence that the court would have wanted to give the employed to begin with, which is a heavier sentence, and then that person could legitimately say that's not right. (Probation officer – follow-up interview)

Interviewees were more receptive to the idea of extending leniency to the first-time offender or to someone for whom the offence was out of character (categories seen as overlapping), although one victim argued that, logically, a crime was not 'out of character' if the person had done it. For others, motivation and the offender's circumstances were relevant considerations; cited examples included offending out of necessity or to feed a drug habit (factors arguably relevant to culpability and therefore the seriousness of the offence). For one offender, a 'callous' repetitive offender might deserve comparatively severe treatment. One magistrate drew a connection between all three factors in saying that she would try to avoid giving someone who had never offended before a prison sentence; it would have a harsher impact on them to acquire a prison record and to be forced to mix with more hardened criminals.

Conclusions

I began this chapter by reviewing how von Hirsch (1993) and Duff (2001) have sought to reconcile retribution with the goal of preventing crime in penal theory, and the role played by the principle of proportionality in their respective schemes. Having considered the application of desert principles to community penalties in England under the Criminal Justice Act 1991, I conclude that it would be technically possible to achieve proportionate community sentences, although more work would need to be undertaken to examine and attribute values to their various dimensions. Of course, this does not address how far proportionality *should* constrain the pursuit of crime prevention, a normative question not yet resolved in the academic literature. However, there seems an emerging consensus in favour of bands containing roughly equivalent and interchangeable sentences, an approach tried – and one that failed – in the 1991 Act. Outstanding questions remain about the relevance of offenders' prior records, their background circumstances and the impact the sentence might have on them: whether and to what extent these factors are consistent with a principle of proportionality or justify deviations from a proportionality scale.

Interviews with and surveys of those with a practical stake in criminal justice reveal a clear priority towards crime prevention as an overall aim of sentencing. However, there was also a commitment to retribution and a strong endorsement of proportionality in deciding amounts of punishment (what might avert further offending weighed as a lesser consideration). On the whole, comparisons between offences were seen as possible. These views seem to favour an approach to punishment that looks both backwards to the offence and forwards to the possibility of change. Indeed, efforts at reform appear to play a more central role in how respondents conceptualised punishment than acknowledged by von Hirsch (1993). Accordingly, tensions between proportionality and crime reduction seemed to be resolved by prioritising what might have a positive impact on the offender even if that failed to match up to the gravity of the offence. Illustrative comments might be taken implicitly to endorse departures downwards from deserved punishments, in other words leniency, to accommodate crime prevention; departures upwards did not feature in people's explanations of their views. In looking at understandings of the messages transmitted in the act of sentencing and how offenders are expected to respond in the next two chapters, I will have an opportunity to consider further the balance between the normative and the instrumental elements in punishment.

Factors particular to the individual offender – his or her background, the circumstances in which he or she was offending and the impact the punishment might have on him or her – were seen as relevant to the amount of punishment, especially by offenders. However, these views cannot be taken as endorsement of the idea of sensibility (Walker 1992) – that offenders' particular perceptions of painfulness should be taken into account. Not only did very low proportions of questionnaire respondents (with the exception of offenders) agree that sentence should be reduced if it would hit the offender very hard, but interviewees also seemed disinclined to extend leniency to the parent or the employed. Culpability, choice and the possibility of discriminating against the already disadvantaged were among the factors that informed people's thinking. Here, it is difficult to reconcile offenders' claims for particularity with the value they clearly attached to fairness, but perhaps it is not surprising for them to want both due acknowledgement of the predicaments that drew them into offending *and* sentences that were fair and just in their particular circumstances. These are challenging expectations.

History, or prior record, was another factor that the vast majority of respondents agreed should count in determining the length of sentence (though less so offenders than other groups). However, it was difficult to disentangle quite *why* prior record was seen as relevant and this is a question that would undoubtedly benefit from further specific exploration of the views of 'stakeholders'. Its popularity with retributivists, together with comments in interview associating first-time offenders with those for whom offending was out of character or a case of necessity, suggests that the level of previous offending was seen to influence judgements about motivation and culpability. There were perhaps intimations here that a 'callous' repetitive offender was seen to have shown a settled 'disposition' towards offending that called for the imposition of the full force of punishment for an individual who had forfeited any personal mitigation. This interpretation would be in keeping with findings by Robinson and Darley (1995) discussed in the previous chapter about the circumstances in which an act is regarded as 'dispositional', an idea whose role in punishment has been considered by Lacey (1988).

Punishment, Lacey argues, is only fair and right when the person's 'breach of a criminal regulation manifests hostility or indifference towards, or rejection of, either that particular norm or the standards of the criminal law in general' (Lacey 1988: 76). In putting forward this formulation, she specifically rejects a 'character' conception of responsibility, on the basis that this might be seen to allow over-intrusive modes of punishment intended to mould offenders' characters. Whether judgements about levels of dispositional responsibility might inform decisions about *amounts* of punishment is not directly addressed by Lacey. On the one hand, she does allude to behaviour being excused on the basis that it was 'out of character' (1988: 68), an idea reminiscent of Wasik and von Hirsch's (1994) 'uncharacteristic lapse' and indicative of the progressive loss of mitigation model. On the other hand, she accords proportionality to socially acknowledged gravity a fairly minor role, the 'central functions of punishment [dictating] that the scale be modified in order to accommodate goals such as deterrence, incapacitation and prevention' (1988: 194). This hardly implies a close relationship between blameworthiness and levels of punishment.

Notes

1 Braithwaite (2003) argues that a republican philosophy of justice (Braithwaite and Pettit 1990) is actually more effective than retributivist theory in assuring that upper constraints on punishment cannot be breached, since the requirement for these upper limits derives from the pursuit of non-domination that is the central aim of republican justice. However, it is not obvious how upper constraints would be preserved in Braithwaite's

(1999) 'enforcement pyramid', in which recalcitrance is met with custodial incapacitation. Dignan (2003) proposes that the proportionality constraint should be linked to the seriousness of the *wrong* that has been done to the victim; this would detach the overall scale of punishment from the particular harm that the victim may have suffered (as often advocated by restorative theorists) but still acknowledge that the victim was entitled to reparation.

2 In this, Duff may have overstated von Hirsch's position. Bottoms (1998) argues persuasively that von Hirsch sees ordinal proportionality as a 'determining' principle, not in the practical sense that it is reasonably easy to determine a rank ordering of crime seriousness, but *technically* as a necessary feature of a desert-based sentencing system. This follows Lucas's (1980) examination of justice as an asymmetrical concept, in that it is very difficult to say precisely what is just but people certainly recognise unfairness when certain boundaries are crossed.

3 A related question is whether it is possible to rank all offences on a single scale of seriousness. Duff argues that such an exercise is feasible in principle, but would entail costs that 'we should not be willing to pay' (2001: 136). I do not address this question here, since my concern is with penal severity.

4 Essentially, Schiff developed a Criminal Punishment Severity Scale (CPSS), which scores the relative severity of intermediate sanctions according to the extent to which they impose constraints within five 'parameters' of restrictiveness. Each parameter would be weighted according to its significance on a scale of 1–5, so that being required to stay at home under a curfew would be worth '5' and CS work '3'.

5 Espoused by Norval Morris (1974) as the least costly way of securing the most good, the parsimony principle derives from Bentham's maxim that no state policy (including punishment) could be justified unless it avoided greater aggregate unhappiness than it caused (e.g. by deterring others from committing similar crimes) – see Tonry (1998c).

6 According to the principle of progressive loss of mitigation, a 'ceiling' to the punishment which can be imposed is determined by the gravity of the offence; while an absence of, or a modest, previous criminal record will justify a reduction in sentence, a long record will not justify a sentence in excess of the permissible ceiling (see Ashworth 2000).

7 The original version of section 29(1) of the 1991 Act provided that an offence was not to be regarded as more serious because the offender had previous convictions or had reoffended after receiving community sentences. It was repealed amid controversy in the Criminal Justice Act 1993, which specifically permits a court to take account of any previous convictions or failure to respond to previous sentences. Sentencing trends (see Chapter 2) suggest that the reform encouraged courts to treat record as an aggravating factor (see Ashworth 2000).

8 Alternatively, victims and members and staff might be articulating an 'ethic of care', which it has been argued women prioritise over the formal logic of fairness (Gilligan 1982).

9 On this point, von Hirsch accepts that exceptional departures downwards might be invoked for cases deserving of special sympathy, but he does not see crime prevention as a plausible justification for reducing sentence as 'it is

difficult to imagine extraordinary losses of prevention stemming from a failure to lower the sentence for a particular type of crime below its proportionate level' (1993: 52). Duff (2001) takes a somewhat similar view: downward departures would only be justified in cases in which mercy was appropriate. Against the objection that insisting that everyone receives their deserved punishment will do unnecessary harm, he argues that the negative principle of proportionality to which he adheres means that 'sentences can be more flexibly and thus less harmfully tailored to the offender's particular situation' (2001: 141).

Chapter 5

Penal messages

Introduction

This chapter and the next draw on what my research participants said about the dialogue that takes place in sentencing and while the offender is serving the sentence ordered by the court. In this chapter, I look at the messages that courts were seen as seeking to convey to offenders whom they were sentencing, and how sentencers were seen to use particular sanctions to reinforce such messages. Chapter 6 will then explore the responses expected from offenders, whether they were seen as responding in these ways, and what might have impeded their readiness and ability to do so.

Again, I have divided the chapter into two sections. The first extends the discussion of sentencing priorities in Chapter 4 to look at how my respondents characterised penal aims and how they understood the four main options available to the court: custody, and community service, probation and curfew orders.[1] These data are interesting in their own right; they also set the scene for the discussion of penal communication that forms the second section of this chapter.

I. Overall aims of punishment

In discussing the aims of punishment, it is convenient to follow a normative-instrumental categorisation to reflect the censuring versus crime prevention debate in the literature. However, it will soon be seen that this distinction offers a crude characterisation of how people understood punishment as an institution. As with the discussion of sentencing priorities, it is also useful to start with questionnaire responses as these provide a structured framework for analysis.

Table 5.1 Moralising: percentage agree (and ranking in list of all statements)

Groups	N	Disapprove 'Show them society does not like what they did'	Victim hurt 'Show them they have hurt the victim'	Persuade 'Make them see why what they did was wrong'
Magistrates	382	81% (1st)	66% (7th)	73% (4th)
Staff	132	69% (7th)	78% (3rd)	82% (2nd)
Offenders	142	59% (10th)	61% (9th)	70% (6th)
Victims	105	76% (5th)	77% (4th)	85% (1st)

Punishment as moralising

The questionnaire asked people the extent to which they agreed with 13 statements about what the court should be trying to do in sentencing offenders (5 being 'strongly agree' and 1 being 'not at all'). One group of statements was intended to explore various aspects of censure (a key element for von Hirsch 1993 and Duff 2001); ratings are presented in Table 5.1.

Table 5.1 suggests that for magistrates, the main point was to demonstrate society's disapproval to the offender. Theirs might be interpreted as a somewhat 'symbolic' approach to sentencing in which the offender is dealt with 'externally', reminiscent of von Hirsch's (1993) model as it has been characterised by Bottoms (1998). By contrast, in prioritising the need to make offenders see *why* what they did was wrong, victims and staff seemed to envisage a greater degree of engagement with offenders. This position implies that the offender is a person with a normative outlook capable, as Duff (2001) argues, of seeing his or her crime as wrongful. Consistent with that perspective, both staff and victims put more emphasis than magistrates on showing offenders that they had hurt their victims. Offenders showed comparatively less support for these moralising messages, although a substantial proportion were open to persuasion about the wrongfulness of their crimes.

Indeed, Table 5.1 and Tables 5.2, 5.4 and 5.5 below show that it was common for more than 50 per cent of any group of respondents to agree with a sentencing purpose listed on the questionnaire (for example, 59 per cent of victims showed positive support for that group's least popular option). This was also the case when it came to the messages that sentencing was seen to convey (see section II below) and how offenders were expected to respond to that communication (discussed in Chapter 6). The fact that respondents were also capable of expressing strong *disagreement* with some statements on the questionnaire (see Tables 4.2, 4.4 and 4.5 in Chapter 4) suggests that this is because a wide range of penal objectives attracted support rather than because the questionnaire prompted indiscriminate agreement from respondents. In considering the rankings indicated in the various tables, it is important to bear in mind that the majority of respondents expressed support for many statements even though some were clearly less popular than others.

In line with the views summarised in Table 5.1, first-round interview participants had identified the expression of censure as an important sentencing aim (the messages by which censure was conveyed are considered in the second part of this chapter). However, the reservations sometimes expressed about the value judgements implied in portraying punishment as 'moralising', in both first-round and follow-up interviews, may explain the mixed support for censure in questionnaire responses. One victim saw the hard treatment element in punishment as conveying disapproval, but did not believe that the law had a 'socialising' role. One offender admitted to being somewhat cynical in seeing sentencing as intended to demonstrate that action had been taken about lawbreaking rather than expressive of moral values.

Another set of statements in the questionnaire envisaged exacting recompense from offenders for their misdeeds, whether in the form of payback (retribution), putting something back into the community, or some personal sense of remorse (see Table 5.2).[2]

The low level of support for 'retribution', even from magistrates, is striking. The same is true of 'remorse'; these respondents might agree with von Hirsch that 'censure is not a technique for evoking specified sentiments' (1993: 10). Similarly, relatively little attention was paid in interviews to remorse as an aim of sentence. However, Chapter 2 showed that feelings of remorse or 'shame-guilt' by offenders are

Table 5.2 Exacting recompense: percentage agree (and ranking in list of all statements)

Groups	N	Retribution* 'Make them pay for what they did wrong'	Reparation 'Make them put something back into the community'	Remorse 'Make them feel sorry for hurting someone'
Magistrates	380	59% (10th)	66% (6th)	51% (11th)
Staff	131	49% (13th)	72% (5th)	58% (11th)
Offenders	142	40% (13th)	48% (12th)	54% (11th)
Victims	108	59% (13th)	77% (4th)	65% (11th)

*See the explanation of this definition given in note 2.

important elements both in Duff's (2001) communicative theory and in restorative theory (Harris 2001), and I will be exploring these specific aspects of offenders' responses to punishment in Chapter 6. 'Reparation' was actually more popular among all groups other than offenders, who seemed reluctant to accept that one aim of sentencing might be to make them pay or offer recompense for their offending.

In interview too, reparation was generally portrayed in a positive light; it was sometimes associated with community service, and seen as a way of ensuring that other people might benefit from the offender's 'paying' for the crime or 'putting right what they'd done wrong' (magistrate – first-round interview). One victim struggled to express how crimes might be repaid in a positive way, and accepted my suggestion of 'reparation':

> I think that when the person sees the effects on the victim and the reparative part of it, they might come to a point where they acknowledge the wrong of it, and the fairness of the punishment. And say 'well, yes, that's my dues, I've done this to that person and I deserve that'. (Victim – first-round interview)

As in prioritising sentencing aims (Chapter 4), some discomfort was expressed with 'pure' retribution (often equated with 'punitiveness'), both in first-round and follow-up interviews. A magistrate interviewed in the first-round recognised that 'if someone has offended, they have to pay for offending'. However, some magistrates preferred the more neutral language of 'restricting liberty', and one commented in follow-up interview that she found 'suffer' a little strong but would not want the person to be rewarded for offending. A probation officer commented:

> The retributive bit underlies everything for me because that's what the system is there for: to give society a sense that this person is being punished, but hopefully in a reasonably humane and en-lightened way. (Probation officer – first-round interview)

Interviewed victims expressed support for punishment in order to make the person pay, but some were wary of society displaying vengeance. One commented that 'society needs to move forward from this punish-ment and revenge culture'; another perceived a need to make offenders 'understand that this is not a good thing to do' (whether as a result of special deterrence or more normative processes was not clear). The need for punishment not simply to 'hurt' but to serve crime preventive goals was a sentiment shared by magistrates and probation staff alike. As one magistrate commented in a follow-up interview, she saw the main point of sentencing as 'whatever it took' to stop that person from offending

Table 5.3 Normative aims: mean scores

Statement	Magistrates	Probation	CS staff	Victims	Offenders
Disapprove	4.19	3.65	4.32	4.14	3.65
Victim hurt	3.85	3.87	4.38	4.07	3.81
Persuade	4.06	4.08	4.57	4.34	3.96
Retribution	3.77	3.25	4.05	3.66	3.47
Reparation	3.82	3.73	4.55	4.04	3.55
Remorse	3.49	3.33	4.05	3.84	3.66

again, whether through an educational or an unpleasant experience. Offenders accepted that they were being 'punished'; for some that merged with crime preventive goals:

> [The aim is] maybe to punish me, and make me look at what I did wrong [. . .] To punish people, to send them away and make them think 'hold on a minute, I don't want this'. (Offender – first-round interview)

A comparison of mean scores given in questionnaires (Table 5.3) for normative aims showed that offenders scored the lowest means on most statements, significantly (p < 0.01) below victims' scores on all three 'moralising' statements and 'reparation', and below magistrates' on 'disapprove' and 'retribution'. However, when staff were separated according to whether they worked in probation or CS, mean scores registered by probation staff were close to those of offenders. By contrast, CS staff had very high mean scores on most statements, even higher than magistrates on 'disapprove' and victims on 'persuade'. Differences between probation and CS scores were all statistically significant (p < 0.01), pointing to a real disparity in view between the two parts of the probation service apparent across much of the questionnaire.

Another significant difference in mean scores was between victims' and magistrates' scores on 'remorse'. Together with magistrates' comparatively low support for 'victim hurt', this may reflect an inclination for magistrates to see a crime more as a wrong against society than against the particular victim. Conversely, victims' agreeing more often than magistrates with 'reparation' may reflect an ability to recognise that a public as well as a private wrong has been committed.

Before moving to sentencing aims that are specifically crime preventive, it is worth comparing views on these statements according to whether questionnaire respondents categorised themselves as retributivists or consequentialists in how they prioritised sentencing. As might be expected, retributivists favoured 'retribution' (76.9 per cent agreed with this statement compared with 50.6 per cent of consequentialists). However, other statements found significantly more agreement among a higher proportion of consequentialists than retributivists, possibly because instrumental goals lay behind the normative communication; interviews certainly suggested that one point of conveying a sense of wrongdoing and harm to offenders was to prompt them to refrain in the future.[3] To a less marked extent, a higher proportion of consequentialists than retributivists also agreed with 'reparation' and 'disapprove', the latter quite possibly because consequentialists saw censure as a moral appeal that promoted desistance (in line with von Hirsch 1993). In relation to 'reparation', there was some comment in interview that it might be crime reducing for offenders to undertake work for the community as it increased their awareness of socially disadvantaged groups and their own sense that they might be socially useful (Johnson and Rex 2002).

Crime preventive aims

Turning now to explicitly consequentialist goals, a group of statements on the questionnaire addressed the contingent aims of deterrence and incapacitation. Ratings of these statements (Table 5.4) show considerable support for 'incapacitation' from magistrates, staff and offenders, and middling levels of support for 'special deterrence' (but more support from victims). Slightly less support is shown for 'general deterrence', although it still gained agreement from the majority of respondents.

Views expressed in interviews (both first-round and follow-up) were indicative of some agreement with the point made by Halliday (Home Office 2001) that there might be some general deterrent effect but not sufficient for its justification as a primary rationale for sentencing. Magistrates were most inclined to express support for deterrence in interview as a means by which they might be able to stop an individual

Table 5.4 Stopping further offending: percentage agree (and ranking in list of all statements)

Groups	N	Special deterrence 'Show them that crime does not pay'	General deterrence 'Show other people they won't get away with crime'	Incapacitation 'Keep them away from offending'
Magistrates	381	67% (5th)	62% (8th)	74% (3rd)
Staff	132	64% (9th)	56% (12th)	73% (4th)
Offenders	141	64% (7th)	61% (8th)	77% (2nd)
Victims	107	78% (3rd)	67% (9th)	65% (10th)

Table 5.5 Variations on reform: percentage agree (and ranking in list of all statements)

Groups	N	Reform 'Get them to change their ways'	Rehabilitation 'Help them with problems behind their offending'	Encouragement 'Get them to do something useful with their lives'	Education 'Teach them how to go on the straight and narrow'
Magistrates	382	79% (2nd)	61% (9th)	44% (12th)	41% (13th)
Staff	132	71% (6th)	86% (1st)	66% (8th)	61% (10th)
Offenders	142	70% (5th)	79% (1st)	72% (4th)	73% (3rd)
Victims	107	82% (2nd)	73% (7th)	74% (6th)	63% (12th)

from future offending, but still expressed doubts about its efficacy. Victims thought that deterrent effects might wear off in the case of multiple offenders, while magistrates and probation staff both saw deterrence as more effective for people with a stake in society or 'mainstream' values (as theorised by Bottoms 2001). Offenders argued that deterrent effects were limited because people believed they were unlikely to be caught in the first place. Similarly, incapacitation was most popular with magistrates, who regularly referred to the public expectation to be offered (even temporary) relief from persistent or serious offenders – usually through short custodial sentences but sometimes through curfew orders. Other groups expressed more scepticism about the efficacy of a curfew order or the usefulness of a prison term.

Finally, four statements on the questionnaire sought views on reform and other indicators of positive change. Ratings, as shown in Table 5.5, show that all these options received comparatively strong endorsement from offenders (whose responses to this part of the questionnaire convey a highly consequentialist view of punishment). Views from other groups were more mixed: relatively low levels of agreement with 'education', but strong support for 'reform' from victims and magistrates and for 'rehabilitation' from staff. It is interesting that magistrates were keen for offenders to 'change their ways' but not through 'education' and 'encouragement' (more so through 'rehabilitation' and 'special deterrence': see Table 5.4), whereas victims expressed considerably more support for 'encouragement'.

For the offender to move away from crime was prominent in discussions about the aims of sentencing in first-round interviews in a multiplicity of ways that defy facile categorisation. One striking finding was the lack of a clear distinction in interviewees' minds between what might be called 'reform' and 'special deterrence'. Wishing to avoid future prison sentences, for example, was seen as just one among many factors that offenders might take into account in decisions to stop offending. Some offenders commented that custody might eventually deter them because of a realisation that it was getting them nowhere or depriving them of family life. I shall consider the implications of this point more fully in Chapter 6, having discussed how offenders respond to the experience of being sentenced.

In envisaging how sentencing might prompt offenders in effect to reform themselves, interview accounts varied around differing themes: practical help or support; treatment through cognitive or substance abuse programmes; educational intervention (either literally or retraining people's thought processes); introducing offenders to self-discipline; and encouraging offenders to see themselves as useful members of society. These ideas are enlarged upon below in considering the role of different disposals. In both first-round interviews and follow-up interviews, magistrates appeared noticeably more 'rehabilitative' than when asked to rate different aims on the questionnaire. Perhaps this was because interviews provided an opportunity to articulate a degree of ambivalence, for example about the notion of administering punishment to people who needed help. One encapsulated the dilemma in presenting the role of the magistracy as quite clearly *not* a 'welfare service':

> We've got to work out what we're here for as magistrates. We're not welfare officers. We're here to do something to people that have committed crime. So we're not really a welfare service that says 'oh, this person needs this, that or the other', we're here to punish them. But, on the other hand, you can see some people who obviously need help rather than punishment. But again that's not our problem. That problem is with society, but it's not our problem in our role as a magistrate. (Magistrate – first-round interview)

A strong belief among probation staff was that offenders themselves had to make the necessary changes to stop offending: by taking responsibility for their behaviour following a period of self-examination as a result of being taken to court or through the work undertaken on probation or community service. To a lesser extent, magistrates made similar points, and some offenders referred to having to bring about these kinds of changes themselves albeit with the help of a probation officer. One probation officer stressed the need for realism about the speed with which this kind of change could be brought about:

> I think it's quite important that, as well as punish people, we make them understand the seriousness of what they've done and try and resolve any difficulties which might be tied into that behaviour . . . You've got to be aware of what you can't achieve as much as what

Table 5.6 Instrumental aims: mean scores

Statement	Magistrates	Probation	CS staff	Victims	Offenders
Special deterrence	3.99	3.44	4.57	4.17	3.87
General deterrence	3.82	3.07	4.30	3.92	3.75
Incapacitate	4.18	4.05	4.23	3.93	4.16
Reform	4.20	3.85	4.38	4.19	3.94
Rehabilitate	3.77	4.25	4.55	4.05	4.24
Encourage	3.19	3.46	4.43	4.13	4.10
Educate	3.13	3.28	4.28	3.83	4.10

you can achieve, and I think we are a bit more realistic now than we were. We see change as a gradual process that can perhaps take place over a number of orders rather than one great wonderful piece of work. (Probation officer – first-round interview)

The theme of self-determination emerged again in follow-up interviews, with one offender stressing that the key aim was to help the person to sort things out themselves: 'just teaching people to deal with things, without using drugs and crime and blaming other people'. A magistrate explained that he had only rated 'reform' (getting the offender to change his or her ways) '2' on the questionnaire because he did not believe that it was possible to *make* people change, as he had interpreted the statement. Only they could do that if steered or guided in the right way.

If we look at mean scores given in questionnaires for instrumental aims (Table 5.6), mean scores from CS staff on all statements were again higher than those given by probation staff, with statistically significant differences ($p < 0.01$) on both types of deterrence and on 'reform', 'encouragement' and 'education'. On 'incapacitation', mean scores were very similar across all groups (just above or below 4.0) with no statistically significant differences between them. Victims' mean score on 'special deterrence' was significantly higher than offenders' ($p < 0.05$), but otherwise there seemed a fair degree of accord between magistrates, offenders and victims on whether the aim of the sentence was to deter the offender or others.

Overall, probation staff were least in agreement with 'reform' and CS staff most in agreement. Magistrates seemed least in favour of 'rehabilitation', with a mean score significantly below all other groups. On 'education' and 'encouragement', mean scores from magistrates and probation staff were similar, and significantly below those of all other groups ($p < 0.01$). Offenders' mean scores were in line with probation staff's on 'reform' and 'rehabilitation', but closer to the more positive view of CS staff on education and encouragement.

Consequentialists expressed more support than retributivists for all these instrumental messages, with the notable exception of 'general deterrence'. This finding leads me to speculate that the wish to make an example of someone is more expressive of a desire to make them 'pay' than a genuine concern to prevent crime. Indeed, a magistrate interviewed in the first-round appeared to be voicing real anger in envisaging what the sentence might communicate to the offender's 'friends and associates'. This may help to explain the continued attachment to general deterrence as part of the rationale for sentencing despite a lack of empirical evidence for its crime preventive efficacy (see von Hirsch et al. 1999). What might be discerned here is similar to Tyler and Boeckmann's (1997) finding that Californians' support for three strikes legislation was more to do with beliefs that the social order was breaking down than with preventing crime.

Finally, there were interesting male-female differences in how the aims of sentencing were rated. One notable finding was that women agreed with all options to a greater extent than men, whether because victims (60 per cent female) tended to be more positive than offenders (10 per cent female) or because women were more amenable than men is not clear. There were statistically significant differences in mean scores given by women and men on 'victim hurt' and 'reparation' ($p < 0.01$), and 'disapprove' and 'general deterrence' ($p < 0.05$). Other than 'victim hurt', this cannot be explained by women's greater membership of the victim subsample. One possible explanation, though it is entirely speculative, is that women are revealing a more 'community' orientation than men, wanting offenders to put something back into the community and seeing sentencing as maintaining the social system by using disapproval and threats to promote law-abiding behaviour. Women showed little preference for 'education', possibly because this option was favoured by offenders but not particularly by other groups. They also showed less agreement with 'persuade' and 'special deterrence' than might be expected from their high level of representation among victims, and more agreement with 'incapacitation'. Perhaps what they are showing here is less faith than men in the possibility of negotiating with (young male) offenders and a correspondingly greater attachment to physical restraints.

Evaluating different disposals

Having reviewed the overall aims of sentencing, I now want to consider how the four main sentencing disposals fit in: prison, community service, probation and the curfew.[4] For each one, the questionnaire listed the 13 statements about sentencing aims and asked respondents to tick those they saw as representing the main purposes of that particular

Table 5.7 Purposes of different orders – top three

	Magistrates (N=385)	Staff (N=132)	Victims (N=111)	Offenders (N=143)
Custody				
1st	Disapproval 90%	Disapproval 77%	Disapproval 69%	Retribution 61%
2nd	Incapacitate 82%	Incapacitate 66%	Incapacitate 66%	Sp. deter 60%
3rd	Gen. deter 79%	Retribution 58%	Retribution 61%	Gen. deter 55%
Community service				
1st	Reparation 97%	Reparation 90%	Reparation 90%	Reparation 78%
2nd	Retribution 85%	Encourage 70%	Encourage 69%	Retribution 63%
3rd	Disapproval 84%	Retribution 68%	Retribution 50%	Incapacitate 48%
Probation				
1st	Rehabilitate 91%	Rehabilitate 92%	Rehabilitate 64%	Rehabilitate 60%
2nd	Persuade 82%	Persuade 75%	Disapproval 55%	Persuade 57%
3rd	Reform 79%	Reform 73%	Persuade 46%	Educate 48%
Curfew (tagging)				
1st	Incapacitate 93%	Incapacitate 88%	Incapacitate 85%	Incapacitate 74%
2nd	Disapproval 81%	Disapproval 66%	Disapproval 69%	Retribution 51%
3rd	Sp. deter 59%	Retribution 46%	Sp. deter 40%	Persuade 45%

order. Table 5.7 presents the three most popular purposes for each order among the different groups of respondents. Respondents could select as many statements as they liked, and they often selected four or more for any given disposal. In fact, some overtly signalled a lack of familiarity with – or support for – a particular disposal by ticking few or no statements. Taking the size of the proportions in this table as expressing the level of confidence in the relevant disposal, then, magistrates conveyed the most confidence overall, offenders the least, and victims showed less faith in custody or probation than in community service or the curfew.

Various points emerge from Table 5.7:

- There was considerable consensus (with the exception of offenders) that prison could be used to express disapproval and provide incapacitation.

- The 'payback' aspect of community service, as both retribution and reparation, was given some prominence by all groups. Staff and victims alike favoured the 'reforming' aim of encouragement, perhaps indicating that they saw offenders as gaining positively from the experience of performing work for the community. Offenders (but only half) saw the obligation as hampering their freedom to offend, while magistrates emphasised moralising rather than crime-preventive benefits.

- All groups portrayed probation in terms of rehabilitation and persuasion, and it was generally depicted as crime reductive.

- It is not surprising that all groups defined the curfew primarily in terms of incapacitation. Otherwise, disapproval was emphasised by magistrates, staff and victims. Offenders were alone in placing 'persuade' within the top three purposes of electronic monitoring (i.e. making them see *why* what they did was wrong), and this is intriguing.

These understandings were developed both in first-round and follow-up interviews in which custody and curfew orders were usually offered as examples of incapacitative measures (though with some reservations about their effectiveness). A few people also saw custody or a curfew as a means to introduce offenders to some sort of structure or, as one probation officer put it, 'a set of tangible rules'. Generally, however, prison was singled out as failing to offer anything constructive, usually because sentence lengths were too short to offer rehabilitation or the prison environment was not conducive to this kind of work. An offender suggested that not having to pay bills or put food on the table encouraged dependency rather than a sense of responsibility among prisoners.

Community service was usually cited as the archetypal way in which to achieve reparation. According to a magistrate interviewed in the first-round, the best form of community service involved the offender 'deliberately putting right what they had done wrong'. One offender argued that it was reasonable to be required to give something back to the community:

I think [community service] is a good idea. If you've done something against the public, then it's giving back. I know it doesn't make right what you've done, but it's like giving back to the community in some way. Obviously the courts are telling you to do it, but if you are genuinely sorry then you shouldn't feel angry. Maybe you do feel angry, but you shouldn't be annoyed at having to do something. (Offender – first-round interview)

Rehabilitation, in the form of assistance with problems underlying offending or offering treatment programmes, was firmly associated with probation in the minds of magistrates and probation staff, who spoke of the move away from welfare or social work with a mixture of approval and regret. One probation officer interviewed in the first-round discussed the consequences of a failure to acknowledge that probation demonstrated that a civilised society cared for its transgressors by trying to get them to cope with life without resorting to offending:

> It is right that we as a community demonstrate publicly that we actually care sufficiently for somebody who has transgressed the law to offer them help. If they don't take it, OK, then we throw the rest of the book at them ... [The probation order] has been confused, because nobody has ever made the explicit statement that this is to demonstrate what a civilised country we are, how much we care for those who have transgressed. So the consequence of never putting that strong message across is that people have assumed that it's just a let off. Now actually trying to work with someone to sort out their ability to cope and problem solve enough to avoid offending and to begin to live a life that is socially acceptable is damned hard work for them. (Probation officer – first-round interview)

Accounts of how offenders might be encouraged to reform (in other words, to bring about change towards lawful behaviour) featured both probation and community service. According to interviewees, probation required offenders to address their behaviour and its impact, and helped them to change their attitudes and thinking; it awakened their 'social conscience' and encouraged their social participation. Community service broadened offenders' horizons, enabling them to develop insight into what their offences might mean for other groups in society such as the elderly or the disadvantaged. Performing work for the community, as well as requiring offenders to pay back to society, also introduced them to a routine of work, and helped them to realise that they had a contribution to make to society. Offenders described finding it motivating to be told they could achieve something, whether on probation or community service. A CS manager recounted the use of pro-social modelling by CS supervisors to educate offenders' 'views and ways of thinking' and to show them how to negotiate with others.[5] A probation officer offered a practitioner's perspective on probation:

> I work with people all the time, and my view is that you actually teach them a new way of behaving, and so it is about learning, about changing their perspective on life, so they don't have the same dysfunctional coping mechanisms. Because that's how, often, crime is committed, because people don't know another way of dealing with things, and they repeat the same patterns. So it's through teaching them new thinking, new behaviour, and new attitudes. Obviously, you have to do it in a pro-social way, so they accept, they learn that as well. (Probation officer – follow-up interview)

In order to compare how the respective disposals were evaluated, I calculated a 'score' based on how the different groups ranked their 'top three' purposes for each order as an overall sentencing aim and then converted the score into a percentage.[6] The results are shown below, with an overall score given in brackets; they should be treated with some caution as very different proportions of the various groups in effect 'voted for' a specific disposal. A more sophisticated calculation would have taken this variability into account, but would also have introduced greater complexity.

- *Custody (51 per cent)* – magistrates: 83 per cent; staff: 44 per cent; victims: 39 per cent; offenders: 39 per cent.

- *Community service (49 per cent)* – magistrates: 69 per cent; staff: 44 per cent; victims: 42 per cent; offenders: 42 per cent.

- *Probation (84 per cent)* – staff: 92 per cent; offenders: 89 per cent; victims: 81 per cent; magistrates: 75 per cent.

- *Curfew (67 per cent)* – magistrates: 92 per cent; victims: 67 per cent; offenders: 58 per cent; staff: 50 per cent.

According to this analysis, the curfew was most highly evaluated by magistrates. Probation served the most popular purposes for the other three groups, and was far more popular overall than any other option. Prison served the least popular purposes for all groups except magistrates (who evaluated community service least favourably), closely followed by community service. That everyone appeared to value the curfew (in terms of sentencing aims) more highly than community service is an unexpected finding.

Before turning to sentencing 'messages', it is worth recapping the findings presented in this section. Magistrates placed considerable emphasis on the role of disapproval in sentencing, as did victims. Victims were particularly keen for the sentence to make offenders see *why* what they did was wrong ('persuade'). This aim also attracted strong support from staff and a substantial proportion of offenders were prepared to accept it (although they were less keen on 'victim hurt'). Overall, offenders expressed more support for consequentialist goals, their top five preferences being rehabilitation, incapacitation, education, encouragement and reform. On these, the views of other groups were more divided, with rehabilitation attracting support from staff and reform from magistrates and victims. Education received comparatively little support from any of these groups, but encouragement received moderate support from staff and victims. Incapacitation was reasonably popular with all groups and special deterrence with victims. Generally, however, deterrence was not greatly favoured;

interviews with magistrates suggested more interest than was apparent in questionnaire responses where they were evaluating deterrence as one of a range of sentencing aims. Retribution and remorse attracted relatively little support from anyone, but reparation secured moderate levels of agreement from all groups other than offenders.

What emerges from this summary is that offenders were keen for the sentence to help them to stop offending, but were less prepared to take 'moralising' on board or to accept that they owed recompense for their offending. Other groups too stressed the role of sentencing in getting offenders to move away from crime, but were more receptive than offenders to the moralising and reparative dimensions in punishment. Indeed, a comparison of retributivists' and consequentialists' views, as well as interview analysis, suggests that one cannot divide sentencing aims neatly into normative or instrumental categories. Instrumental goals lay behind normative communication (such as 'persuade') and it was hoped that performing reparative acts would prove a crime-reducing experience for offenders. Similarly, the wish to make an example of a particular offender seemed expressive of retributive sentiments rather than genuinely crime preventive aspirations. Provisionally, it might be argued that the popularity of probation lay in its strong status as a crime preventive sanction, a role that was not ascribed to community service to nearly the same extent but was seen as a major aspect of electronic monitoring.

II. Sentencing as communication

In discussing sentencing specifically in terms of communication, I once again divide penal messages into normative or 'moral' expressions of disapproval of wrongdoing and 'instrumental' messages intended to secure a particular reaction from the offender. However, this distinction proved somewhat artificial. Indeed, the difficulty of maintaining it in practice lends immediate support to a formulation of punishment that is both normative and forward-looking, as proposed by Duff (2001) and von Hirsch (1993). In reporting these findings, I start with my exploratory analysis of the first-round interviews as this formed the basis upon which I identified the key penal messages to include in the questionnaire and how they might be phrased.

Normative messages

Most interviewees saw punishment communicating what von Hirsch (1993) would understand as censure: disapproval, and disavowal of the behaviour, in some cases with specific reference to the harm or suffering caused. What theorists characterise as 'hard treatment' (something that was painful or inconvenient) needed to be imposed, to bring home the fact that the behaviour was wrong, and to make that message impinge on offenders. But views could be classified as 'vindicative' rather than 'vindictive'.[7] Too much punishment was seen as excluding and likely to propel the offender into further offending. As Duff (2001) has argued, punishment is something we do, not to an implicitly excluded 'them', but to ourselves as full if imperfect members of the community. Conversely, too little punishment would allow the offender to 'get away with it', and one victim argued that this would prevent someone in her position from overcoming the experience of victimisation.

One magistrate thought it sometimes necessary to make it clear in relation to the offender that we 'dislike your type extremely'; by contrast, another recoiled from the idea of expressing abhorrence. Disapproval was often portrayed as containing an implicit instrumental message, to the effect that society cannot condone or will not tolerate this behaviour – the last implying a boundary that the offender was expected to observe in future. However, the doubts expressed by staff, offenders and victims alike about the efficacy of the moral communication of disapproval hinted at some unease with its underlying values. Probation staff saw a potential for disapproval to become offender-focused rather than offence-focused, and therefore to be excluding or to imply that the person was unable to change. Victims had reservations about the meaningfulness of such a message, one pointing to the contradiction of the court asserting, on the one hand, that the person had done something horrendous but then, on the other hand, letting them off. Offenders recognised the message that they had done something wrong but some queried its justification; one commented 'in my eyes I didn't think there was anything wrong with it'. For another, the lack of respect shown to him undermined the legitimacy of the court as an institution to which he should defer:

> How am I supposed to give [respect], if they don't show it in the first place? Yeah, I've done something wrong, but why don't I still deserve respect from someone who doesn't know me, doesn't know the circumstances and they sit there, they walk out, everyone stands up for them, they sit down and say 'take them away'. (Offender – first-round interview)

The questionnaire asked respondents to indicate the extent to which they agreed with various statements about what the court should be saying to the offender in the act of sentencing (as before, 5 being 'strongly agree' and 1 being 'not at all'). One group of statements addressed the

95

Table 5.8 Normative messages: percentage agree (and ranking in list of all statements)

Groups	N	*Censure* 'We do not like what you did'	*Hurt* 'What you did hurt someone else'	*Harm* 'What you did harmed the community'	*Boundary* 'We can not put up with this kind of behaviour'
Magistrates	377	80% (3rd)	88% (1st)	84% (2nd)	72% (5th)
Staff	131	75% (3rd)	88% (1st)	83% (2nd)	64% (8th)
Offenders	132	50% (9th)	58% (4th)	44% (10th)	55% (5th)
Victims	106	75% (5th)	88% (1st)	76% (4th)	77% (3rd)

normative dimensions of this type of communication as discussed in first-round interviews, and ratings are presented in Table 5.8.

It is immediately striking that this kind of moralising was much less popular with offenders than with other groups, mirroring offenders' comparative reluctance to take disapproval on board as an aim of sentencing (see Table 5.1 above). As one offender explained in follow-up interview, he had refrained from ticking 'hurt' or 'harm' because he did not see them as applying to an offence that he regarded as victimless. As against the views expressed by offenders and as with moralising as a sentencing aim (see Table 5.1), consensus among the other groups was high, each ranking the four statements within their top five (except staff on 'boundary'). It is interesting that when it came to sentencing messages as opposed to sentencing aims, the emphasis for magistrates as well as staff and victims was on communicating the damage that the offence had caused rather than simply signalling censure (or disapproval) for what the offender did. Perhaps unsurprisingly, victims gave considerably more support to 'hurt' than to any of the other normative messages. A victim commented in follow up interview that the impact of an offence on the victim was far greater than its impact on the community.

A comparison of mean scores bears out these findings (Table 5.9). Differences were statistically significant in all cases ($p < 0.01$), with offenders usually producing the lowest and magistrates (or CS staff) the highest means. As before, important differences emerged between staff according to whether they worked in probation or CS, with probation officers rating 'boundary' even lower than offenders and censure almost as low. Here, women produced significantly higher mean scores than men on 'hurt' ($p < 0.01$) and 'harm' ($p < 0.05$), quite possibly following offenders' lack of support for these two statements.

Table 5.9 Normative messages: mean scores

Statement	Magistrates	Probation	CS staff	Victims	Offenders
Censure	4.21	3.75	4.26	4.10	3.43
Hurt	4.48	4.25	4.50	4.49	3.71
Harm	4.35	4.11	4.35	4.12	3.37
Boundary	4.06	3.27	4.25	4.12	3.63

Instrumental messages

One very clear finding from first-round interviews was that the message seen as transmitted in the act of sentencing often implied the expected response, whether through the language of threats or couched in the more positive terms of a second chance or encouragement. Indeed, an important element in much of the communication discussed in interview was the anticipation of a positive reaction on the part of offenders to the experience of being sentenced, as will be seen below.

Around half the interview participants described the court using threats to secure the desired outcome. This was an idea that resonated particularly with magistrates, who saw a need to make it clear to offenders that nasty consequences would follow continued offending. Offenders, too, detected the message that continued offending would lead to a harsher response, implicitly or explicitly custody. They seemed to regard being given what von Hirsch (1993) has called a 'prudential disincentive' to further offending as an inevitable and unobjectionable part of being sentenced:

> What the magistrates are saying is 'if you go out and burgle this bloke's house and you get caught for it, we're going to put you in prison. And if you do it again, we'll step up a little bit, or we'll put you in prison if you haven't been in before'. (Offender – first-round interview)

A popular variation on the 'threat' theme, conveying both censure and the expectation that the behaviour would stop, was that the court was indicating that the offender had crossed a boundary into unacceptable behaviour, some probation officers specifically referring to boundaries. In referring to society's inability to tolerate offending behaviour, some magistrates implied that offenders should therefore refrain and perhaps be assisted in doing so. However, the following magistrate doubted offenders' capacity to comprehend the point:

I'm trying hard to say 'your behaviour is anti-social. If you want to live in our community then we expect you to abide by some reasonable guidelines'. I suspect that's probably a bit deep for most of our offenders. (Magistrate – first-round interview)

Another prominent idea along similar lines, particularly popular among magistrates, was that of giving the offender a second chance. Portrayed almost as a 'positive' threat, this was expressed in varying ways. According to some magistrates, the offender was being told 'don't step out of line again', 'it's almost the end of the line', 'if you trip up again . . .'. More frequently, however, the sentence was presented as a chance 'for a new beginning', 'to put something right' or 'to prove that this isn't your normal behaviour'. The latter expressions implied that the offender should live lawfully in the future or even make some form of apology or reparation. The fact that this function was usually ascribed to a conditional discharge suggests that magistrates were thinking here of first-time offenders. Victims too tended to apply the idea to cases where the offence might be seen as out of character: the first-time offender or someone whose offending was the product of a poor environment:

There is almost a 'we'll give you a second chance' approach to the first-time offender: 'you've got to choose now whether you are going to commit yourself to a life of crime or choose to go back the other way, and we'll try and help you do that'. (Victim – first-round interview)

Much communication anticipated that the offender would respond positively: making amends for his or her behaviour by putting the harm right in some way or putting something back into society through community service or a reparation order. More broadly, the intention might be to encourage the offender to move forward in a positive way, perhaps to improve themselves by making a 'go' of their life or seeking to become a better person. Some people saw punishment as seeking to 'educate' or 'persuade' offenders to change their behaviour, though Duff's (2001) distinction between moral persuasion and education was hard to detect. These aspirations were often associated with a non-custodial penalty, as discussed later in this chapter.

Drawing on these interview discussions, six statements in the questionnaire addressed instrumental communication (ratings are shown in Tables 5.10 and 5.11). On the whole, and consistent with their view of sentencing aims (see Tables 5.4 and 5.5 above) these instrumental messages carried more meaning for offenders than the normative messages discussed above. In some cases, offenders' responses showed considerable consistency across different questions. For example, a

Table 5.10 Instrumental messages I: percentage agree (and ranking in list of all statements)

Groups	N	Rules 'If you want to live in the community you have to follow the rules'	Threat 'If we see you here again it will be worse for you'	Amends 'We expect you to do something to make up for what you did wrong'
Magistrates	377	78% (4th)	48% (9th)	61% (7th)
Staff	129	69% (5th)	46% (10th)	69% (4th)
Offenders	132	52% (7th)	60% (3rd)	52% (8th)
Victims	107	78% (2nd)	66% (6th)	63% (7th)

Table 5.11 Instrumental messages II: percentage agree (and ranking in list of all statements)

Groups	N	Lawful 'We are giving you a chance to show that you can live a lawful life'	Improve 'This is your chance to show you can make something of your life'	Learn 'This is to help you learn the difference between right and wrong'
Magistrates	375	61% (6th)	56% (8th)	40% (10th)
Staff	129	68% (6th)	66% (7th)	56% (9th)
Offenders	134	65% (1st)	63% (2nd)	53% (6th)
Victims	106	59% (8th)	53% (10th)	59% (9th)

similar proportion of offenders agreed with the idea of a 'threat' as had favoured deterrence as a sentencing aim (Table 5.4), and a similar proportion agreed with 'amends' as had shown support for 'reparation' as a sentencing aim (see Table 5.2 above). Generally, though, these messages attracted less support from offenders than the corresponding sentencing aim: 'lawful' and 'improve' were top of their ranking overall, but lower proportions agreed with the respective statements than had supported 'reform' and 'encouragement' as sentencing aims (see Table 5.5 above). Indeed, the proportions of offenders agreeing were very similar to other groups that had ranked these messages lower, so that 'lawful' ranked 1st with offenders and 6th with staff, and 'improve' 2nd and 7th respectively, but a higher proportion of staff actually agreed with the two statements. Finally, 'learn' attracted less support from offenders as a message than had 'education' as a sentencing aim, possibly because its connotation was more 'moral' (see Table 5.5).

Compared with normative communication, consensus seemed lower among groups other than offenders about these instrumental messages (it will be recalled that their support for consequentialist goals had also been more mixed – see Tables 5.4 and 5.5 above). Magistrates and victims expressed comparatively little support for 'improve', and magistrates and staff likewise for 'threat'. Looking back at the corresponding sentencing aims, 'encouragement' attracted considerably more support from victims, and 'special deterrence' from magistrates and staff. 'Lawful' was less popular as a sentencing message with magistrates and victims than 'reform' was as a goal (staff responses were more consistent as between the two). The fact that 'learn' carried relatively liitle conviction with anyone (as had education as a sentencing aim) might reflect a view expressed in interview that if offenders were not already aware of the difference between right and wrong, it was too late for them to be taught it through being sentenced. 'Amends' received less support than might be expected, given that Table 5.2 (above) indicated that 'reparation' was comparatively popular as a sentencing goal.

Comparisons of mean scores (Table 5.12) revealed that CS staff expressed considerably more support for these instrumental messages than did probation staff (whose views, again, were closer to those of offenders than to those of their colleagues). Differences in means were statistically significant in the case of 'rules', 'threat' and 'learn' ($p < 0.01$) and 'amends' ($p < 0.05$), with CS staff at the top of the range in all cases. Probation staff produced the lowest means of all groups for 'rules' and 'threat', magistrates for 'learn' and offenders for 'amends' (and on the latter, the mean score produced by men was significantly below that produced by women, $p < 0.01$).

Reinforcing the sentencing message

As discussed in Chapter 2, it is central to Duff's (2001) theory that the communication in sentencing continues through the sanction, which should be intrinsically appropriate to the penal aim of moral persuasion.

Table 5.12 Instrumental aims: mean scores

Statement	Magistrates	Probation	CS staff	Victims	Offenders
Rules	4.22	3.49	4.44	4.15	3.58
Threat	3.33	2.76	3.93	3.71	3.71
Amends	3.72	3.70	4.04	3.80	3.43
Lawful	3.84	3.82	4.04	3.58	3.92
Improve	3.67	3.52	3.98	3.59	3.87
Learn	3.13	3.23	4.09	3.61	3.53

How penal messages were reinforced in the delivery of the sentence was most often discussed in interview by probation officers and magistrates. One probation officer saw contact with a penal agent (whether prison or probation) as reinforcing the message that this was a court sentence – a responsibility to be taken seriously. By contrast, a curfew order – where such contact was absent (or restricted to staff monitoring the electronic tag) – might fail to convey that expectation. More generally, merely being on a court order was seen to remind the offender that he or she was being punished for doing wrong. This point was brought home by the fact that the order might be enforced through breach proceedings bringing the offender back to court, although probation officers saw this effect fading over time. Magistrates expressed considerable faith in enforcement, backed by the ultimate sanction of imprisonment, as ensuring that the sentence was taken seriously. One magistrate described encountering in her capacity as a housing adviser an offender who was far more worried about the impact of losing his accommodation on his ability to comply with a curfew order than he was about the prospect of becoming homeless.

Interviewees were aware of the difficulties of getting offenders to see an order as a continuation of a process that began at court, partly because the court hearing might become a distant memory for people on longer orders. Indeed, offenders themselves seemed not to make strong links between what happened to them in court and what happened afterwards, and appeared to see the court and supervisory stages as discrete processes. This account from an offender provides an insight into why the threat of imprisonment might fail to motivate offenders:

> I was supposed to go to court one day but I didn't go. I got my dates muddled up, and I got arrested, spent the night in cells and then got taken to court. I got breached for the [curfew] again, breached for probation and community service and they sent me to prison. [When you didn't manage to keep the curfew going, did you think that you were going to end up in custody?] No. Well I had a little suspicion in the back of my head that I could end up in prison but it wasn't a reality. (Offender – first-round interview)

Both magistrates and probation staff made the point that the sentencing message would be most effectively reinforced where efforts to engage the offender began immediately after sentence. How supervisory staff used their authority and their level of experience or expertise were seen to have an impact on the extent to which offenders took the order seriously and were prepared to take on board its underlying message. An over-authoritarian style was described as counter-productive, but laxness or a lack of interest or commitment was equally ineffective. The following offender questioned why she should be expected to take the process seriously when the pre-sentence report author seemed not to be listening to her:

> But I wish people would listen. Just in one ear, through the empty space and out the other. For instance, I have three sons and a daughter. [According to this probation officer], in the next sentence I had two sons and two daughters. The sentence after I had one son and three daughters. [So you were getting quite confused?] No. I was getting annoyed. Because if she expects me to listen to her, I expect the same courtesy. (Offender – first-round interview)

Several participants suggested how the direct linkage between court and what happened afterwards might be strengthened. An idea inspired by the court's role in Drug Treatment and Testing Orders was for the court to have a review function, to enable sentencers to continue communicating after pronouncing sentence or to learn about the 'successes' instead of just the 'failures' encountered in breach proceedings. An offender argued that the route from court to drugs rehabilitation was too lengthy, and that closer liaison was needed between court, probation and rehab. One probation officer thought it would be helpful for comments to be made by magistrates when passing sentence, so that these could be discussed with offenders at various points during their orders. Another described the ideal implementation of a probation order:

> The order should [continue a process that started in court]. The information from the pre-sentence report about the circumstances of the offence and the factors that motivated it should form the foundation of the supervision plan. (Probation officer – first-round interview)

There was some discussion of how supervisory processes might continue specific elements of the communication started in court, for example that behaviour was wrong and harmful. Again, these ideas came mostly from probation staff and magistrates. Magistrates believed these post-sentence processes might act as a reminder that reinforced their sentencing aims. They sometimes saw probation as involving a demanding review of the offender's lifestyle and pattern of behaviour. According to the following magistrate, the inconvenience of a curfew order both indicated that the behaviour was wrong and encouraged offenders to change by bringing home to them the need to avoid creating problems for others:

> I think it's the only way that really brings it home to them that what they've done is wrong and perhaps acts as a deterrent. You know,

'my mates are out drinking tonight and I've got a curfew order and that's inconvenient to me. I don't really want this and I'll do something about it'. Perhaps it does bring home to them that there is a different life rather than creating problems for other people. (Magistrate – first-round interview)

A process of moral reasoning was depicted by some probation officers, which carried strong similarities to 'moral persuasion' (Duff 2001). However, they were only too well aware of the sheer difficulty of getting some offenders to attend to the wrongfulness of their behaviour or its impact on the victim. Offenders themselves recounted receiving helpful advice or 'straight talk', or having their thinking endorsed (for example, in groupwork programmes). However, as portrayed by offenders, discussions about 'reasoning' were rational rather than 'moral' dialogues. The following offender seems to be referring to the provision of clear advice about decision-making rather than an attempt to persuade him about the nature of his offence as a public wrong and the need to modify his future behaviour:

I can come and talk to my probation officer, I've known her for a long time and she's straight with me and she'll tell me what I need to hear not just what I want to hear. (Offender – first-round interview)

The role of different disposals

This brings the discussion to a consideration of the role played by specific sanctions in transmitting penal messages. The questionnaire asked respondents to tick up to three instrumental messages that the court should be saying in using each of four disposals (as before, prison, probation, community service and the curfew). Table 5.13 shows the top three messages selected by the different groups for each order. The level of consensus between the different groups about the main messages conveyed by each order is striking. On three out of four occasions on which just one group selected a particular sentencing message among its top three, a disposal was interpreted as communicating a threat: custody and CS by offenders, and curfew by staff. Otherwise, magistrates were alone in seeing custody as communicating an expectation that offenders would make up (possibly they meant 'pay') for what they did wrong.

As before, in order to compare how the different groups evaluated the respective disposals in terms of the messages conveyed, I calculated a 'score' based on where each group ranked their 'top three' messages for each order as an overall penal message and converted this to a percentage.[8] The results are shown below, with an overall score in

Table 5.13 Messages conveyed by different orders (up to three selections invited)

Ranking	Magistrate	Staff	Victim	Offender
Custody says by respondent				
1st	Rules 81%	Rules 59%	Rules 76%	Rules 48%
2nd	Learn 53%	Learn 42%	Learn 53%	Learn 47%
3rd	Amends 37%	Improve 36%	Threat 37%	Improve 36%
Average no. of selections	2.13	1.72 probation 2.39 CS	2.41	2.11
Probation says by respondent				
1st	Lawful 71%	Lawful 70%	Lawful 72%	Lawful 45%
2nd	Improve 57%	Improve 58%	Rules 52%	Improve 40%
3rd	Learn 53%	Learn 56%	Improve 44%	Rules 36%
Average no. of selections	2.69	2.57 probation 2.63 CS	2.59	2.10
CS says by respondent				
1st	Amends 73%	Amends 80%	Amends 65%	Amends 40%
2nd	Rules 58%	Lawful 48%	Lawful 52%	Lawful
3rd	Lawful 49%	Rules 44%	Rules 50%	Threat 38%
Average no. of selections	2.63	2.22 probation 2.63 CS	2.61	2.13
Curfew says by respondent				
1st	Rules 77%	Rules 59%	Rules 61%	Rules 50%
2nd	Lawful 46%	Lawful 48%	Lawful 49%	Lawful 43%
3rd	Learn 41%	Threat 33%	Learn 43%	Learn 34%
Average no. of selections	2.28	1.91 probation 2.38 CS	2.41	2.08

brackets; they should be treated with some caution as different disposals received differing numbers of selections or 'votes' from the various groups (as shown in Table 5.13 above). As a rule, disposals received fewest selections from offenders. A more sophisticated calculation would have taken this variability into account, but it would have introduced greater complexity.

- *Custody (73 per cent)* – victims: 87 per cent; magistrates: 80 per cent; offenders: 67 per cent; staff: 60 per cent.

- *Community Service (87 per cent)* – magistrates: 100 per cent; staff: 100 per cent; victims: 80 per cent; offenders: 67 per cent.

- *Probation (65 per cent)* – offenders: 87 per cent; staff: 60 per cent; victims: 60 per cent; magistrates: 53 per cent.

- *Curfew (77 per cent)* – magistrates: 80 per cent; victims: 80 per cent; offenders: 73 per cent; staff: 73 per cent.

The widest diversity of view emerges in relation to probation, which scored lowest overall and which offenders appeared to value considerably more than other groups, while the curfew attracted the highest level of consensus. Otherwise, magistrates and staff both awarded community service 'ten out of ten' and overall it scored highest as a communicative sentence. These findings are the reverse of those reported above, where probation scored highest in terms of the sentencing purposes that it was seen to pursue and community service lowest. It seems that community service carried far more conviction as a communicative sentence than it did in terms of the aims that it was seen to pursue. While it was seen primarily as a retributive and reparative sanction (neither particular popular as a sentencing aim), community service was generally seen to convey the expectations (living lawfully, following the rules and making amends) in which people expressed most faith. Probation, on the other hand, was seen to be communicating less convincing messages (learning the difference between right and wrong, making something of one's life), but was clearly valued as a sanction aimed at reducing offending. I shall discuss the implications of these findings in Chapter 7.

Community service and probation were often cited in interview as examples of how different sanctions might contribute to penal communication. The experience of undertaking community service was seen by magistrates and probation staff as encouraging in people a sense of self-belief or self-efficacy, and the realisation that they had a contribution to make to society.[9] It was suggested that probation and community service might be used to explain or to develop the offender's awareness of the impact of his or her behaviour, or the needs of other people, an understanding that seems close to the idea of 'moral persuasion'. Participants also expressed what might be seen as an 'educational' perspective – variously referring to the 'law as teacher', likening probation to going back to school, and describing CS supervisors as having the opportunity to show offenders that others were worse off than they. This is how one probation officer portrayed what the court was saying in sentencing someone to probation:

'We feel you need to examine your offending, and you need assistance to do so. Therefore we're still judging you. We're still saying you're culpable but we feel you can be helped and this is the means to do it.' (Probation officer – first-round interview)

Conclusions

When it came to the particular penal messages that were being communicated to offenders, views seemed reminiscent of 'dialectically defensible censure' (Bottoms 1998). Offenders should be shown why what they did was wrong and they should come to appreciate the resulting hurt to the victim and harm to the community. There was an element of deterrence in the 'instrumental' messages put across to offenders, though often couched in positive language – giving someone a chance to put the harm right or to adjust their behaviour. Indeed, the expectation was often of a positive reaction from offenders – making amends or moving forward in a positive way as a result of encouraging or educational experiences. In line with the view of offenders as autonomous, self-determining agents, it was seen that they would make decisions to reform themselves – this was not a process that could be foisted upon them.

The penal messages described in interview often anticipated a positive reaction from offenders, and community orders figured quite prominently in explanations of how particular disposals could be used to reinforce those messages. For example, community service enabled offenders to make amends by putting something back into the community, although understandings did not appear to extend to Duff's (2001) model of apologetic reparation (which he accepts might be formal rather than sincere). More broadly, the aspiration that sentencing could be used to encourage the offender to achieve positive change was quite strongly associated with a community sentence. Community service enabled offenders to see that they had something to contribute to society, and therefore to gain 'grounded increments in self-esteem' (Toch 2000), and offenders described themselves as gaining a sense of achievement through probation as well as community service. Reasoning was part of the process of supervision on a probation order, but in offenders' eyes it did not extend to the moral dialogue described by probation officers or envisaged by Duff (2001). This is a discussion that I will take further in the light of the findings presented in the next chapter about how offenders were seen to respond to penal communication.

The above findings indicate that offenders were much less receptive than other groups to any form of penal communication. This is perhaps troubling from a public policy perspective, suggesting a real gap in aspiration and understanding between criminal justice personnel (and victims) and offenders. Findings reported in Chapter 4 suggested that offenders believed that sentencing failed to take sufficient account of their backgrounds and the impact that the punishment might have on them. One might speculate that offenders' perceptions that their circumstances were not being adequately considered may account for some resistance on their part to receiving, or simply an inability to comprehend, what was being conveyed to them. Perhaps what is being expressed, in the lack of support for 'rules', 'amends', 'censure' and 'harm', is disenchantment with a 'community' whose values they do not share or from which they feel excluded. Offenders seemed slightly more supportive of sentiments that centre on the individual – either the victim who has been 'hurt', or the offender who needs to lead a 'lawful' life or 'improve' that life. They also seemed more amenable to the language of 'threat' than to a moral appeal. Criminal justice personnel, on the other hand, clearly aspired to speak in the language of morality.

Notes

1 I called this order 'tagging' on the questionnaire as respondents were likely to have heard of the tag, but defined it as 'the offender is under curfew to stay at home for part of each day'.
2 The dictionary definition (Oxford Concise) of 'retribution' is: *recompense or requital (repay with good or evil)*. I chose to define the term as 'Making them pay for what they did wrong' as a relatively neutral way of expressing the underlying idea. It was a phrase used in first-round interviews and its meaning did not present difficulties in piloting the questionnaire. There was a risk that it might be interpreted literally as a 'financial payment', but a word like 'revenge' with its connotations of illegality was even more likely to be misleading. The fact that exactly the same phrase was used in seeking views about different disposals, both custody and community orders, should have reduced the risk of misinterpretation by making it clear that the meaning was symbolic rather than literal.
3 These differences were significant ($p < 0.01$) in relation to 'victim hurt' (70.3 per cent versus 54.8 per cent), 'persuade' (78.1 per cent versus 64.5 per cent) and 'remorse' (57.1 per cent versus 42.2 per cent).
4 I omitted the combination order (now the combined order) on the basis that it was covered through its components of community service and probation. Nor did I ask about the fine or the discharge, as these are not personally restrictive (although people did refer to them in interview).
5 See Johnson and Rex (2002) for a discussion of pro-social modelling and its development in community service, a topic to which I will return in Chapter 7.
6 I awarded 13 points for a purpose ranked 1st by that group, 12 points for one ranked 2nd, and so on. Thus, custody scored 30 points $(13 + 11 + 6)$ with magistrates out of a maximum possible score of 36 (i.e. 83 per cent). This is because 'disapproval' received top ranking as a sentencing purpose with magistrates, who ranked 'incapacitation' third and 'general deterrence' eighth.
7 As discussed by Bottoms (1998), Lucas (1993) draws a distinction between a vindictive form of retributivism, in which the central objective is to pay

people back for having done wrong, and a vindicative kind, the aim of which is to vindicate the law and the victim and to disown responsibility for the deed.

8   I awarded 6 points for a message ranked 1st overall by that group, 5 points for one ranked 2nd overall, and so on. By this calculation, custody scored 12 points ($6+1+5$) with magistrates out of a maximum possible score of 15.

9   A perceived impact in line with Toch (2000), who argues that 'grounded increments' in self-esteem can be gained by assisting the underprivileged, possibly with rehabilitative implications.

Chapter 6

Responding to punishment

Introduction

Having looked in the last chapter at the penal messages communicated to offenders during sentencing, in this one I turn to the responses expected from offenders. The bulk of the chapter is devoted to this discussion, structured according to the same normative-instrumental categorisation as before. It also examines a subsidiary question that has intuitive appeal but on which there is some debate in the literature: whether an offender who shows remorse or tries to put the damage right in some way deserves a reduced sentence.

In conducting this study, it became obvious that research participants perceived numerous barriers to an effective communication with offenders, with the result that offenders often failed to respond in the ways envisaged. Indeed, the majority of those who completed questionnaire thought that fewer than 50 per cent of offenders did respond as, ideally, they should like them to. The chapter would be incomplete, therefore, without a consideration of why sentencing might fail to live up to the ideal in prompting the desired responses from offenders, and I address that question in the final section. But, first, what did people see as the ideal?

I. Responding to the penal message

As this chapter will show, the people I surveyed and interviewed saw the ideal as being for the penal messages discussed in Chapter 5 to prompt offenders to take responsibility, to realise the harm they had caused, and to accept that it was justified for them to be punished. As in Chapter 5, such aspirations seem close to 'dialectically defensible censure', as theorised by Bottoms (1998). However, in the view of research participants, offenders' reactions should go well beyond a mere acceptance of the legitimacy of the court's sentence. Their acknowledgement that punishment was warranted, it was hoped, would prompt offenders to take positive steps to make amends or to engage in processes of reform. Incidentally, participants' choice of phrases to express what they were looking for from offenders – 'learning a lesson', 'thinking twice' or realising the 'error of their ways' – made it difficult to draw a clear distinction between reform and individual deterrence. This point was touched on in Chapter 5 and it arises again during the course of this chapter.

In discussing below how offenders were seen to respond to punishment, I use the same moral-instrumental categorisation as in Chapter 5, with a similar caveat about the tendency for the distinction to evaporate under scrutiny. A useful starting point is the first-round interviews as these enabled me to explore the themes incorporated in the questionnaire.

Responding to the 'moral' messages

A dominant idea in first-round interviews was that offenders should accept responsibility, both for the offence and for the behaviour in which it was implicated. A sense of responsibility was not expected necessarily to come as an instant response to the sentence: its development was a process that might start or continue *after* the court hearing, perhaps during supervision or from 'mature' reflection. A probation officer commented that some people already knew they had done something wrong, but might not be prepared to admit it even to themselves. Others came to that realisation by being brought to court, but for others 'you will need to work at [it] during supervision'. There was much discussion by magistrates of offenders' taking responsibility and the court being willing to give credit where they showed they had done so. One cautioned against taking the 'hardened' minority as the model for what to expect from others. A victim wanted the offender to be accountable, not just to society, but 'to me as a person'. Offenders recounted how they had come to recognise their own responsibility, sometimes before the court case. A first-time offender saw herself as letting herself down and letting other people down. Another commented:

> One has to admit one's own guilt I think. For us to recognise the things we have done wrong. (Offender – first-round interview)

For some interview participants, offenders' accepting responsibility led logically to their coming to accept the punishment, because they recognised they had done wrong and deserved to be punished. These were processes that both magistrates and offenders saw as occurring over time. Offenders described coming to recognise that they had 'done the crime' so had to 'do the time', and that they might even benefit from an experience that was enjoyable or useful but still clearly a punishment. It seemed important to magistrates that offenders accepted the punishment as fair, proportionate and deserved; this was seen as promoting compliance and perhaps law-abiding behaviour.[1] In recounting real or imagined incidents, some seemed desirous of a subsequent encounter in which the person or his or her immediate family accepted the punishment that the court had handed down.

Probation staff injected a sense of realism about the barriers that might impede acceptance of the punishment by offenders, who might find it difficult to acknowledge the court's authority or experience resentment, alienation or denial (especially if they received a sentence of imprisonment). However, magistrates were also aware that offenders might feel resentful if they did not understand the process leading to sentence or perceived the sentence as unfair. Victims thought a sentence (whether prison, curfew or CS) that the offender perceived as purely punitive rather than useful in any way might breed resentment and possibly a desire for revenge against society (possibly against the victim). Offenders provided interesting insights into the kinds of experiences that might provoke their resentment, whether it was the receipt of a custodial sentence (one protesting 'I haven't got a grudge against the magistrate for sending me down') or the sense that the 'system' simply did not care about them.

It was also recognised by a number of participants that offenders' experiences within the criminal justice system might militate against their ability to take responsibility. Probation staff spoke of the contradiction inherent in trying to get people to take responsibility for themselves, while at the same time controlling their lives through supervision or other restrictions. Prison, in particular, was seen as enabling offenders to avoid responsibility, both for their behaviour and for other aspects of their lives. Specifically in prison, people adapted and became institutionalised, avoided family responsibilities and attended offending or other programmes primarily to pass the time or to secure parole. Prison meant not putting something back into the community; it could leave offenders with no sense of further obligation and with a sense of victimisation. Magistrates, too, spoke of the inadvertent consequences of custody, where offenders had all their decisions made for them and had the slate wiped clean. Worse, it produced a sense of grievance, and of no longer owing anything to society. Echoing views expressed by Lord Woolf (2001), one magistrate saw the short prison sentence as a poor alternative to a community order, achieving neither punishment nor rehabilitation. For another magistrate, the logic of this argument was that magistrates required stronger powers than the maximum six months sentence currently available for a single offence. Offenders repeated similar arguments (with the exception of the last):

> I had no responsibilities. I think that's why I preferred it in there than I did outside because all the responsibility is gone. (Offenders – first-round interview)

Around half the interview participants discussed how the offender came to realise the harm he or she had caused as an aspect of accepting responsibility. Probation staff saw this as part of the process towards rehabilitation; it required insight into one's behaviour and induced feelings of remorse. It was a less prominent theme for magistrates, but some thought that the cold light of day, or community reparation, might cause the impact of the offence on other people to dawn on offenders. Offenders reported coming to admit in a variety of ways the harm caused to victims, to themselves, and to their families – some before the court case, others as a result of experiences on probation. One commented of probation 'it does make you sit back and think: "would I like my things to be smashed or taken" '. Unsurprisingly, it was particularly important to victims that the impact on them should be brought home to offenders; demanding work might help offenders realise the value of what they had taken or damaged (for example how long it took to earn the money to buy a car). In the opinion of one victim, what they had done to others should outweigh offenders' concern about their own plight:

> Well firstly [the offender should] be obviously sorry for what they've done, realise what they've done and not worry about what's actually going to happen to them. It's what they've done to another person that matters. (Victim – first-round interview)

Implicit in the above quote is the hope that the realisation that one had done wrong and harmed others would stimulate feelings of remorse. This was a response that was widely seen as propelling decisions to change one's behaviour, partly because it indicated a readiness to take other people into account in formulating one's actions. Offenders saw remorse as a natural process, which could not be 'forced' yet might promote acceptance of the sentence where it did take place. Magistrates discussed signs of remorse in court, such as body language or some act of reparation, which were more credible from the first-time offender, and discussed how they might respond to such a display. The fact that an offender appeared remorseful might inform sentencing decisions, prompting a conditional discharge or a community service order rather than a combination or probation order because the offender was not seen as needing to be deterred from or persuaded to stop offending. Victims saw remorse as indicating that offenders had punished themselves, had learnt their lesson or might be 'easier to reach', and sometimes as a prerequisite to change. For probation staff, remorse was indicative of a lower risk of reoffending or provided a basis for rehabilitation; therefore it might justify a probation order. One probation officer discussed using remorse in post-sentence processes:

> I think there is room for using remorse in sentencing after the event ... Yes I do think that [the process of remorse is a necessary part of people not offending in the future]. I think that our responsibility is to motivate them to get to that point where they can start to look at what they did and why they did it. (Probation officer – first-round interview)

Clearly, the above discussion begs the question whether a display of remorse justifies a reduced sentence (the classic case being an early guilty plea). This is known to be a vexed question, on which Duff (2001) opposes a reduced sentence, partly because it encourages dishonesty and sends the wrong messages about crime, but more significantly because repentance and reparative apology need to 'complete' the process begun by remorse. It is a point on which the views of interview participants were divided. One probation officer thought that magistrates might be inclined to show leniency towards the remorseful, deferential offender who displayed the right reactions in court; another argued that society's expectation of punishment minimised the amount by which the sentence could be reduced. Such reservations seemed symptomatic of a reluctance to make judgements about what were seen as profoundly intimate and internal processes. People expressed discomfort about having to distinguish the genuinely 'remorseful' offender from one that was merely self-pitying. Probation staff cited the difficulties of making an accurate assessment, partly because of the incentives to show remorse in the pre-sentence report interview to elicit sympathy and a reduced sentence. One was less convinced, the greater the display:

> In my experience, the ones that have felt genuinely terrible about the things they have done, somehow don't feel the need to go around telling everybody how bad they feel. (Probation officer – first-round interview)

Magistrates were also aware of the difficulties of judging sincerity, one saying they believed it occasionally and another that it failed to convince them in 75 per cent of cases. Defence lawyers clearly inspired scepticism in some magistrates by an over-reliance on remorse in pleas in mitigation. One victim saw real remorse as inducing a deep sense of shame that was difficult to articulate – the person getting drunk at a party who was unable to face anyone the following day.

Despite such doubts, the quality of the remorse experienced by some offenders seemed to invite compassion and what might be seen as an exercise of mercy. Certainly, it is difficult to identify a principled judicial rationale for the reduced sentence that some interview participants seemed to envisage for offenders who exhibited particularly strong emotions. Bottoms (1998) suggests that normative penal theory, such as that postulated by von Hirsch, might accommodate what Lucas (1980) describes as the 'rational exercise of mercy' based on a set of rules applied consistently to exactly similar cases.[2] Lucas uses the example of the genuinely remorseful offender to illustrate his argument that leniency in such a case is not unfair, so long as similarly culpable and similarly penitent offenders are treated in the same way.[3] The people I interviewed implied that an extra element, beyond the mere expression of remorse, was required to demonstrate genuine contrition. Clearly, this is a contentious proposition to the extent that it suggests that whether one receives leniency might depend upon one's ability to manifest the desired emotional reactions.

One way in which offenders were seen as displaying genuine remorse was through experiencing obvious shame or fear, an experience that one or two victims thought might be useful for young offenders (though another argued that shaming processes were likely to inspire resentment rather than guilt). Magistrates sometimes expressed sympathy towards the person who was clearly petrified to find themselves in court or incoherent with tears in the dock. The experience recounted by one offender of being too ashamed to tell her parents or friends, and therefore going through the court hearing without their support, made it possible to comprehend the sympathetic reactions she encountered from probation and court staff. Indeed, probation staff described their feelings of compassion towards remorseful offenders who felt self-disgust or a need to suffer in order to absolve their guilt. One community service officer had been prompted to mitigate the impact of the punishment on someone who had already paid his dues through the suffering imposed on himself:

He felt if he could suffer personally, it would make it a bit better. He just wanted to do anything he could to try and make things better ... I suppose with this guy, if he'd come here saying 'I don't care, I don't give a damn', I'd have probably stuck him on a group with seven or eight other offenders and a supervisor, and he'd have had a slightly harder time. Whereas, because of the way he was in the interview, I found him a nicer – wasn't cushy – but a nicer placement . . . So I think that must have some impact on the sentencer . . . I did feel sorry for him. (Probation officer – first-round interview)

More problematically, the offender might experience a sense of shame (or shame-guilt according to Braithwaite and Braithwaite 2001 – see Chapter 2) or humiliation. The few offenders who mentioned these experiences saw them as an uncontentious part of going to court or being made to perform community service where 'it might be good for your mates to see that you're having to paint this school 8 hours a day'. Some magistrates believed that feeling shamed might prove crime-reductive as the person who was ashamed might never commit another crime again. The reasoning offered by one magistrate seemed quite reminiscent of reintegrative shaming (Braithwaite 1989): 'naming and shaming' was desirable to make offenders accountable to the community, not in a stigmatising sense but to make other people aware that they had been in trouble and were doing something to recompense society. Victims also seemed inclined to support a 'humiliating' process in order to deter the offender or make him or her experience guilt. However, one victim (an ex-offender) saw attempts to make someone feel guilty as more likely to provoke resentment than a sense of shame. Probation officers, too, had mixed feelings. One described being sent to prison as shaming because 'ultimately, [it was] saying "you cannot control yourself so we are going to control you" '; this was not a message that should be conveyed too soon.

I drew on the above analysis in formulating twelve statements in the questionnaire to encapsulate the ways in which offenders might be expected to respond after being sentenced, to which respondents were invited to indicate the extent of their agreement ('5' being strongly agree and '1' not at all). Six of these statements addressed the offender's taking on board the normative messages underlying sentencing (explored in Chapter 5). (The others dealt with instrumental responses and will be discussed in the next section.) For ease of presentation, ratings of these statements are presented in Tables 6.1 and 6.2.

One point that emerges from these data is that the proportions agreeing with the statements were markedly lower in the case of offenders than for other groups. Together with the similar findings discussed in Chapter 5, this indicates a lack of engagement on the part of offenders with penal communication, a finding to which I shall return in the next section of this chapter.

The fair degree of consensus that offenders should 'take responsibility' was hardly surprising given the prevalence of this idea in first-round interviews. Otherwise, offenders' views were somewhat out of line with

Table 6.1 Accepting behaviour was wrong: percentage agree (and ranking in list of all statements)

Groups	N	Take responsibility 'Accept that what they did was wrong'	Accept hurt 'Accept that they hurt the victim'	Accept harm 'Accept that they have harmed the community'
Magistrates	372	95% (2nd)	94% (3rd)	86% (6th)
Staff	127	88% (2nd)	87% (3rd)	78% (6th)
Offenders	139	74% (4th)	58% (9th)	48% (12th)
Victims	108	89% (4th)	93% (3rd)	77% (7th)

Table 6.2 Taking disapproval on board: percentage agree (and ranking in list of all statements)

Groups	N	Feel ashamed 'Feel ashamed for what they have done'	Show remorse 'Show that they are sorry for what they have done'	Accept punishment 'Accept that it is right for them to do the punishment'
Magistrates	372	67% (12th)	76% (8th)	83% (7th)
Staff	127	45% (12th)	65% (10th)	72% (7th)
Offenders	137	52% (11th)	71% (5th)	65% (6th)
Victims	106	73% (10th)	76% (9th)	77% (8th)

those of other groups: 'accept hurt' came 9th with offenders but 3rd in other rankings; and 'accept harm' was least popular with offenders but middling in its other rankings. Conversely, 'show remorse' was 5th with offenders but ranked much lower by others, possibly reflecting the doubts expressed in interview about the sincerity of such a response. In keeping with the somewhat mixed views expressed in interviews, there was much less consensus about the value of 'feel ashamed'. A probation officer explained in follow-up interview that she had been unable to rate 'feel ashamed' because she did not believe that sentencing should be a 'shaming' experience; treating the offender with respect was more likely to produce the desired sense of shame. I shall look at how mean scores compared for these and instrumental messages below.

The impact of 'instrumental' messages

It was clearly the hope of participants in first-round interviews that their taking the normative messages on board and experiencing feelings of remorse might prompt offenders to take positive steps or to refrain from certain activities, and ultimately to stop offending. Similar views were expressed in follow-up interviews, where this offender saw an acceptance of the punishment as a prerequisite to future restraint:

> I think, fundamentally, if somebody doesn't accept that what they did was wrong, or doesn't actually accept that the punishment that's been given out to them was right, then it actually can't be in their own heads that they wouldn't do it again. (Offender – follow-up interview)

Interviewees were only too well aware of the obstacles to discontinued offending: that their own social circumstances or the 'system' might make it more difficult for offenders to stop. Nonetheless, those who discussed it still saw continued offending as warranting a more severe penalty, a view endorsed by the many questionnaire respondents who agreed that prior record should influence sentence length (see Chapter 4 above). There were various rationales put forward to justify this position: 'prison' was the only way to protect society; society had lost sympathy; disappointment needed to be signalled at the offender's failure to heed the warning or to respond as expected. In envisaging what might happen where an offender *failed* to stop offending, even against the odds, such accounts were very telling about the level of expectation upon offenders not to offend in the future. One probation officer recounted in a follow-up interview it being quite galling when a quite serious offender had failed to respond to the chance offered by being given a probation order. When asked how he had dealt with that, he continued:

> Well I kept trying with him, but in the end I gave up, because it was evident that he was just not interested. And he let it be known that he wasn't interested and that he held me, and the probation service, in contempt. That's why it springs to mind, I think, it wasn't just that he wasn't really interested, cause there are lots of people who aren't really interested, but it was his hostility and contempt that sprung to mind. (Probation officer – follow-up interview)

One positive response, discussed by around a third of interview respondents across all groups, was for the offender to want to make amends. Probation staff linked this to processes of rehabilitation, through which efforts the offender might demonstrate amends-making for his or her offence. Magistrates reflected on offenders' wish to go to some lengths to clear their conscience. Victims saw a need for offenders to make some recompense (possibly symbolic) to make up for the damage caused, while 'hard treatment' might provide the offender with a chance to expiate guilt and atone for his or her offence. One quite graphically illustrated the point by imagining a dialogue in which a judge asked the offender what he or she could do to *'make it better'*, to which the offender might respond 'I won't have bananas' or 'I'm going to eat less ice cream'. Offenders, too, expressed similar sentiments in wanting to do something right to make up for the wrong and to put something back into the community.

Linked to this was the idea of paying one's dues, others recognising the point made by this probation officer about prison impeding such a process:

> You certainly hear offenders say 'well I've been to prison. I've paid the price. I've paid for that. I don't see why that should be brought up again'. So they feel this paying a price. You do something wrong and you pay for it and then it's finished with. So there's that kind of message that's given to them. (Probation officer – first-round interview)

A more introspective reaction, again mentioned by around a third of respondents, was for offenders to 'think twice' as a result of the punishment. Some were quite obviously referring to deterrence, but for others the phrase seemed to signify a more reflective process leading towards self-reform – itself an important idea that was discussed by around two-thirds of the participants. Almost all offenders referred to the possibility of reforming themselves; they placed varying degrees of emphasis upon the role of external factors. Probation staff recognised that offenders had to be prepared to change – it was patronising, punitive and ineffective to do things *to* people – but expressed different views as to how the sentence might signal that expectation. For one, the offender had to prove an ability to live legally in the community; another saw custody as inevitable in the absence of a prospect of change. The following probation officer was relieved not to be able to penetrate people's internal states:

> I suppose there is an expectation that, by receiving a sentence, the person will review and reflect and examine themselves and what has contributed to their being in that place and how they can take steps to change their attitudes. [Have you encountered people who have gone through that sort of process would you say?] I've had experience of people who have said that they have. You can't see inside a chap's soul, thank God. (Probation officer – first-round interview)

Magistrates portrayed a rational, thinking offender with responsibility to change him or herself in response to varying stimuli – avoiding custody, family responsibility, becoming aware that they could live without causing harm to others. There was an element of deterrence in this thinking, coupled with the awareness that 'you can take someone to court but only they can change themselves'. Victims gave the idea of reform less prominence, but one expressed the view that a compulsory attendance might draw someone to a position where they recognised what they had done and wanted to be different. Offenders emphasised that the decision, and the effort, was for them to make, albeit in response to a variety of factors including the wish to make something of their lives:

> So it wasn't what the courts did to me, it was within me that I wanted to stop all the stuff that I've done, petty things, criminal damage and drink driving ... [And what makes you think it's got to stop, what's the important consideration?] Because I want to get somewhere in life. I didn't want to be in and out of prison. (Offender – first-round interview)

In the eyes of around a quarter of interview participants, feelings of remorse might excite repentance – a determination not to reoffend. However, this determination might not always be realised, as one offender put it 'because you don't know what stands in line six months later'. Probation staff, too, recognised that people who were determined to behave differently or avoid custody might fail because of their social circumstances or an inability to change. Magistrates saw repentance as relevant to sentencing, seeing a person who was really sorry as less likely to offend again, but expressed different views about by how much the sentence should be reduced. One victim was clearly discomforted by the religious connotation associated with repentance, but could not think of a more appropriate word:

> It's more than remorse because remorse can just mean feeling sorry for yourself, so it's the feeling sorry for what you've done and its effects on others. The word repentance means changing, a giving up of one side and moving to another, that sort of change, whereas remorse can mean you are still stuck in feeling sorry for yourself. I can't think of a word that doesn't have any religious connotation. (Victim – first-round interview)

Some participants referred specifically to the offender's making an apology, raising similar doubts about its sincerity to those discussed above in relation to remorse. They also foresaw occasions where words alone would be insufficient to reflect the gravity of the behaviour for which the offender was apologising, and saw a need in such cases for an apology to be accompanied by specific reparative activity. Positive steps towards reparation for the victim or community or to reform oneself, then, were seen as ways in which offenders might both prove that they meant it and simultaneously give their apology appropriate weight. As in the case of remorse, it seemed that offenders would have to make extra efforts if they were to dispel scepticism about their sincerity. This kind of ambivalence is reminiscent of the analysis by Tavuchis (1991), in which he explores the sociological significance of an apology as an acknowledgement of responsibility and expression of genuine regret and remorse. Of the impact of bringing third parties into what is more naturally a private realm he observes, '[third party] intervention ... typically militates against a mutually acceptable and morally satisfying resolution insofar as it interferes with the normal unfolding of the process' (1991: 51). This might illuminate the dissatisfaction expressed by interview participants with processes of remorse and apology within the criminal justice setting, where such reactions might be 'forced' or inspired by considerations other than a wish to acknowledge one's responsibility and assuage one's guilt.

On the basis of the above analysis, I included six statements in the questionnaire about offenders' readiness to change their behaviour; ratings are presented in Tables 6.3[4] and 6.4. Table 6.3 shows that 'repent' and 'prepared to change' were popular with all groups. The fact that 'deterred' topped the list for offenders suggests that this was a significant incentive for them to want to change their behaviour, a point to which I shall return below.

It is interesting that no group showed strong support for a reparative response from offenders (Table 6.4). Beyond 'pay dues' achieving a middling ranking with offenders and 'make up' with victims, low proportions agreed with these statements compared with other state-

Table 6.3 Avoiding future offending: percentage agree (and ranking in list of all statements)

Groups	N	Deterred 'Want to avoid being punished again'	Prepared to change 'Be willing to change their behaviour'	Repent 'Try to avoid offending in the future'*
Magistrates	375	89% (4th)	88% (5th)	97% (1st)
Staff	128	80% (5th)	82% (4th)	95% (1st)
Offenders	139	86% (1st)	77% (3rd)	84% (2nd)
Victims	105	86% (5th)	94% (2nd)	98% (1st)

*See the explanation of this definition in note 4.

Table 6.4 Offering recompense: percentage agree (and ranking in list of all statements)

Groups	N	Pay dues 'Be ready to pay their debt to society'	Make up 'Be ready to make up for what they have done wrong'	Compensate 'Try to put right the harm to the victim'
Magistrates	373	70% (11th)	75% (9th)	75% (10th)
Staff	128	63% (11th)	70% (9th)	71% (8th)
Offenders	136	63% (7th)	61% (8th)	54% (10th)
Victims	104	73% (11th)	80% (6th)	70% (12th)

ments (although two-thirds or more of most groups still showed support for them). The fact that 'compensate' was the least popular statement with victims seems indicative of a high level of public spiritedness, or perhaps a wish so to present themselves, consistent with their emphasis in interview on the need to protect other potential victims. What we do not seem to be seeing here is a strongly restorative paradigm – other accounts seemed to have more resonance.

The emerging picture is that offenders were less able to identify and receive penal messages than other groups were to transmit them (see Chapter 5). However, they were reasonably responsive to those messages: their top 5 options attracted over 70 per cent of agreement, and it was only 'accept harm' that attracted support from less than 50 per cent of them. Indeed, the comparison of mean scores in Table 6.5 shows that it was in fact probation officers who often produced the lowest mean scores overall, and CS staff the highest (in line with findings presented in Chapter 5). Amongst other groups, the level of consensus was remarkably high; the only statistically significance difference in the mean scores produced by magistrates, CS staff and victims related to 'deterred', more popular with magistrates than CS staff or victims ($p < 0.01$).

Relatively speaking, probation officers' views were in tune with offenders', but there were six statistically significant differences between their respective mean scores: 'accept harm', 'feel ashamed', 'show remorse' and 'deterred' (all $p < 0.01$); and 'accept hurt' and 'pay dues' ($p < 0.05$). Offenders were actually more receptive than probation officers to the idea that they should 'feel ashamed', 'show remorse' and 'pay dues'; they were also much closer to or even slightly above the other groups on 'deterred'. On the other hand, probation officers showed more support than offenders for 'accept hurt' and 'accept harm', a finding in keeping with the emphasis in current probation practice on confronting offenders with the consequences of their offending.

Table 6.5 Responses: mean scores

Statement	Magistrates	Probation	CS staff	Victims	Offenders
Take responsibility	4.69	4.00	4.53	4.55	4.19
Accept hurt	4.65	4.16	4.46	4.67	3.83
Accept harm	4.43	3.99	4.34	4.24	3.46
Feel ashamed	3.99	2.97	3.91	4.14	3.55
Show remorse	4.13	3.39	4.29	4.19	3.94
Accept punishment	4.33	3.62	4.47	4.25	3.88
Deterred	4.62	4.03	4.43	4.37	4.45
Prepared to change	4.58	4.16	4.54	4.64	4.15
Repent	4.78	4.53	4.72	4.81	4.38
Pay dues	4.12	3.44	4.42	4.01	3.81
Make up	4.16	3.64	4.42	4.19	3.81
Compensate	4.14	3.77	4.23	4.00	3.69

In fact, mean scores for all groups (including probation officers and offenders) were high for 'repent', 'take responsibility' and 'deterred'. This raises the question whether offenders were seen as trying to avoid offending in the future (repenting) because they were deterred or because they had taken the normative messages on board, or indeed because of a mixture of the two as suggested by von Hirsch (1993). If the latter, do respondents agree with von Hirsch that the normative reasons outweighed the 'prudential discentive' to further offending? Here, comparative rankings suggest that normative considerations weighed more with other groups but that offenders saw themselves as responding primarily to a wish to avoid being punished in the future.[5] In follow-up interview, one probation officer described how she saw the process working:

> I think the sentence should be a vehicle for a person to recognise that they need to change. I think that's one of the aims of sentencing: through the sentencing process, the person has time to reflect 'I need to change that, because I have done this and that wrong'. Very often, people go to court without realising how serious the offence was, and through the process of sentencing they may actually learn that what they've done is much more serious than their understanding of the situation. (Probation officer – follow-up interview)

It is possible to test further the association between the wish to avoid future offending and taking responsibility on the one hand or being deterred on the other by examining the extent to which scores correlated on the pairings *deterred/repent* and *take responsibility/repent*. These tests produced the following results:

- Overall, the correlation on *take responsibility/repent* was remarkably similar to that on *deterred/repent* (0.468 and 0.467, both statistically significant at $p < 0.01$).

- The strongest correlation on *deterred/repent* was with offenders (0.648, $p < 0.01$), but it was also fairly strong in the case of probation officers (0.551, $p < 0.01$).

- The correlation between the two statements was moderate in respect of both magistrates and CS staff (0.414 and 0.417 respectively, $p < 0.01$), but low with victims (0.235, $p < 0.05$).

- *Take responsibility/repent* achieved a moderate correlation in the case of both probation officers and offenders (0.427 and 0.524 respectively, $p < 0.01$), as well as victims (0.436, $p < 0.01$) and magistrates and CS staff (0.399 and 0.422, $p < 0.01$).

It can be seen from these findings that the strength of correlation on each pair is very similar in the case of magistrates and CS staff. It is not altogether surprising that offenders' scores correlated to a greater extent on *deterred/repent* than on *take responsibility/repent*. However, it does seem surprising that the same applied in the case of probation officers. Conversely, victims appeared to correlate 'take responsibility' with 'repent' considerably more strongly than they did 'deterred' (the *deterred/repent* correlation also achieved a lower level of statistical significance). This suggests that victims put more emphasis on the normative considerations, but that instrumental incentives actually weighed more heavily with offenders, as probation officers may have been aware. Magistrates and CS staff appeared to weigh normative and instrumental factors about equally.

Finally, when comparing male-female mean scores, women produced higher mean scores than men for all statements except 'deterred'. None of the differences on instrumental responses reached statistical significance, nor did 'show remorse', whereas all the differences on the normative statements were statistically significant ($p < 0.01$ for 'take responsibility', 'accept hurt' and 'accept harm'; $p < 0.05$ for 'feel ashamed' and 'accept punishment'). In general terms, this pattern seems likely to mirror the views of offenders, who were predominantly male (and less in favour of the normative statements than other groups, with the exception of 'show remorse').

II. Leniency for the remorseful offender?

As discussed above, a question on which sharply differing views were expressed in first-round interviews, as in the literature, was whether

Table 6.6 Response justifies reduced sentence: percentage agree

Groups	N	*Sorry* 'They show they are sorry for the crime'	*Put right* 'They have tried to put some of the harm right'	*Change* 'They have already tried to change their ways'
Magistrates	379	56%	76%	70%
Staff	130	45%	76%	67%
Offenders	135	53%	84%	68%
Victims	108	37%	65%	64%

offenders who showed remorse should receive a reduced sentence. I tested this further in another part of the questionnaire by asking respondents the extent to which they agreed that factors indicating a response from the offender should elicit a reduced sentence.

The ratings in Table 6.6 show a fair degree of consensus as to the relative weight of these factors – with offenders giving them slightly more support than other groups and victims slightly less. In line with more general reservations about remorse expressed both in interviews and in questionnaire responses, little support was given to an offender's showing that he or she was sorry. As one offender argued in follow-up interview, 'anyone can come up with a sob story', doubts echoed by others. In explaining why she was not impressed with statements in court about feeling sorry or ashamed for having committed the offence one magistrate exposed thinking somewhat similar to the arguments put forward by Duff (2001):

> The way that they can show me that they're sorry and they understood what they've done is not to do it again. If they can't do that, then I don't think that they were truly remorseful. (Magistrate – follow-up interview)

There was far more support for 'put right' and 'change', perhaps indicating that people were looking for an active demonstration of remorse on the part of the offender of the kind discussed in the last section. In follow-up interviews, respondents illustrated the kind of action they might be looking for: a supervised dialogue with the victim or undertaking certain steps to change their ways (victims); doing voluntary community work or extra CS hours (offender); and embarking on an addictions programme (magistrate).

This is a point on which Duff (2001) might disagree, arguing that repentance – like remorse – does not justify a reduce sentence. In part this is because of the requirement that the severity of the sentence should reflect the seriousness of the crime, which is not lessened by virtue of repentance unless it indicates that the offence was an aberration and the offender therefore less culpable. Perhaps more importantly, Duff presents the whole sentence as serving the dual purpose of inducing and expressing repentance; for the already repentant offender, it acts as apologetic reparation from the start. Dignan (2003) offers a slightly more sympathetic position from a restorative perspective, in which he suggests that the 'wrongfulness' of a crime may be determined in part by the extent to which the offender may be willing to engage in reparation, perhaps by participating in a restorative process.

III. The efficacy of the message

As Duff (2001) argues, his theory represents an ideal; it does not describe or justify criminal justice processes as they operate in practice (see Chapter 2 above). I was very conscious that I had been asking respondents to talk about the 'ideal': what they thought the court *should* be trying to achieve in sentencing, what messages it *should* convey and how offenders *should* respond to those messages. First-round interviews contained much discussion of the limitations of sentencing, why it might fail to live up to this ideal picture. In the questionnaire, I therefore invited respondents to indicate what percentage of offenders they thought actually did respond as they had indicated (eight gradations between 0 and 100 per cent were offered as well as 'no idea').

Responses, summarised in Table 6.7, show that staff and offenders were considerably more optimistic than magistrates or victims (the views of probation officers and CS staff were quite similar, with CS staff being the slightly more positive). Differences between the views of offenders and both magistrates and victims were statistically significant ($p < 0.01$). Indeed, victims seem particularly pessimistic, with the vast majority believing that no more than a third of offenders would be prepared to take the normative messages on board, to avoid offending or to offer recompense.

Table 6.7 How many offenders 'respond' to penal message

Groups	N*	Up to 33%	50% to 66%	75% plus
Magistrates	305	230 (75%)	59 (19%)	16 (5%)
Staff	118	72 (61%)	36 (31%)	10 (8%)
Offenders	99	54 (55%)	28 (28%)	17 (17%)
Victims	89	75 (84%)	11 (12%)	3 (3%)

These differences raise the question whether the staff view was actually more in tune with how offenders react and magistrates and victims unduly cynical. Alternatively, offenders and staff may be presenting a rosier image, so that magistrates and victims are actually being more realistic. However, it remains the case that the majority of all groups of respondents thought that fewer than 50 per cent of sentenced offenders responded in the ways discussed in this chapter, and it is worth investigating why views were quite so negative.

For illumination, it is necessary to turn to accounts given in interviews (on which there has already been some discussion in Chapter 5). Here, I focus on how offenders' experiences in the courtroom or their wider experiences of criminal justice might detract from the efficacy of the sentencing message. This is not to deny the importance of wider questions relating to offenders' experiences of social 'justice', i.e. exclusion and disadvantage (as discussed by Raynor 1997 and Hudson 1998). However, I do not see myself as competent to contribute to those questions given the focus of my research on the processes of sentencing and punishment.

A major impediment was that one party to the communication – the offender – was not seen as receptive or participating. Their preoccupation with the threat of receiving a custodial sentence and their relief when this proved not to be the case was seen to restrict offenders' ability to absorb any other information. According to offenders, the only thing on their mind was whether they were going to get a custodial sentence; everything else went over their heads. Probation officers and magistrates both realised that this was the case. For probation officers, it meant that offenders might leave court without 'a clue' as to what a community order involved, so that it was imperative to start making that clear as soon as possible after the court hearing. A magistrate graphically described the moment sentence was handed down:

> When the Chairman's announcing what the punishment is to be, all the offender hears is the first couple of words which tell him whether he's going to prison. Whether he's going to be on probation. Whether he's going to be fined. After that they don't hear a single word. (Magistrate – first-round interview)

Another factor was offenders' resistance to the messages conveyed in sentencing. Sometimes this came across as bravado, used to conceal more fearful reactions or to maintain street credibility. On other occasions, offenders simply seemed to lack interest or motivation. This was of particular concern to probation officers; offenders, they suggested, might appear amenable in court but have no real intention of taking the order seriously. They might be resistant to the idea that they needed someone to help them achieve change, or they might technically comply with the terms of an order but with no real engagement. The following probation officer was frank about her failure to get a heroin addict to address his offending:

> So I stopped that and started talking more about the drug problem. When somebody answers in monosyllables the whole time, it is really difficult. Essentially it deteriorated into monitoring his behaviour and where he was living and his drug intake. His drug intake had a big impact on his offending, so I thought I was doing something meaningful, even though it wasn't what I would have liked to be doing. Maybe it takes a better officer than me, and also one that's got more experience. I discussed it with colleagues. He just would not engage with it at all. So, basically probation was a waste of time and what he was doing that week was none of my business. Yet he came into the office, so technically he was complying. (Probation officer – first-round interview)

A magistrate described being similarly inhibited in court when faced with a group of 'fairly uncooperative young men':

> And I prodded very hard to try and get them to say something, they didn't. They were surly. They weren't actually rude, but they were damned near. In the end I got up in a hurry, said 'right, let's go, sort this out'. Whether that left the right message or not, I don't know. (Magistrate – first-round interview)

Added to this, courtroom processes were seen to impede communication in a number of respects. Magistrates described the experience as frightening, confusing and punishing, for first-time offenders in particular. This might act as a deterrent, but it also made it difficult for the offender to take anything on board. Offenders recounted feeling excluded, confused about what was going on and anxious about the outcome. The following offender discerned a complete failure to appreciate his predicament on the part of the 'professionals' in court:

> It was the second-time I've ever been in court in my life. Even the solicitor, he said 'oh don't look so worried' and everybody else was all laughing and joking. It's water off a duck's back to them, I'll be here again next week and it didn't worry them. Whereas I had sleepless nights. (Offender – first-round interview)

Part of the confusion experienced by offenders was attributed to the technical language and ritualistic nature of the proceedings, in which offenders saw themselves as playing no role. To some extent, the process was seen as a game in which a certain amount of 'acting' was demanded. Offenders' own lawyers were seen as adept at 'playing the game': speaking on their behalf and translating their words into the appropriate legal jargon, and sometimes appearing flippant or over-friendly with the prosecution. All this intensified offenders' feelings of exclusion and alienation. A probation officer described breach proceedings in which the offender clearly had no idea as to what was going on:

> They said 'Do you admit or deny the breach?' The defence looked at him: 'I don't know'. The solicitor just said 'Admit. Admit'. And so the guy said 'Yeah I admit it'. It just makes a mockery of the whole thing really. If he doesn't understand what is going on at that level. Whether he was admitting or denying [the breach]. (Probation officer – first-round interview)

Against these conditions, magistrates acknowledged the difficulties in getting offenders to understand or to engage with the sentencing process, although some were at pains to describe their efforts to explain what the sentence meant or to get the offender to think about what the proposed sentence might achieve. Probation officers suggested that their ability to get offenders to engage with community orders might be enhanced by courts' providing written statements of the expectations of the sentence which could be used with offenders afterwards. One magistrate believed that the requirement in the Human Rights Act 2000 to give reasons for sentence would help to reinforce the rationale behind sentencing:

> Sometimes I think we ought to say a bit more, like 'what you've done to the community is not acceptable, and for this reason you're being given a sentence', instead of just blandly reading out an announcement. The new Human Rights requirement, I think, will be great because [...] when we're giving the sentence, we're going to have to give a bit more reasoning about 'the seriousness of your offence, the effect it's had on your victim' and so on. We'll have to give reasons for why we're giving the sentence and I think that's really much better. (Magistrate – first-round interview)

Another set of problems was created by the role of magistrates' courts in dispensing 'inexpensive justice' within a criminal justice system in which the various agencies still failed to work well together (so that offenders were not dealing with a system that appeared coherent or well-integrated). Magistrates and probation officers alike referred to the pressures to get through heavy caseloads, and to make the system more efficient by combining Petty Sessional Divisions or by magistrates' making decisions without retiring for discussion, and the resulting costs to the quality of local justice. Some magistrates saw the options available to them as too restricted or ineffective: fines were counter-productive for people with multiple debts; curfews could not be used for people lacking stable accommodation; and probation or drugs programmes were ineffective for people with intractable problems. The following magistrate regretted the routinised approach to which he sometime resorted in sentencing a repeat petty offender for whom previous sentences had not 'worked':

> I quite often just take the view 'give him three months'. And it's sad really that I should do that. But I'm being honest with you and that is what I do. And perhaps I shouldn't. But the reason I do it is because you look at the number of cases we deal with in a day and there just isn't the time, energy, or will left any more by the time you get to that particular type of case to give it any more than a cursory look and pass it on. (Magistrate – first-round interview)

Conclusions

Research participants hoped that offenders would respond to the experience of being sentenced by accepting that their behaviour had been wrong and merited punishment, thereby being prompted to take steps to make amends and change their behaviour. Indeed, a failure to stop offending was seen to justify a more severe sentencing response, usually for reasons (losing sympathy or being disappointed) that seem consistent with the principle that a repeat offender should progressively lose mitigation (Ashworth 2000). Although the view was also discernible that society had an additional claim to protection in the case of a persistent offender, findings presented in Chapter 4 suggest that the accumulation of previous convictions was associated primarily with questions of culpability.

An important point to emerge from the findings discussed above is the extent to which deterrence blurred with more normative incentives to desist from offending in people's thinking. Quantitative analysis of questionnaire responses suggested that a wish to avoid offending was more closely associated with deterrence for offenders (and probation officers), that CS staff and magistrates weighed deterrent and normative considerations roughly equally, but that victims placed more emphasis on normative factors. Relating these findings to the literature discussed in Chapter 2, it is difficult to find in them support for von Hirsch's (1993) insistence that the 'prudential disincentive' to offending must be secondary to the normative reasons. Duff (2001) too resists too strong a reliance on individual deterrence as a means to secure lawful behaviour because it undermines the claim to address offenders as members of the normative community who are obligated by laws whose values they share.

In the light of the understandings I encountered, it seems necessary to revisit the argument that individual deterrence is inconsistent with, or can only play a minor role in, a normative theory of punishment in which offenders are treated as rational moral agents. It does not seem acceptable merely to dismiss the views expressed in interviews as muddled or incoherent; these were people with a strong interest in, and real experience of, criminal justice who were thinking carefully about the questions I put to them, and their answers deserve serious consideration. In arguing that it is possible to deter a rational agent by giving reasons against a course of action that he or she will regard as cogent, Lucas seems to get close to the kind of reasoning I heard:

> One man may be deterred by the thought that his action will cause another some pain, another by the fear of doing wrong, another by the fear of public rebuke, and another only because of some adverse effect on his own interests. (Lucas 1980: 145)

Lucas (1980) warns of the dangers of sliding into a more manipulative understanding of deterrence that applies equally to animals, but this did not seem to be how deterrence was understood by the people I interviewed, whose portrayals of offenders were imbued with a strong sense of agency. Offenders were clearly seen as thinking and active, as reacting to what was happening to them and making decisions about what to do as a result. Bottoms (2001) may shed further light on the possible interactions between the normative and the instrumental factors associated with compliance. He theorises that instrumental compliance (secured through deterrence) is enhanced for people with strong attachments to family or social groups who disapprove normatively of the behaviour at which a deterrent sanction is aimed. In a similar way, my interviewees seemed to see instrumental and normative consider-ations as reinforcing each other in offenders' thinking and to contemplate that the respective factors might weigh differently depending on the circumstances in which offenders were placed.[6] However, this does not mean that they would support an increase in the severity of a sentence in order to maximise its deterrent impact on a particular offender; proportionality was regarded as overriding unless crime prevention warranted a departure downwards (Chapter 4).

So what did participants make of remorse, repentance and what Duff (2001) might call a reparative apology? Some certainly accorded these ideas considerable importance, although remorse and reparative actions were ranked comparatively low in questionnaire responses. Coupled with this, the discomfort expressed about the unsatisfactory nature of these intimate processes as acted out within a criminal justice setting argues against their characterisation as central to the purpose of punishment (even in an idealised sense). Respondents might share von Hirsch's (1999) doubts about whether the state is authorised or required to impose secular penance, as envisaged by Duff. Nor, however, would they seem likely to agree with von Hirsch that efforts to encourage offenders to reform (or otherwise to secure a positive response) are merely 'additional permissible activities' and not a justification for punishment. The anticipation of a certain kind of response from offenders, though in many cases it might not be forthcoming for a whole variety of reasons, seemed central to accounts given in interview of the penal messages conveyed in sentencing. Accordingly, that offenders should try to avoid offending in future was given top ranking in questionnaire responses.

It was seen in Chapter 5 that community sentences were prominent in descriptions of how their experiences of penal sanctions might reinforce the communication that had started in court and assist offenders to respond as desired. According to these accounts, undertaking community service or being supervised on probation both had the potential to help offenders take on board the adverse impact that their behaviour might have on other people. In relation to probation, this idea seems close to Duff's (2001) conceptualisation of the aims of the conditions attached to a probation order as communicating to offenders the character and implication of their offences as public wrongs, and therefore to persuade them to modify their future conduct. In the case of community service, a similar process was seen to operate through work site supervisors' showing offenders that others were worse off than them, a possibility posed by McIvor (1998) in reflecting on her study of community service in Scotland (McIvor 1992). This might actually offer a richer and more subtle understanding than that offered by Duff, who portrays community service as 'constituting an attempt to persuade [the offender] to face up to the wrong she has done' (2001: 105).

In keeping with the current vogue for probation programmes to 'confront offending behaviour', probation officers perceived their task as promoting offenders' acceptance of responsibility, both for the offence and for the behaviour in which offending was implicated. They made a link between offenders experiencing remorse and resolving not to offend in the future, and saw their role as helping to stimulate the necessary processes of self-examination. In Duff's words, probation officers seemed to see themselves as getting offenders to attend to the wrongfulness of their behaviour. However, consistent with their more general resistance to what might be summed up as 'penal moralising', offenders themselves portrayed a more morally neutral process in which they received advice or were assisted in their decision-making. Moreover, although probation supervision might help them realise the harm caused by their offending, offenders placed considerable emphasis on their own development of a sense of responsibility, and saw remorse as a natural – rather than an induced – process. The understandings expressed by offenders seemed far short of a conception of probation as aiming to secure their penitent understanding of their wrongs and therefore their repentance (Duff 2001). But they could see probation supervision as helping them to develop a better understanding of their offending and its consequences, and as helping them to engage in processes of change and reform. In the next chapter, I shall consider more fully the possibilities offered by people's understandings of probation and community service.

Notes

1   A view reminiscent of the proposition discussed by Bottoms (2001) that rules promulgated by an authority seen as legitimate are more likely to generate normative compliance than where the authority lacks legitimacy.

2   An idea that seems very close to the criteria for mercy outlined by Walker (1999).

3   Indeed, applying leniency as part of a consistent pattern of sentencing might be seen as a particularised form of justice rather than 'mercy', which suggests the exceptional use of discretion on humanitarian or compassionate grounds.

4   I found it particularly difficult to define 'repent' adequately in the questionnaire. The dictionary definition (Oxford Concise) is 'think with contrition of … be regretful about … wish one had not done, resolve not to continue wrongdoing in', ideas that, as acknowledged by the interviewee quoted above, are difficult to express in straightforward terms. In trying to distinguish between 'repent' and 'remorse', which seems to encapsulate regretting one's actions or wishing one had not done something, I focused on the 'giving up' element in repentance but have to admit that I have failed to do justice to its meaning.

5   'Take responsibility' was ranked above 'deterred' by magistrates, staff and victims, but offenders gave 'deterred' the highest ranking of all 12 statements.

6   In fact, they might be seen as 'integrat[ing] prudential and moral reason [for desisting from offending], by committing himself to pursue his good together with others through moral norms' (Matravers 2000: 264–5).

Chapter 7

Towards a framework for community penalties

Introduction

This chapter brings together the research findings presented in the previous three chapters to consider what they mean for community penalties. Its key concern is whether a communicative theory of punishment offers a promising approach for community penalties and if so how the relevant processes and material forms of these sanctions might be developed to bring out their full communicative potential. In addressing that question, the chapter takes account of recent developments and initiatives relating to community-based interventions.

The chapter comprises four sections. In the first, I discuss the role of communication in punishment in the light of views expressed in interviews and surveys before going on in the next section to look at the role of proportionality in drawing a balance between exacting retribution and pursuing the goal of reduced offending. The third section considers the particular utility that research participants ascribed to community penalties, so laying the ground for moving towards a possible framework for communicative community penalties in the concluding section. Before embarking on the substantive discussion in the chapter, I want to return to the issues raised in Chapter 3 about the relationship between normative theory and the kind of empirical work reported in the three previous chapters. How might people's views elucidate penal theory?

The first point to re-emphasise is that my aim in interviewing and conducting surveys of people who might be seen as having a practical stake in the kinds of questions that penal theory is seeking to address is not to 'prove' or disprove the theory. With Bottoms (2000), I do not believe that 'ought' questions of the kinds to which penal theory seeks principled answers are susceptible to 'proof' in the same way as explanatory theory dealing with social reality. Where I believe my work might be useful is in promoting a dialogue between normative theory and empirical research in which the latter can advance normative analysis (Bottoms 2000) and strengthen its relationship with practical decision-making (Raynor 1997). From a strictly philosophical point of view, discordance between penal theory and ground level thinking, or what Robinson and Darley (1995) might call 'community standards', exposes a tension that requires analysis and possibly the penal theorist to re-examine his or her position. This might lead the theorist either to modify his or her view or to find stronger and more persuasive arguments, especially if she or he was hoping to influence public policy. Moreover, as discussed in Chapters 2 and 4, there is contested ground between different theoretical positions that the views of relevant actors and decision-makers might elucidate. Although not necessarily a con-clusive argument, a finding that a particular approach makes sense to those involved in the criminal justice system might make that approach more plausible or attractive. So might a finding that the approach was seen to have useful practical applications.

From a practical or utilitarian point of view, a penal theorist might be interested in whether his or her theory is likely to 'work', under what conditions and against what possible obstacles. To take just one example, if offenders show some resistance to the idea of penal 'moralising', should we take this into account in developing ways in which to get them to change their behaviour? If courtroom processes are seen to impede effective dialogue, what – if anything – can we do to change those procedures? More widely, as has been pointed out by a number of commentators, how criminal justice is dispensed requires a level of consensus if they are to secure cooperation and prove effective. It seems relevant, therefore, if people see a particular approach as wrong or unfair (or are simply ill-informed or for other reasons lack confidence in the system). Ultimately, whether what people think about punishment 'matters' is a question of opinion, but as was pointed out in Chapter 3 the more recent emphasis on public confidence means that a poorly informed public or misguided assumptions about what the public think can have a deleterious impact on policy. In such a climate, it seems more useful to attempt to conduct research into the kinds of values that people hold than to dismiss their views as irrelevant. At the very least, it is reassuring that people can respond sensibly to various kinds of theoretical ideas even if the theories themselves seem remote from everyday practice. The research reported in this book cannot possibly provide definitive answers to the theoretical questions that I was seeking to explore, or even to address all the aspects to those questions (for example, I have not examined offenders' experiences of exclusion and disadvantage beyond the criminal justice system).[1] However, I hope it will be seen as a starting point, stimulating interest in this line of enquiry as well as further and more sophisticated research than I have been able to conduct.

Punishment as a communicative enterprise

One point to have emerged clearly from the findings discussed in the previous three chapters is that a conceptualisation of punishment as communication accorded with people's everyday understandings. To recap on the findings presented in Chapter 5, all four groups (magistrates, probation and CS staff, offenders and victims) were able to discern normative or 'moralising' messages in the court's sentencing of an offender. Views also supported a 'hybrid' approach to punishment that looks both backwards to the offence and forwards to the possibility of change, as envisaged by both von Hirsch (1993) and Duff (2001). Indeed, 'instrumental' messages played a key role. The messages conveyed in sentencing were clearly intended to elicit a positive response from offenders, usually in the form of making efforts to refrain from offending in the future.

Sentencing as moralising

When asked about the aims of sentencing, magistrates, staff and victims all seemed to see the communication of censure as a key element. This idea is central to penal theory of the kind put forward by von Hirsch (1993) and Duff (2001) in which retribution plays a major role. However, different groups appeared to place the emphasis somewhat differently. For magistrates, the main point seemed to be to demonstrate society's disapproval to the offender. Theirs might be interpreted as a somewhat 'symbolic' approach to sentencing in which the offender is dealt with 'externally', reminiscent of von Hirsch's model as characterised by Bottoms (1998). By contrast, victims and staff seemed to envisage a greater degree of engagement with offenders, in prioritising the need to make offenders see *why* what they did was wrong. This position implies that the offender is a person with a normative outlook who, in Duff's terms, can be persuaded of the wrongfulness of his or her crime. It is consistent with such a view that one should seek to show offenders that they had hurt their victims, an aim also prioritised by staff and victims to a greater extent than magistrates. Generally, people seemed comfortable with the notion that an offence is a *wrong* requiring censure (as opposed to the less 'blaming' conceptualisation of a harm requiring repair, popular among restorative justice theorists – see Chapter 2). However, retribution (making someone pay for wrongdoing) attracted

135

little support as a sentencing aim, and interviews indicated some discomfort with the idea of simply being punitive.

Needless to say, offenders are an important audience for what might be described as penal 'moralising'. It is significant therefore that, as a group, offender participants seemed less convinced by it than other groups (although, when interviewed, other groups too expressed reservations about what underlying value judgements were being implied). Certainly, offenders were less receptive to the expression of disapproval as an aim of sentencing, although more than two-thirds did seem open to persuasion about the wrongfulness of their offences. On both points, the views expressed by probation staff were actually closer to those of offenders than to those of their colleagues in CS.

Prompting remorse was not especially favoured as an aim of sentencing, although Chapter 6 showed that there was rather more support for remorse as a suitable response to sentencing. A possible inference is that participants did not see sentencing as a 'technique for evoking specified sentiments' (von Hirsch 1993: 10), but did consider it desirable for offenders to come to feel a sense of remorse as a result of being taken to court and sentenced. However, reactions to the 'remorseful' offender were qualified by reservations about the scope for dishonesty and manipulation and there was little support for a display of remorse as justifying a reduced sentence. In interview, whether the offender felt sorry for what he or she had done seemed to be seen as a matter for the private 'internal' realm rather than for the formal criminal justice setting. In the latter context, it seemed to be regarded as fitting to retain a certain distance between offenders and criminal justice personnel. Certainly, people expressed some discomfort about delving too deeply into what were seen as intimate processes, trying to penetrate someone's soul or the religious connotation of repentance.

The picture described above was largely confirmed when I asked specifically about the messages that the court was seeking to convey in sentencing an offender. Here, the emphasis was on communicating the damage that the offence had caused rather than simply signalling censure for what the offender did. Again, it seemed important to persuade offenders by making them see *why* what they did was wrong rather than simply to express disapproval. Accordingly, magistrates as well as staff and victims all rated communicating the hurt to the victim right at the top of the list of all statements – both normative and instrumental – that might be communicated to offenders (88 per cent of each group agreed with the relevant statement on the questionnaire). Overall, offenders showed far less support for these normative messages, being distinctly less receptive than other groups to the communication of censure, hurt to the victim or harm to the community. There were some indications that this might be because offenders did not believe that what Duff (2001) describes as the pre-conditions for this normative communication had been met. Chapter 4 suggested that they certainly believed to a greater extent than other groups that sentencing decisions should take account of their peculiar circumstances: what they saw as the predicaments that drew them into offending and the hardship that the punishment might inflict on them personally. The offenders quoted in Chapter 5, who recognised the moral message behind their punishment but disputed its content or the court's authority, might be seen as accepting a communicative account of punishment as a moralising dialogue but wanting to have their say or being concerned with its preconditions. Here, courtroom processes as depicted in Chapter 6 did not appear conducive to offenders' active participation in a moral dialogue, a point on which more is said below.

Sentencing to prevent crime

Chapter 4 showed that all groups quite clearly prioritised crime prevention as *the* overall aim of sentencing, and the pursuit of instrumental goals was accordingly seen as an important element in sentencing. Indeed, offenders placed far more emphasis on those aims associated with their desisting from offending than on more normative aims. Their top five aims of sentencing were all preventive (including incapacitation, but not deterrence). Other groups, too, prioritised certain aspects of prevention as an aim, but not always the same ones. Staff – both probation and community service – rated rehabilitation (tackling the problems behind offending) highest, as did offenders. However, it received considerably less support from magistrates or victims. The last placed more emphasis on getting offenders to reform themselves, perhaps influenced by special deterrence and to a slightly lesser extent assisted by encouragement and rehabilitation. As before, there were significant differences between the views of probation and CS staff, with the latter showing far more support than the former for the idea that sentencing should be used to encourage and educate offenders.

Again, much of the above was confirmed when the questionnaire asked what instrumental messages the court should be seeking to convey in sentencing an offender. Here, other groups placed less emphasis on these than on the normative messages referred to above, but offenders seemed to see sentencing primarily in instrumental terms. Their views painted a picture in which the court was communicating an expectation that they could live lawfully and make something of their lives, backing that up with the threat of dire consequences should they reappear in court. Conversely, neither magistrates nor staff agreed greatly with the sentence being used to convey a threat; despite my impression from interviews that this was an

137

idea with particular resonance for magistrates, it gained comparatively less support when evaluated against the full range of possibilities. As was also suggested in interview, questionnaires prompted a preference for communicating expectations in more positive terms.

Responding to penal communication

Given that the messages seen as conveyed in sentencing often implied the expected response, the strong endorsement of statements (in the questionnaire) encapsulating how offenders should respond to the experience of being sentenced came as no surprise. Magistrates, staff and victims seemed fairly unanimous that offenders should try to avoid offending in the future; they also agreed that offenders should be willing to change their behaviour. Offenders tended to agree that such was the expectation upon them, although their support was more muted. Like von Hirsch (1993), people expected a 'moral' response from the offender in terms of an acknowledgement of wrongdoing and an effort at better self-restraint. Indeed, they seemed highly critical when such a response was not forthcoming, a reaction that does not seem to accord with the position argued by von Hirsch (1999) that efforts at reform are peripheral or 'additional permissible' aspects rather than at the core of sentencing.

When it came to how offenders might reach a position by which they were prepared to avoid offending, the analysis presented in Chapter 6 suggested that the 'prudential disincentive' of punishment (von Hirsch 1993) – its deterrent value – weighed more heavily with offenders than the more normative reasons for desistance. They clearly did not see it as only a supplement to the law's moral appeal. Indeed, victims were the only group for whom normative considerations appeared the more telling, in that they seemed to believe that offenders' avoidance of future offending should follow from their taking responsibility rather than a wish to avoid future punishment. Even then, very few victims believed that a sizeable proportion of offenders would actually respond as they thought desirable. Overall, such findings challenge the notion that individual deterrence should not play a prominent role in a normative penal theory in which offenders are treated as rational moral agents, as argued by both von Hirsch (1993) and Duff (2001). In interviews, it was clear that offenders were seen as capable of understanding a 'moral appeal'; they were certainly portrayed as self-determining agents who themselves had to make the decision to reform. Accordingly, it was not seen as objectionable for an offender to be deterred by the sanction that he or she received or might receive. Indeed, this was just one of a number of considerations that a rational person might take into account in deciding against a course of action (Lucas 1980). The views I collected suggest that people did not draw a sharp distinction between the normative and the instrumental reasons for stopping offending, nor did they see either as acting alone. Rather, they saw them as interacting and mutually reinforcing in ways that suggest that the kind of analysis sketched by Bottoms (2001) warrants further attention and that more nuanced understandings of the aims of punishment would get closer to everyday thinking.

As well as taking responsibility, offenders were receptive, comparatively speaking, to the idea that they should show remorse and accept that punishment was justified. However, they were less inclined to agree that they should accept that they had hurt the victim or harmed the community, making it difficult to see what the 'wrong' consisted in for which they believed remorse was due. On the other hand, offenders' views of the penal messages coming from the courts as summarised earlier suggested that they saw living lawfully and making something of their lives as legitimate goals. This implies some acquiescence with social norms in favour of being useful and law-abiding members of the community.

The general tenor of these findings – together with what appeared to be a resistance to 'penal moralising' – could be taken as suggesting that it might be more effective to appeal to offenders about what they might be capable of in the future than to dwell on their past behaviour. This conclusion would be consistent with emerging findings from the desistance literature. Looking at how ex-convicts reform and rebuild their lives, Maruna (2001) identified a process of 'making good' in which the individual selectively and creatively reinterprets past events to suit his or her future aspirations, so justifying one's past while also rationalising the decision to go straight. This is a process that Maruna suggests may be necessary in order to reconstitute oneself as a non-offender while preserving 'psychological and cognitive continuity'. From the desistance-related perspective, Farrall (2002) urges a future-orientation for probation work rather than an exclusive focus on what offenders have done wrong in the past. I come back to these points below in looking at how the communicative potential of community-based interventions might be developed.

Levels of support for what might be seen as restorative responses were comparatively disappointing. Consistent with their resistance to acknowledging that a victim had been hurt, offenders were disinclined to agree that they should try to put right the harm they had caused to the victim; interviews suggested that this was because they had some difficulty accepting that they had victimised someone. Other groups too, including victims, agreed with this to a lesser degree than other possible responses. The ideas that offenders should 'pay their debt' or make up for what they had done wrong also received relatively low levels support. This fits in with the lack of prominence given to getting offenders to make reparation to the community as a sentencing aim (which was distinctly unpopular with offenders), or to communicating an expectation that offenders would make amends for their wrongdoing (both reported in Chapter 5). Also relevant is the lack of support expressed in the questionnaire for the idea of the victim's having a say in the choice of punishment (Chapter 4). Interviews suggested that a particular victim was not seen as qualified to speak for other victims, the implication being that this was rightly a matter for the state acting through trained 'professionals'. At the same time, the victim's point of view was seen as important and people who were aware of them expressed support for restorative and mediation schemes.

Communication failure

A discussion of penal communication would be incomplete without considering the circumstances in which it is *not* seen to work as intended. Here it is interesting that, as Chapter 6 suggested, the higher their ideals, the more pessimistic were people's views of offenders' actual responses to punishment. Explanations given in interview fit in with Braithwaite's portrayal of traditional criminal justice procedures as putting offenders on 'an assembly line populated by lawyers who are anything but moralising about what the offender has done' (1989: 181). One particular problem was seen as a lack of integration between the pronoucement of sentence in court and its administration or delivery afterwards. Restorative justice theorists would see the solution to such problems as lying in establishing restorative processes (either within criminal justice or through alternative arrangements) in which offenders and victims play more active roles, such as reintegrative shaming (Braithwaite 1989). Less ambitiously, there seems scope to make what currently happens in the courtroom a less excluding and more comprehensible experience for offenders and I return to this issue in Chapter 8.

Balancing retribution with crime prevention: what weight proportionality?

The priority given to crime prevention as the overriding aim of punishment is in line with the public opinion research reported in Chapter 3, where in one study 'changing behaviour to prevent reoffending' was found to be the most popular main aim of sentencing (Chapman et al. 2002). However, Chapter 4 showed that it would be a mistake to equate the emphasis on crime prevention with a purely consequentialist position. Research participants displayed a commitment to retribution, and prioritised proportionality in deciding amounts of punishment. This accords with factorial surveys of public views in the US, which found a high degree of association between crime seriousness and penalty severity (Roberts and Stalans 1997). Arguably, the views of the English public on proportionality have yet to be researched thoroughly (see Chapter 3).

The above is consistent with what appears to be a hybrid approach towards sentencing, in which normative goals (and thus penal messages) blended with instrumental ones. It argues that a false dichotomy between consequentialist and retributive theories of punishment is unlikely to be in keeping with everyday understandings of sentencing. Those responding to my interviews and surveys wanted punishment to be socially useful; they also wanted it to be fair. This seems to be the case whether they were retributivist or consequentialist in how they prioritised punishment in the questionnaire. Equally, interviews suggested that retribution (or justice), alone, was not seen as a sufficient goal; there should be positive gains for society from the exercise, and this meant that a constructive approach was required towards the offender concerned. Indeed, victims were capable of articulating quite positive ambitions in interview, consistent with their support for the aims of rehabilitation and encouragement as expressed in the questionnaire. Offenders, too, clearly saw that criminal justice could offer them rehabilitation, education and encouragement. Interestingly, it was magistrates who seemed least convinced by these kinds of sentencing aims.

It is particularly interesting that when interviewees were asked how they would react if obliged to chose between the need to prevent crime and the need to do justice to the gravity of the offence, they gave examples in which departures from proportionality limits were downwards. They did not seem even to contemplate departures upwards in order to stop that person offending, quite possibly because I was asking them to think about offenders convicted of mid-range crimes rather than people who might be seen to pose a danger to the public. In relation to the non-dangerous offender, their position seemed to be that an insistence upon punishment should not impede efforts to rehabilitate. This does not seem to be a position that argues for a principle of cumulative sentencing by which punishment escalates until a recidivist stops offending (Ashworth 2000), or for levels of intervention to be determined by 'risk' as proposed by Carter (Carter 2003). Both von Hirsch (1993) and Duff (2001) oppose downward departures from proportionality other than exceptionally in cases deserving of mercy. However, Duff makes the point that the negative principle of proportionality that he advocates would allow sentences to be more flexibly tailored to an offender's particular circumstances without the need to build in departures.

Among the people participating in my research, adherence to proportionality did not seem absolute in the sense that they were prepared to accommodate other factors. It would be difficult to interpret the views reported earlier as indicative of support for a 'positive' principle of proportionality, and it might even be said that people were looking for a punishment that was 'substantially apt' (Duff 2001). Indeed, attitudes towards the offender seemed somewhat personalised, in that his or her background and the impact that the punishment was likely to have on that individual (in the sense of stopping them from offending in the future) were both seen as important. This was particularly so in the case of offenders, who rated these statements on the questionnaire at the top of their list, followed by the statement that all offenders are different and should receive different punishments. But it was also true of other groups. In interview, for example, magistrates seemed keen to avoid setting an offender up to fail, and they showed some awareness of the kinds of predicaments that might cause offenders to get into trouble.

In the light of this, the comparative lack of support for offender-related mitigation from questionnaire respondents other than offenders might seem surprising. In interview, there was a distinct lack of sympathy for the parent who received a prison sentence or the employed person who might have to give up precious spare time to perform community service.[2] The rationale seemed to be, according to offenders as well as others, that people had exercised choice in taking a decision to offend and deserved to suffer the consequences. This might accord with a view of offenders as rational agents in charge of their destinies. However, it seems at odds with the evident recognition of the many factors militating against someone's determination not to offend again in the future. Where an individual did lapse in the face of these odds, tolerance seemed scant.

History – or the offenders' previous convictions – was also given some priority by victims, magistrates and staff (less so by offenders) when asked what the court should take into account in deciding the amount of punishment. This seemed to be because the level of previous offending influenced judgements of motivation and culpability. The need to prevent further offending was not seen to be a major consideration in deciding the amount of punishment (with the exception of victims, possibly arising from their preoccupation with public protection). There were indications in interview that a repetitive 'callous' offender was seen to have showed him or herself to have a settled 'disposition' in favour of offending (Lacey 1988), which called for the full force of the law in response. Again, this would fit in with what we know about public opinion – see Robinson and Darley (1995).

Somewhat speculatively, these views might be seen as consistent with a principle of progressive loss of mitigation, as explained by Ashworth (2000). However, it is not absolutely clear whether less severe treatment was being advocated for the first-time offender or more severe treatment than warranted by the gravity of the offence for the recidivist. One clue might be that some support was expressed both in interviews and on questionnaires for leniency for the first time offender or the offender for whom the offence was out of character. On the other hand, the level of intolerance for repeat offending might be interpreted as indicative of a premium for the recidivist. Against that interpretation was the lack of evident support for cumulative sentencing; as discussed above, it was departure downwards from desert that seemed to be envisaged to accommodate crime-preventive goals rather than departures upwards. This is an area that would benefit from further illumination by research specifically into stakeholders' views on the role of offenders' prior record in sentencing.

Using community penalties to communicate

As discussed in Chapters 5 and 6, community penalties figured quite prominently in explanations of how people saw penal messages as being reinforced by particular disposals and desired responses encouraged from offenders. Below, I focus on two particular examples in comparing how community service and probation were portrayed in people's accounts with how Duff (2001) has conceptualised the communicative potential of the two disposals.[3] As we saw in Chapter 2, von Hirsch (1993) has little to say about the material forms that particular sanctions might take, as his main concern is with the correspondence between their size and the gravity of the offence.

Probation: its persuasive power

Dealing with probation first, it will be recalled from Chapter 2 that Duff (2001) sees this disposal predominantly in terms of transparent persuasion. Its aim is to bring home to the offender the character and implication of his or her offence(s) as public wrongs and to persuade the offender of the necessity to change his or her behaviour. A certain amount of emphasis is placed on offending behaviour programmes, not as therapeutic interventions, but as a means to help offenders to recognise the wrongfulness of their past conduct (to 'confront offending behaviour') and so to bring about change. As Duff correctly points out, this is very close to the current official view of probation. The general offending programmes accredited by the Joint Accreditation Panel (now the Correctional Services Accreditation Panel) are based on cognitive-behavioural techniques. Based on social learning theory, the aim of such programmes is to teach offenders cognitive skills to enable them to think about the consequences of their actions and develop alternative strategies for dealing with relevant situations (as explained in, for example,

Lipton et al. 2002; Raynor 2002; Rex 2001). In addition to problem-solving and social skills training, an important element in such programmes is victim empathy or empathy-building intended to develop the offender's awareness of the victim perspective.

In response to the questionnaire, magistrates and staff expressed a great deal of confidence in probation as a means to help offenders with the problems underlying their offending (rehabilitation) and to persuade them of the wrongfulness of what they had done (see Chapter 5). Over half of offenders also selected both statements, and nearly two-thirds of victims help with problems (a large minority persuasion). For magistrates and staff, another aim was to get offenders to change their ways (to reform), and a large minority of offenders saw the point of probation as to teach them how to go on the straight and narrow. What comes across in these accounts of probation is a disposal used actively to engage offenders, helping them both to gain an understanding of why their offences were wrong and to overcome the underlying circumstances. When it came to sentencing messages, the clear emphasis was on the opportunity for offenders to show that they could live lawfully (though much less for offenders than for other groups). A majority of magistrates and staff also saw probation as communicating an expectation that offenders could make something of their lives and a substantial minority of offenders and victims agreed.

In the light of the practice initiatives referred to earlier, it is not surprising that reasoning was given a certain amount of emphasis by probation officers in discussing in interview how they worked with the offenders they supervised to reinforce the penal messages conveyed in sentencing. The processes depicted by some probation officers might be seen in terms of 'moral reasoning' as understood by Duff (2001), in that they saw their task as getting offenders to take responsibility and to experience the sense of remorse associated with a resolve not to reoffend. However, they did not always see offenders as receptive to discussion about the wrongfulness of their crimes or the impact on the victims. There was some awareness that offenders might be resistant to the normative – or moralising – aspects of the sentencing message, as discussed above.

In view of that resistance, it is equally unsurprising that offenders should portray the discussions with their supervisors in more neutral terms, in which they received advice or 'straight talk'. For offenders, the focus seemed to be much more on what might be in their self-interest or what might help them achieve non-offending goals in life rather than on the wrongfulness of their past conduct. Offenders might not see probation as aiming to secure their penitent understanding of their wrongs and therefore their repentance (Duff 2001). Nor, incidentally, were probation officers inclined to describe their work in such intimate, almost spiritual terms. However, offenders could see probation as helping them to develop a better understanding of what caused them to offend, with what consequences and how to avoid the same pitfalls in the future. They could also see the experience as helping them to engage in processes of change: they could learn something and receive encouragement from their probation officer; and they could gain a sense of achievement from engaging in or refraining from certain activities while on probation.

Community service: apologising by making reparation

Community service, according to Duff (2001), consists primarily of apologetic reparation of a public nature. Even if these are not the terms in which the offender recognises his or her performance of compulsory work for the community, Duff argues that other citizens should accept that the offender has sufficiently apologised for the offence. It also enables the offender to express his or her understanding of what he or she has done and his or her renewed commitment to the community. Furthermore, where the offender is required to undertake work relevant to his or her offence (for example, the vandal having to repair damage caused by vandalism), she or he is confronted with a rich and substantial censure that says in effect 'look what you have done' (Duff 2001: 105).

Again, this portrayal largely fits in with, and enriches, how community service has traditionally been seen – primarily as a 'fine' on time (a punishment) that offers incidental reparation to the community (Pease 1985). However, since the late 1990s that image has been changing, with the re-emergence of a rehabilitative agenda in the light of evidence that their experiences of community service may have an impact on offenders' recidivism.[4] This has culminated in Pathfinder projects sponsored by the Home Office under the Crime Reduction Programme with the aim of developing the reintegrative potential of community service through pro-social modelling and awards for guided skills learning (Johnson and Rex 2002). Most recently, the Correctional Services Accreditation Panel has given Recognised status to an Enhanced Community Punishment scheme based on the Pathfinder projects, which is due to be implemented nationally from October 2003 (Rex and Gelsthorpe 2003).

Indeed, its capacity to bring about change could be glimpsed in the accounts of community service that I heard. As reported in Chapter 5, community service was characterised on the questionnaire chiefly in terms of reparation and retribution, enabling the offender to make amends for what he or she had done wrong. However, it was also seen by over two-thirds of victims and staff as a means to encourage offenders to do something useful with their lives, and a large minority of offenders agreed that community service kept them away from offending while they were on the order. Among the messages conveyed by a community service order, according to a large minority of questionnaire respondents, were the expectations that offenders would follow the rules and show that they were capable of living a lawful life.

Descriptions in interview, too, portrayed community service as the archetypal way in which offenders could make reparation. This is an interpretation in keeping with Duff's (2001), albeit perhaps without the connotations of penance conveyed by 'apologetic' reparation. In addition, quite rich and complex accounts were given of the mechanisms by which performing work for the community might help offenders to live lawful and useful lives, understandings that seemed to go beyond Duff's idea of a renewed commitment to the community. While Duff seems to confine himself to what the offender might be expressing in actually undertaking the work, the people I interviewed seemed to be contemplating the impact of that experience on other aspects of offenders' lives. Thus, for example, offenders were seen to gain an insight into what existence was like for particularly vulnerable groups, such as the elderly and disabled. In addition, community service was seen as a motivating – even as an educational – experience, which enabled offenders to see that they might have a useful contribution to make to society and to gain 'grounded increments in self-esteem' (Toch 2000). Such aspirations seem very close to the aims of the CS Pathfinder projects referred to above, where CS supervisors acting as pro-social models used reinforcement and rewards to encourage socially responsible attitudes and behaviour.[5]

Comparing questionnaire ratings of different disposals

Table 7.1 brings together the analysis presented in Chapter 5 of how various disposals were rated in terms of penal aims and messages. It is interesting that probation scored highest according to how respondents rated its aims as a punishment, whereas community service scored highest in terms of the penal messages that it was seen to communicate (although there was a narrower range of scores for penal messages). Tagging was rated second in both analyses. Why might this be the case?

To a large extent, probation's popularity in terms of its aims was due to the level of confidence expressed by staff and offenders, with whom

Table 7.1 Levels of confidence in different sanctions

Sanction	Penal aims	Penal messages
Custody	51%	73%
Community service	49%	87%
Probation	84%	65%
Tagging	67%	77%

it gained over double the score of custody or community service. However, it was also rated highly by victims and magistrates; at 75 per cent, the latter gave probation the lowest score of all groups. Probation's success can be attributed to the fact that it was seen primarily in terms of rehabilitation and persuasion, sentencing aims that were especially popular with staff, victims and offenders. Tagging was seen primarily in terms of incapacitation and disapproval; both were popular with magistrates but victims gave comparatively little support to incapacitation and offenders to disapproval. By contrast, the aims attributed to community service (reparation and retribution) were not highly regarded as general sentencing aims.

When it came to the messages communicated in the act of sentencing, there was a fair degree of consensus about the utility of community service; at 67 per cent, the score awarded by offenders was the lowest of all groups. In short, community service was seen to convey the expectations in which, overall, most faith was expressed: living lawfully or otherwise facing the consequences so far as offenders were concerned; following society's rules according to victims and magistrates; and making amends in the view of CS staff. By contrast, probation was seen to convey expectations that attracted less support overall: learning the difference between right and wrong; and making something of your life (although the latter carried some conviction among offenders). Thus, it seems, community service offered a straightforward appeal that people could comprehend. To a slightly lesser extent, the same could be said of tagging, seen primarily as conveying an expectation that offenders will follow the rules and live lawfully.

A communicative framework for community penalties?

In this concluding section, I will be considering how the findings summarised above bear on the possible future development of a stronger framework for community penalties. Does the idea of communication offer a promising approach for community penalties, and how might the relevant processes and material forms be developed to maximise their communicative potential? Could this provide a firmer grounding for community penalties, and give them a more central, stable and secure role in our penal practices? Could it help to resolve the tension discussed in Chapter 4 between, on the one hand, community punishments as proportionate responses to crime, and on the other, community-based intervention as a means to pursue crime prevention.

One of the most positive findings to emerge from the research summarised above is the level of support for community penalties and their credibility with each of the groups contributing to my research.

This is in keeping with the public opinion research reported in Chapter 3, which showed that members of the public support community penalties once they are reminded or made aware of them. Indeed, the professionals contributing to the research reported by Halliday (Home Office 2001) may have been unduly pessimistic about the profile of non-custodial sanctions with the public as 'soft options'. Here, it is interesting that Sanders and Roberts (2000) found that support for the community-based conditional sentence more than doubled among Canadians when the nature of the conditions was made clear to them.

It will be clear from the discussion in the preceding section that this confidence arose from the key role that community penalties were seen to play in giving offenders the opportunity, or positively assisting them, to respond appropriately to the expectations placed upon them not to offend in the future. In this regard, community penalties were often compared favourably with custody, particularly when it came to encouraging offenders to take responsibility for their offending and for related aspects of their lifestyles. This was not an aim that imprisonment was seen to promote. Variously, being in prison: separated offenders from domestic responsibilities; denied them their capacity to make decisions; relieved them of a sense of further obligation; and produced a sense of grievance according to which they were the victims rather than the victimisers. The sentencing aims that custody was seen primarily as delivering – disapproval, retribution and incapacitation – conjure up a picture of the offender as someone to whom things are done rather than someone whose active engagement is sought. Unfortunately, however, alongside the frequently expressed view that custody failed to offer anything constructive, there were also plenty of hints that it was the only way to deal with offenders who persisted in offending despite being given opportunities to desist.

As I commented above, the centrality of reform in accounts of punishment suggests a far stronger role than the peripheral one identified by von Hirsch (1999). On this point, my findings were consistent with public opinion research in the UK and US, in which people have been found to place considerable emphasis upon crime preventive and rehabilitative goals. The desire for punishment to be directed at socially useful goals is hard to dismiss, given the frequency with which it is expressed when people are asked for their views. It seems to go beyond the mere expression of censure – even dialectically defensible censure – as a normative appeal to desist supplemented by the prudential disincentive of hard treatment (von Hirsch 1993, as refined by Bottoms 1995). Indeed, in conceding that there would be grounds to criticise the offender who reacted with indifference to being punished, von Hirsch (1993) seems to struggle with the limitations imposed by his own definition. Granting grounds for criticism implies that society has a stake in how offenders respond to the experience of being punished; if that is so, it seems to follow that punishment should promote responses that are considered desirable. As Duff (2001) argues, this means that material forms of punishment should cohere with the aims of sentencing, and this is an aspect of punishment in which theorists have a proper interest. In other words, if we want offenders to stop offending, it is not enough to appeal to them to do so and back this up with threats; we should be looking to penal agents to reinforce those messages and assist offenders to meet the implicit expectations. We should also be looking for congruence between what happens in court and how the sentence is delivered. In pursuing these aspirations, community penalties appear to have much to offer.

What comes out of the findings rehearsed above is that a conceptualisation of punishment in terms of communication commanded considerable support. There was also strong confidence in community penalties as being particularly apt for the pursuit of communicative penal aims, with the capacity to combine an appeal to offenders' sense of moral agency (or citizenship) with practical help in overcoming the obstacles to their moving away from crime. This supports the case for giving community-based sanctions a central place in a sentencing framework whose focus is on persuading offenders of the nature of their offences as public wrongs, encouraging them to take responsibility and assisting them to move forward in a positive, law-abiding way in the future. As portrayed by the people participating in my research, community penalties clearly have rich communicative potential; their accounts also suggest that there is further scope to develop that potential.

The views reported in the previous section reveal a fair degree of consensus that probation is intended to meet sentencing aims at the core of the whole punishment enterprise: making offenders see why what they did was wrong and helping them with the problems behind their offending. Quite clearly, offenders were not to be let off the hook in the sense that the wrongfulness of their behaviour was to be brought to their attention. At the same time, a constructive outcome was to be sought in which offenders were engaged as individuals capable of understanding a moral appeal and worthy of assistance in overcoming what caused them to offend (in the technical language, their 'criminogenic needs').

To a large extent, as discussed above, current approaches within probation focus on confronting offending behaviour and teaching offenders cognitive and problem-solving skills. According to Raynor (2002), there are strong prospects of 'What Works' interventions being extended to meet offenders' 'social integration' needs, with Pathfinder projects being implemented in basic skills, resettlement and hostel-based work. This may be an overoptimistic prediction. True, the Correctional Services Accreditation Panel has widened its remit beyond a focus on programmes to encompass 'integrated systems' such as case management, assessment and resettlement (see Rex et al. 2003; Joint Prison/ Probation Accreditation Panel 2002). However, it is not clear yet that enough is being done to deal with offenders within their social environments, and to complement work on their thinking and behaviour by attempts to help them with the problems they encounter in the community (Rex 2001; Raynor and Vanstone 1997). Until that happens, studies of the effectiveness of accredited programmes may continue to produce mixed results.[6]

I suggested earlier that a future orientation towards desistance might be more productive than a backwards-looking preoccupation with confronting offending behaviour. As seen above, offenders showed a certain amount of resistance to what might be described as penal 'moralising'. For one, they were not particularly receptive to disapproval (indeed, other groups disclosed doubts about the value judgements being expressed), nor were they as ready to take on board that they had hurt the victim or harmed the community as other groups perhaps thought they should be. Part of the explanation may be that such censure often failed to carry legitimacy in offenders' eyes; it was not 'dialectically defensible' (Bottoms 1998) or tempered by an adequate understanding of their particular difficulties. Moreover, dwelling on their past misdeeds may not be the most effective way in which to get offenders to go through the processes of self-reinvention that Maruna (2001) associates with 'making good'. This is not to suggest that any discussion of offending is counter-productive or that the offence should never be mentioned: offenders were open to persuasion about the wrongfulness of their offences and saw themselves as learning from thinking about what caused them to offend and with what consequences. However, it does suggest that a consideration of why certain kinds of offending are wrong – how other people might be damaged – would provide just the starting point for an intervention in which the emphasis would be pro-social rather than condemnatory. The focus would be on how the individual might be helped to overcome the problems behind his or her offending to live lawfully in the community – whether this meant tackling drugs dependency, a lack of basic skills or access to employment and stable accommodation.

When it came to community service, the experience of making reparation to the community (in itself not greatly prioritised as a sentencing aim) was seen to have the potential for a positive impact on offenders by encouraging them to live lawful and useful lives. Such a view goes well beyond the image of community service as a classic punishment that can be equated with a 'fine' on time. Here, research participants seemed to be anticipating the rehabilitative and reintegrative aspirations encapsulated by the recent CS Pathfinder projects. This approach was implemented on a national scale in October 2003, in the form of the Enhanced Community Punishment scheme, providing an opportunity to see whether those aspirations can be achieved in practice. For the implementation of this approach within CS practice creates significant challenges, not least how to ensure that offenders experience the kind of work placements and supervision that can help them see themselves as capable of making a useful social contribution (see Johnson and Rex 2002; Rex and Gelsthorpe 2004).

Finally, it is necessary to consider the role of proportionality: whether it is possible to develop community penalties that, while being communicative, have a sufficient relationship with the gravity of the offence to meet the requirements of justice. Although the views summarised earlier were not entirely clear cut, they indicated strong endorsement of proportionality in deciding amounts of punishment. Where departures from that principle were contemplated, they seemed to be downwards. This was because the desirability of taking the opportunity to prevent that individual from offending again in the future was seen as more important than the compulsion to punish him or her. At the same time, the requirement for justice seemed to be seen as overriding in that what was not contemplated was the imposition of more punishment than justified by the seriousness of the offence in order to stop that person offending (whether through deterrence or some other means). Within that constraint, the approach might be characterised as somewhat 'individualised', taking account of the offender's background and the likely (positive) impact of the punishment. Although this is an area that would benefit from further research into stakeholders' views, the views I encountered would not contradict the model around which some consensus appears to be emerging, by which community penalties are ranked into several bands from which the penalty that is likely to have the desired impact is selected. This would allow the community penalty to be imposed that was 'communicatively apt' (Duff 2001), while ensuring that proportionality acted as a real constraint on the amount of punishment that could be imposed. Ranking community penalties into bands of roughly equivalent sanctions would require comparable punitive values to be attributed to their various dimensions. I suggested in Chapter 4 that this task is possible and that it would seem suitable for the Sentencing Guidelines Council established under the Criminal Justice Act 2003.

Conclusions

This chapter brought together the findings presented in earlier chapters to argue that community penalties were seen to have rich communicative potential and to suggest how community penalties might be framed in terms of communication. In the next chapter, I bring the book to a conclusion by asking how in practical terms we might be able to use the idea of communication to make punishment more constructive, particularly as delivered in the community setting. In doing so, I consider the possible role of restorative processes in community penalties, and the possible implications of the provisions in the Criminal Justice Act 2003 for custody and the customised community order.

Notes

1 This is a significant omission since these wider experiences are likely to have a substantial impact on the kinds of messages offenders hear and what kinds of responses they can be expected to make. Research into this question would require detailed exploration of offenders' experiences both outside and within the courtroom and the connections and interrelations between them. In addition to 'life history' interviews, observation and an ethnographic component would be helpful.

2 Although there was some recognition of the need to consider the possible impact on children of their mother being jailed, as Lord Woolf has indicated in a case where a woman is the sole supporter of young children (*The Times*, 25th February 2002).

3 Although the respective orders were renamed community punishment and community rehabilitation by the Criminal Justice and Courts Services Act 2000 and will form various elements of the new generic sentence under the Criminal Justice Act 2003, I have retained the original names still familiar in the English jurisdiction and overseas.

4 McIvor's (1992) study of community service in Scotland found that finding community service very worthwhile (because of the opportunities to acquire skills or do something useful for the community) was associated with higher rates of compliance and lower rates of reconviction. Various studies showed community service with a slight advantage over other disposals in comparisons of reconviction rates as against rates predicted on the basis of offenders' prior records (Lloyd et al. 1995; Raynor and Vanstone 1997; May 1999). Unable to attribute this to background social factors or differences in criminal histories, May concluded that the sentence itself had a positive impact on reconviction.

5 As explained in Rex and Gelsthorpe (2004), the thinking behind the CS projects is that the practical setting in which CS occurs, and the nature of the contacts into which it brings offenders, offer learning experiences at least as powerful as the cognitive-behavioural approach used in general offending programmes. The theory is that the performance of community service may engage offenders in the kind of altruistic activity that produces 'teaching points' similar to those in cognitive skills training, which 'emerge, however, from experience rather than academic training' (Toch 2000: 275). McIvor

(1998) suggests that particularly 'rewarding' community service placements entail some reciprocity and exchange in which the offender both offers service to others and has the opportunity to acquire skills.

6 Although Friendship et al. (2002) found reduced reconviction following participation in pre-accreditation cognitive skills programmes in prisons, this positive finding was not replicated in the subsequent studies of accredited programmes by Falshaw et al. (2003) and Cann et al. (2003).

Chapter 8

Conclusions

Introduction

In the previous chapter, I used my research findings to sketch out a possible communicative framework for community penalties. My question in this final chapter is whether such a framework could be made to work in practice: what would need to be changed and what benefits might accrue. I start by distilling from the research findings presented in earlier chapters the implications for how punishment might be understood and developed in terms of communication.

Communicative penalties – a summary

Communicative penal theory in a nutshell envisages a dialogue in which certain messages are transmitted to the offender through the act of sentencing, to which the offender is expected to respond in particular ways. Duff (2001) puts a considerable amount of emphasis on the response, seeing it as the central function of punishment to persuade offenders to repent of their crimes, to express their reparative apology and to undertake to reform their future conduct. From a more 'external' perspective, von Hirsch's (1993) main concern is with the expressive function of the punishment in holding the offender to account and conveying disapproval for the wrong done to the victim. There is also an appeal – to other people's sense of the conduct's wrongfulness as a reason for their restraint, and for some 'moral response' from the offender. However, von Hirsch is neither specific nor prescriptive as to what the offender's response might be. While reform might be desirable, it is not a justification for imposing punishment, a point on which Bottoms (1998) agrees. Nonetheless a response is expected; the offender's indifference would provide grounds for criticism.

At the risk of oversimplification, I attempt below to derive from the views expressed by the people participating in my research some principles for how communicative penalties might be developed. In keeping with what was said in the last chapter about the relationship between empirical research and normative theory, I do not put these principles forward as some kind of definitive statement on punishment, as if I had somehow 'proved' or 'disproved' one theory or another. Rather, they provide a convenient means by which to summarise my research findings, to bring out their implications and to offer suggestions for how the relevant theoretical debates might be taken forward. In doing so, my motivation is to reinvigorate those debates by moving them closer to practical decision-making.

1. Censure and consequentialism as equal partners

Normative and instrumental messages both played a key role in portrayals of punishment, and views supported a 'hybrid' approach looking both backwards to the offence and forwards to the possibility of change. The idea of moral persuasion was prominent, with the aim of making offenders see *why* what they did was wrong. It was central to people's understandings of punishment that it should seek to elicit a response from the offender, ultimately in the form of desisting from offending, and they seemed highly critical when this was not forthcoming. In short, efforts at reform seemed to lie at the core of sentencing; they were certainly not portrayed as peripheral. However, normative goals were seen as equally important. Proportionality was strongly endorsed, and the view expressed that punishment should be just as well as socially useful. Crime prevention might be given priority as the overall goal of punishment, but it was seen as being pursued as much through normative as instrumental means.

2. Proportionality as a real constraint

Proportionality in deciding amounts of punishment was prioritised, particularly by magistrates and staff, and gained equal levels of support among retributivists and consequentialists. Crime prevention was not seen as a major consideration in the quantum of punishment; furthermore, in reconciling the need to prevent crime with the desirability of doing justice, people did not seem to contemplate a greater sentence than deserved in order to stop someone offending. However, within that constraint, they seemed prepared to accommodate other factors and to be looking for a punishment that was substantially apt rather than one that met the requirements of justice in a merely formal sense. An offender's previous convictions were seen as relevant to the amount of punishment imposed because they influenced judgements of motivation and culpability. Views might be seen as consistent with a principle of progressive loss of mitigation, with the full force of the law being brought to bear on someone who had revealed a settled 'disposition' in favour of offending.

3. Censure to be dialectically defensible

One reason why offenders were not entirely receptive to the more moral aspects of penal communication seemed to be because they did not see certain prerequisites as having been met. There was some disparity between their views and those of other groups about the extent to which sentencing should take account of their background, circumstances and the impact of the punishment on them. Nor were courtroom procedures seen as conducive to offenders' participation in a moral dialogue, with offenders' depicting themselves as excluded and alienated from proceedings in which their future liberty was being determined. In short, courts were not delivering dialectically defensible censure, in which offenders believed that their points of view were fully considered. Admittedly, offenders had high expectations that the sentence they received should be both just and responsive to their particular circumstances. Nonetheless, seeing themselves as largely excluded from what was going on around them in court hardly reassured offenders that there was much interest in whatever expectations they might have.

4. Content matters

If, as people seemed to believe, society has a stake in how offenders respond to the experience of being punished, it follows that punishment should promote responses that are considered desirable. This means that the form punishment takes should be consistent with the aims of sentencing. It is not enough to appeal to offenders to stop offending and to back that up with threats. Those administering sentences should be reinforcing penal messages and assisting offenders to meet the implicit expectations. This requires congruence between what happens in court and how the sentence is delivered, which would help to make sentencing more dialectically defensible (or legitimate) by making it clearer what sentences mean and what they involve for offenders.

5. Neither 'denunciation' nor 'repentance' to be overstated

Although censure was seen as a necessary part of punishment, support for denunciatory messages was qualified and reservations were expressed in interview about the value judgements implied in the communication of disapproval. Retribution was not greatly favoured, nor was being punitive for its own sake. Prompting remorse was not popular as an aim of sentencing, and there was some unease with playing out the intimate processes of remorse and apology within the criminal justice setting (and with the religious connotations of repentance). Both probation officers and probationers depicted a process of 'moral' reasoning, the latter in rather more neutral terms than the former, but neither seemed to portray probation supervision as about securing penitence or repentance. Nor were such understandings evident in descriptions of community service, seen as the archetypal means by which offenders could make reparation.

6. *Future orientation better than preoccupation with 'confronting offending behaviour'*

Offenders saw living lawfully and making something of their lives as legitimate goals, and could see probation as helping them understand what caused them to offend and with what consequence, and to engage in processes of change. They saw themselves as able to learn something, receive encouragement and gain a sense of achievement from both probation and community service. Together with a certain amount of resistance on their part to penal 'moralising', this suggests that discussions about offending are useful within the context of a forward-looking focus towards desistance rather than a backward-looking preoccupation with offenders' past behaviour. Dwelling on their past misdeeds does not seem the best way in which to help offenders to become contributing, law-abiding members of society (to 'make good').

7. *Individual deterrence is not inappropriate*

The fact that deterrence weighed more heavily with offenders than the more normative reasons for desisting challenges the view that individual deterrence should not play a prominent role in a normative penal theory in which offenders are treated as rational moral agents. Offenders were seen as capable of understanding a 'moral appeal' and were portrayed as self-determining agents who themselves had to make the decision to reform. Accordingly, it was not seen as objectionable for an offender to be deterred by the sanction that he or she received or might receive, and offenders themselves seemed quite comfortable with the notion of the sentence as a threat. Rather, this was just one of a number of considerations that a rational person might take into account in making a decision about a course of action. It certainly did not rule out the use of more constructive means to encourage people to move away from offending, as appeared to be preferred by magistrates and staff as well as offenders.

An important question is whether the above ideas could become a practical reality. The people who contributed to my research identified significant obstacles to punishment operating in this way, as a result of which only a small minority thought that offenders would respond as desired. This raises several question that I seek to address in the next section: what those obstacles are, how they might be overcome, and what opportunities might be created by seeking their removal in order to promote a communicative understanding of punishment.

Obstacles and opportunities

One major impediment perceived by interviewees to an effective dialogue with offenders was the routinised nature of court proceedings, particularly in magistrates' courts (where the part of my research involving sentencers was focused). The impression gained from interviews, and during my own observation of magistrates' courts, was of pressure to process a heavy caseload as quickly and efficiently as possible. From an admittedly limited amount of personal observation, defendants appeared to play a fairly incidental role in proceedings dominated by exchanges between the representatives from the various agencies (defence, prosecution, court service and probation) about procedures and paperwork. Rarely, it seemed was the defendant addressed; even when the bench retired, informal conversation usually related to the technicalities of other cases or more trivial matters. On one occasion, defender and prosecutor discussed their holidays, inadvertently playing out complaints I heard from offenders of an over-friendliness between defence and prosecution that they took as indicative of a dismissal of their own plights. No doubt partly as a consequence of their adjudicatory role of pronouncing on guilt and sentence, magistrates depicted themselves and appeared in court as somewhat 'remote' figures. Certainly, as was seen in Chapter 5, a real disjunction was perceived between the act of sentencing in court and the administration of the sentence afterwards, which was not seen as helping to reinforce whatever messages the sentence was being used to transmit.

All of the above served to confirm offenders' preconceptions and preoccupations – primarily with the possibility of a custodial sentence, against which all other options were perceived as a 'let off' to which offenders paid scant regard once they learnt that the outcome was not to be custody. In this, they seemed merely to be reflecting the predominance of custody in public thinking about crime and punishment as revealed in the public opinion research discussed in Chapter 3. That research also shows a fair amount of support for community penalties and for rehabilitative and restorative approaches once the public is made aware of them, although raising public awareness may well stimulate people's appetite for 'tough' community penalties with reliance upon custody as the 'back-up' sanction. To some extent, it is difficult to disentangle the preoccupation with custody in what are admittedly punitive times from current preoccupations with 'public protection' evident in the emphasis on 'risk' in assessment. In such a climate, it has been pointed out, the public clamour for punitive responses to crime will continue to take precedence in the absence of more convincing or reassuring alternatives for offering security (Freiberg 2001). In other words, there is no easy route if one wants to move community penalties beyond their subordinate role in relation to custody. The most promising if not the only way forward is to develop community-based interventions that earn public support in their own right because they are widely seen as constructive and effective.

There seem to be major benefits to be derived from achieving the closer integration between the sentence announced in court and the sentence delivered in the community that a communicative approach would promote. As reported in Chapter 5, a number of interviewees clearly thought that more could be done to reinforce sentencing messages and to clarify what sentences meant. Indeed, the requirement resulting from the Human Rights Act 2000 to give reasons for sentence was presented by some magistrates as a helpful development that would give offenders a clearer idea of the intentions of the court. However, I observed signs that courts were resorting to giving formulaic reasons that seem unlikely to elucidate the underlying meaning of the sentence.

Many of the ideas put forward for how communication might be improved and offenders more engaged in the sentencing process were inspired by initiatives that had come to participants' attention. One suggestion was for sentencers to have a higher profile during the administration of the sentence, whether through the use by supervising probation officers of statements and explanations made at the time of sentence or through courts having the power to review an offender's progress on an order. For some, the latter proposal was suggested by the Drug Treatment and Testing Order model, where the evaluation of the pilots has found that court review was welcomed by staff and offenders as making a positive contribution to treatment (see Turnbull et al. 2000). In one pilot site in particular, where the original sentencer conducted 80 per cent of reviews, the clear oversight and growing relationship between the drug-using offender and sentencer were seen as beneficial in reinforcing positive progress and allowing problems to be swiftly addressed.

Provisions that would take us in this direction are contained in the Criminal Justice Act 2003. For example, the Act gives the court a more wide ranging duty to give reasons for and to explain the effect of the sentence in ordinary language, which could be used to prepare offenders for community orders and as the basis for a continuing dialogue during supervision. A proper explanation of the sentence might enhance its legitimacy with offenders and promote their compliance with requirements that they perceive as justified and fair (Bottoms 2001). Although the government did not take up Halliday's proposal for courts to be given a power to review community sentences (Home Office 2001), the provision of a review function for the new suspended sentence will allow the cautious expansion of a power that has significant implications for the judicial role (McKitterick and Rex 2003). Its value will depend on how such a power is used in practice. Halliday envisaged that most reviews would be paper-based, with full hearings reserved for cases likely to result in new restrictions being imposed. Whether a paper-based review will achieve much in terms of helping to engage and motivate the offender is doubtful. The benefits of the drug treatment and testing procedures are surely that they bring the offender into face-to-face contact with the judge or magistrate during the course of the sentence, strengthening the links between the judicial and the administrative elements of the sentence. 'Rewarding' the offender who is making good progress under a suspended sentence through lifting some of its penal measures (e.g. discounting a certain number of hours of compulsory work) may well motivate him or her. However, it seems likely to lose some of its impact – and become a routine expectation – if not accompanied by a court appearance.

A communicative understanding of community penalties looks forward towards the possibility of positive change. This provides a constructive framework for assisting offenders to become law-abiding members of the community, within which it follows that more emphasis should be placed on 'rewards' for compliance and progress than on 'punishments' for failures. This is not to argue that community orders should not be enforced; to allow offenders to evade obligations ordered by a court is hardly conducive to their taking responsibility. However, it does suggest that what should be emphasised is what offenders have to gain rather than what they might lose (i.e. their liberty). As was recognised at a gathering of academics and practitioners at Cambridge University in June 2000, current practice relies on deterrent-based approaches for securing compliance with the requirements of community orders. That group concluded that a more imaginative incentives-based approach might be more effective, focusing on the offender as a citizen based on an understanding of what motivates people to adopt law-abiding choices and lifestyles.[1] This could incorporate 'redemption rituals', which Maruna (2001) suggests provide a psychological turning point for desisting offenders, in which a penal agent (perhaps a judge or magistrate) formally certifies the offender as having reformed. Such an approach would be consistent with the use of pro-social modelling to encourage offenders to become active citizens and to learn more socially responsible behaviour, in which 'rewards' are used to reinforce pro-social statements and actions.[2]

Using community penalties to restore

Communicative penal theory accords a role to the victim. For von Hirsch (1993), this is a limited role: the victim is one of the audiences that the punishment addresses as someone who has been wronged by the crime. For Duff (2001), the victim is more actively involved in the process: as someone to whom the offender has to make reparative apology, and as a wronged individual who can only be restored through retributive punishment possibly in the form of victim–offender mediation (Duff 2003). Inspired by debate with restorative theorists, von Hirsch has very recently developed a theoretical 'making amends' model in which courts would refer a convicted property offender to a victim–offender conference for a negotiated 'punishment' subject to the limitations that term implies (see von Hirsch et al. 2003). However, for writers in the restorative tradition such as Christie (1982), Walgrave (2003) and Braithwaite (2003), such models would not go far enough in recognising the victim's stake in conflict resolution following crime; this requires a system of restorative justice entirely separate from traditional criminal justice.

What was perhaps surprising was the conservative nature of my research participants' views about the role of the victim, and the comparatively limited extent to which they saw punishment as offering opportunities for offenders to offer reparation or to make amends. Possibly, this arose from a lack of familiarity with a restorative paradigm and an inclination to interpret 'punishment' in more traditional terms of 'blaming' and preventing reoffending. On the other hand, interviewees regularly expressed the opinion that criminal justice neglected the victim's point of view, and volunteered support for mediation and restorative schemes when they were aware of them. That said, for the victim to have a say in the choice of punishment was universally unpopular, both because – according to interviewees – this might well prove an artificial exercise and because one particular victim was not seen as qualified to speak for other victims. As a rule, people were content for the state to represent the needs of all victims and to express the harm that the crime had caused. Within this arrangement, they perceived opportunities for victims to describe what they had suffered and to receive compensation or reparation from offenders.

There seems support here for the development of restoration within the traditional retributive paradigm, using community penalties to promote those kinds of processes. It would not be a radical step to improve the quality of reparation offered through community service, perhaps to people who have experienced victimisation. One of the aims of the CS Pathfinder projects discussed in the previous chapter was to enhance the usefulness of the work undertaken for the community and offenders' contact with beneficiaries. This was seen as yielding reparative as well as reintegrative benefits, with the potential to strengthen the exchange between offender and beneficiary – and that between criminal justice agency and community (Johnson and Rex 2001). It remains to be seen whether Enhanced Community Punishment will deliver those kinds of benefits on a national scale (see Rex and Gelsthorpe 2004). For offenders on probation, awareness of the victims' perspective has been developed as a component of accredited offending behaviour pro-grammes. The account of probation presented in the previous chapter could be interpreted as a version of reintegrative shaming (Braithwaite 1989): censure plus reintegration through assistance in overcoming offending-related needs. However, I encountered difficulties with the concept of 'shaming'; for offenders to 'feel ashamed' attracted compara-tively little support on the questionnaire and mixed feelings were expressed in interview about the impact of a sentence as a 'shaming' experience.

More radical would be Duff's (2001) proposal that victim–offender mediation should be built into every probation order or Raynor's (2002) for every community sentence to contain a reparative element. However, steps in such directions can be discerned in the introduction of the reparation order and the probation service's developing contact with victims of crime, and the Criminal Justice Act 2003 makes it possible for reparation to be included in every customised community order.[3] Whether the people who participated in my research would support Raynor's (2002) suggestion for victims to be involved in the choice of rehabilitative work to be undertaken by offenders is more doubtful. There are indications that they might find such an exercise somewhat artificial; in any event, their views do not point to a need to repackage rehabilitation as 'restorative' in order to win it public support.

New forms of custodial and community provision

Much of the above could be taken as overlooking the fact that community penalties are just about to undergo another major upheaval with the enactment of provisions in the Criminal Justice Act 2003 for the customised community order, custody plus and the new suspended sentence. As we saw in Chapter 2, the first of these replaces the various kinds of community orders with a single order in which sentencers will be able to combine any of a wide range of requirements. The custodial provisions in effect erode the distinction between a community and a custodial sentence, by allowing a suspended or short prison sentence to be combined with community-based conditions. In principle, choices between these varying provisions will be governed, first, by the legislative criteria that an offence must be 'so serious' that only custody can be justified or 'serious enough' for a community sentence, and second, by whatever guidance comes from the Sentencing Guidelines Council. In practice, however, fine judgements will be required as to when to select a purely community order and when to use the threat or reality of custody, for which it will be difficult if not impossible to provide sufficiently exhaustive guidance.

Turning specifically to the customised community order, what we know about offering sentencers a wider menu of conditions suggests that the effect is to increase the number of conditions imposed (Hedderman et al. 1999). This makes it more likely that offenders will fail to comply with the requirements, which will hardly enhance the credibility of the 'stand-alone' community order and may well provide further encouragement for sentencers to use custody to ensure a sentence has real 'bite'.[4] Of course, the Sentencing Guidelines Council will have the opportunity to minimise those risks by introducing an outline tariff as proposed by Halliday (Home Office 2001). But there remains a real danger that community orders will slip further down tariff, being used for progressively less serious offenders, as a credible 'punishment' becomes one that contains a custodial element. This makes the recent proposal by the Chief Inspector of Probation (HMIP 2003a) for the probation service to contract out its supervision of low-risk offenders all the more relevant.

So what are the implications of these developments for communicative community penalties? A concern raised in Chapter 2 seems particularly pertinent here: that the use of the generic term 'community sentence' will detract from rather than advance offenders' understanding of what the disposal means; a better starting point might be for its name to describe what an order entails. A possible consequence might be that offenders will start community sentences even less prepared that they are now for the demands placed upon them (and those demands might be more numerous and more varied than currently). It will then become yet more challenging for probation personnel to motivate offenders to comply with community-based requirements. Counteracting that effect will be the fact that the aims of sentencing will be set out in legislation for the first time, and courts will be required to give reasons for the sentence imposed. It might also prove easier to develop a strong coherent idea of what a community sentence is intended to achieve and its place in the sentencing framework if one is dealing with a single order rather than what appears currently to be a multiplicity of disparate orders with different aims. To reiterate the findings summarised in the previous chapter, understood in communicative terms, that aim might be to get offenders to become law-abiding citizens through combining a moral dialogue with practical assistance in overcoming what stands in their way.

Conclusions

This chapter started by presenting a set of principles distilling how the idea of communication might be applied to punishment. It acknowledged that there were formidable obstacles to making communicative penalties a practical reality. However, I hope it also showed that there might be significant benefits in seeking to overcome those obstacles. Not least would be the prospect of developing a strong coherent idea of what community penalties are intended to achieve, in which a balance is found between their role as just or 'deserved' punishments and their capacity to bring about positive change. This, it seems to me, offers the most promising way forward to securing a clearer and more enduring place in the sentencing framework for community penalties that command public – and political – support in their own right.

Notes

1   See Appendix in Bottoms et al. (2001), drawing on the framework developed by Bottoms (2001) for understanding the mechanisms (instrumental, normative, constraint-based and based on routine) underpinning compliant behaviour in proposing a more holistic approach towards compliance in the field of community penalties.

2   In relation to community supervision, the use of pro-social modelling has been most fully developed through the work of Christopher Trotter in Australia (Trotter 1993, 1996, 1999). It is in community service rather than probation that it has been most systematically developed in the UK (see Rex and Gelsthorpe 2004 for a discussion of how pro-social modelling might promote inclusive citizenship).

3   The *New Choreography* (National Probation Service 2001) makes a commitment to a 'victim-centred' approach in which restorative justice and reparation will be encouraged where appropriate, and HM Inspectorate of Probation has recently made proposals for the development of victim work (HMIP 2003b).

4   Completion rates for the combined order are, for example, lower than those for either the CP or CR order (see Probation Statistics for England and Wales 2001). Reporting very low completion rates (30 per cent) for DTTOs, Hough et al. (2003) pointed to the importance of applying standards of enforcement that maximised the chances of retaining a drug-dependant offender in treatment.

Appendix

The questionnaire

The meaning of punishment
What do *you* think?

Deciding what to do with offenders is an important job for society. People have different ideas about punishment and this is a chance to say what you think. It is likely to take you 20 minutes to answer these questions. At the end, I ask for some information about you so that I can see what men and women of different ages and experiences say. All answers will be completely confidential. I will *not* use your name in any report that I write.

In answering these questions, please think about offenders who are being sentenced for crimes such as theft, car crime, break-ins and minor fights or assaults. And don't think only about a prison sentence.

The purpose of sentencing

1. When sentencing offenders, a court should be trying to . . .
(Do you agree? 1 = 'not at all'; 5 = 'strongly agree')

                                                                1 2 3 4 5

Make them pay for what they did wrong
Show them that crime does not pay
Make them see why what they did was wrong
Make them put something back into the community
Show them society does not like what they did
Help them with the problems behind their offending
Get them to do something useful with their lives
Keep them away from offending
Make them feel sorry for hurting someone
Get them to change their ways

Show other people they won't get away with crime
Show them they have hurt the victim
Teach them how to go on the straight and narrow
Anything else?   *Nothing*=0; *Comment*=1

2. **What do *you* see as the most important aim when a court is sentencing an offender?**   (*Please chose one*)

To make the offender pay for the crime   1
To stop the offender committing another crime   2
Not sure   0

3. **Here are some orders that the court can use. For each one, please say what *you* see as its main purposes (tick as many as you like).**

   Thinking about offenders who are being sentenced for crimes such as theft, car crime, break-ins and minor fights or assaults . . .

   Prison   (*Blank*=0; *Ticked*=1)
   Makes offenders pay for what they did wrong
   Shows them that crime does not pay
   Makes them see why what they did was wrong
   Makes them put something back into the community
   Shows them society does not like what they did
   Helps them with the problems behind their offending
   Gets them to do something useful with their lives
   Keeps them away from offending when in prison
   Makes them feel sorry for hurting someone
   Gets them to change their ways
   Shows other people they won't get away with crime
   Shows them they have hurt the victim
   Teaches them how to go on the straight and narrow
   Anything else?   *Nothing*=0; *Comment*=1

   Community service   (*Blank*=0; *Ticked*=1)
   (*The offender has to do unpaid work for the community*)
   Makes offenders pay for what they did wrong
   Shows them that crime does not pay
   Makes them see why what they did was wrong
   Makes them put something back into the community
   Shows them society does not like what they did
   Helps them with the problems behind their offending
   Gets them to do something useful with their lives
   Keeps them away from offending
   Makes them feel sorry for hurting someone
   Gets them to change their ways

Shows other people they won't get away with crime
Shows them they have hurt the victim
Teaches them how to go on the straight and narrow
Anything else?   *Nothing* = 0; *Comment* = 1

Probation   *(Blank* = 0; *Ticked* = 1)
(The offender is supervised by a probation officer)
Makes offenders pay for what they did wrong
Shows them that crime does not pay
Makes them see why what they did was wrong
Makes them put something back into the community
Shows them society does not like what they did
Helps them with the problems behind their offending
Gets them to do something useful with their lives
Keeps them away from offending
Makes them feel sorry for hurting someone
Gets them to change their ways
Shows other people they won't get away with crime
Shows them they have hurt the victim
Teaches them how to go on the straight and narrow
Anything else?   *Nothing* = 0; *Comment* = 1

Tagging   *(Blank* = 0; *Ticked* = 1)
(The offender is under curfew to stay at home for part of each day)
Makes offenders pay for what they did wrong
Shows them that crime does not pay
Makes them see why what they did was wrong
Makes them put something back into the community
Shows them society does not like what they did
Helps them with the problems behind their offending
Gets them to do something useful with their lives
Keeps them away from offending during curfew hours
Makes them feel sorry for hurting someone
Gets them to change their ways
Shows other people they won't get away with crime
Shows them they have hurt the victim
Teaches them how to go on the straight and narrow
Anything else?   *Nothing* = 0; *Comment* = 1

Amount of punishment

4. How the court should decide how much punishment to give an offender:
(Do you agree? 1 = 'not at all'; 5 = 'strongly agree')

1 2 3 4 5

The court should aim to match the punishment to
how serious the crime was

The court should give enough punishment to stop
that person offending

The court should take account of the offender's
background

The court should take account of the impact of the
punishment on that person

All offenders are different, and they should get
different punishments

All crimes are different, and we can't compare how
serious they are

People should know exactly how much punishment
they will get for an offence

The victim should have some say in the choice of
punishment

It is unfair for, say, a small theft to get more
punishment than a larger theft

The court should take account of the offender's
previous convictions

Anything else?   *Nothing* = 0; *Comment* = 1

**5. Offenders should receive less punishment than they otherwise
would if:**
(Do you agree? 1 = 'not at all', 5 = 'strongly agree')

1 2 3 4 5

It is their first time in court

They show they are sorry for the crime

The crime was out of character for them

The punishment will hit them very hard

They have tried to put some of the harm right

They have already tried to change their ways

Anything else?   *Nothing* = 0; *Comment* = 1

What is punishment saying

6. **In the act of sentencing, the court should be saying to the offender:**
   (Do you agree? 1 = 'not at all'; 5 = 'strongly agree')

                                                          1 2 3 4 5

   'We do not like what you did'
   'What you did hurt someone else'
   'What you did harmed the community'
   'We can not put up with this kind of behaviour'
   'If you want to live in the community you have to
       follow the rules'
   'If we see you here again, it will be worse for you'
   'We are giving you a chance to show that you can live
       a lawful life'
   'This is your chance to show you can make something
       of your life'
   'We expect you to do something to make up for what
       you did wrong'
   'This is to help you learn the difference between right
       and wrong'
   Anything else?   *Nothing* = 0; *Comment* = 1

7. **Here are some orders that a court can use. For each one, please tick
   up to *three* things you think the court should be saying:**

   Prison (one, two, three)
   1 'If you want to live in the community you have to follow the rules'
   2 'If we see you here again, it will be worse for you'
   3 'We are giving you a chance to show that you can live a lawful life'
   4 'This is your chance to show you can make something of your life'
   5 'We expect you to do something to make up for what you did
      wrong'
   6 'This is to help you learn the difference between right and wrong'

   Community service (one, two, three)
   1 'If you want to live in the community you have to follow the rules'
   2 'If we see you here again, it will be worse for you'
   3 'We are giving you a chance to show that you can live a lawful life'
   4 'This is your chance to show you can make something of your life'
   5 'We expect you to do something to make up for what you did
      wrong'
   6 'This is to help you learn the difference between right and wrong'

   Probation (one, two, three)
   1 'If you want to live in the community you have to follow the rules'
   2 'If we see you here again, it will be worse for you'

3 'We are giving you a chance to show that you can live a lawful life'
4 'This is your chance to show you can make something of your life'
5 'We expect you to do something to make up for what you did wrong'
6 'This is to help you learn the difference between right and wrong'

Tagging (one, two, three)
1 'If you want to live in the community you have to follow the rules'
2 'If we see you here again, it will be worse for you'
3 'We are giving you a chance to show that you can live a lawful life'
4 'This is your chance to show you can make something of your life'
5 'We expect you to do something to make up for what you did wrong'
6 'This is to help you learn the difference between right and wrong'

How offenders respond to punishment

8. **How offenders should come to think or act after being sentenced:**
(Do you agree? 1 = 'not at all'; 5 = 'strongly agree')

1 2 3 4 5

They should accept that what they did was wrong
They should accept that they hurt the victim
They should accept that they harmed the community
They should feel ashamed for what they have done
They should show that they are sorry for what they
   have done
They should accept that it is right for them to do the
   punishment
They should want to avoid being punished again
They should be ready to pay their debt to society
They should be ready to make up for what they have
   done wrong
They should try to put right the harm to the victim
They should be willing to change their behaviour
They should try to avoid offending in the future
Anything else?   *Nothing* = 0; *Comment* = 1

9. **What % of offenders do you think react as you would like?**
0 **0**; 10% **1**; 25% **2**; 33% **3**; 50% **4**; 66% **5**; 75% **6**; 90% **7**; 100% **8**; no idea **9**
Please say why:

_____

_____

_____

10. And now a few questions about you:
  A. How old are you? ____ years (16; 20; 30; 40; 50; 60 plus)
  B. Are you Male or Female? 1M/2F (please ring)
  C. How long ago/have you
    been mag/po? ____ years (1, 2, 3, etc.)
D. What kind of experience? (see individual codes)

_____

_____
_____

Thank you very much

References

Allen, F. A. (1981) *The Decline of the Rehabilitative Ideal: Penal Policy and Social Purposes*. New Haven, CT: Yale University.

Ashworth, A. (1998) 'Restorative Justice', in A. von Hirsch and A. Ashworth (eds), *Principled Sentencing: Readings on Theory and Policy*, 2nd edn. Oxford: Hart.

Ashworth, A., von Hirsch, A., Bottoms, A. E. and Wasik, M. (1995) 'Bespoke Tailoring Won't Suit Community Penalties', *New Law Journal*, 145, 970–2.

Bandura, A. (1997) *Self-Efficacy: The Exercise of Control*. New York: Freeman.

Bazemore, G. and O'Brien, S. (2003) 'The Quest for a Restorative Model of Rehabilitation: Theory-for-Practice and Practice-for-Theory', in L. Walgrave (ed.), *Restorative Justice and the Law*. Cullompton: Willan Publishing.

Bentham, J. (1789) 'Introductions to the Principles of Morals and Legislation', in A. von Hirsch and A. Ashworth (eds) (1998) *Principled Sentencing: Readings on Theory and Policy*, 2nd edn. Oxford: Hart.

Bottoms, A. E. (1981) 'The Suspended Sentence in England', *British Journal of Criminology*, 21, 1–26.

Bottoms, A. E. (1987) 'Limiting Prison Use in England and Wales 1967–1987', *Howard Journal*, 26, 177–202.

Bottoms, A. E. (1989) 'The Concept of Intermediate Sanctions and Its Relevance to the Probation Service', in R. Shaw and K. Haines (eds), *The Criminal Justice System: A Central Role for the Probation Service*. Cambridge: Institute of Criminology.

Bottoms, A. E. (1995) 'The Philosophy and Politics of Punishment and Sentencing', in C. Clarkson and R. Morgan (eds), *The Politics of Sentencing Reform*. Oxford: Clarendon Press.

Bottoms, A. E. (1998) 'Five Puzzles in von Hirsch's Theory of Punishment', in A. Ashworth and M. Wasik (eds), *Fundamentals of Sentencing Theory: Essays in Honour of Andrew von Hirsch*. Oxford: Clarendon Press.

Bottoms, A. E. (2000) 'Theory and Research in Criminology', in R. D. King and E. Wincup (eds), *Doing Research on Crime and Justice*. Oxford: Oxford University Press.

Bottoms, A. E. (2001) 'Compliance and Community Penalties', in A. E. Bottoms, L. Gelsthorpe and S. Rex (eds), *Community Penalties: Change and Challenges*. Cullompton: Willan Publishing.

Bottoms, A. E. and Dignan, J. (2004) 'Youth Crime and Youth Justice: Comparative and Cross-National Perspectives', *Crime and Justice: A Review of Research*, 31, 21–183.

Bottoms, A. E. and McWilliams, W. (1979) 'A Non-treatment Paradigm for Probation Practice', *British Journal of Social Work*, 9, 159–202.

Bottoms, A. E., Gelsthorpe, L. and Rex, S. A. (2001) 'Introduction', in A. E. Bottoms, L. Gelsthorpe and S. Rex (eds), *Community Penalties: Change and Challenges*. Cullompton: Willan Publishing.

Bottoms, A. E., Rex, S. A. and Robinson, G. (2004) *Alternatives to Prison*. Cullompton: Willan Publishing.

Braithwaite, J. (1989) *Crime, Shame and Reintegration*. Cambridge: Cambridge University Press.

Braithwaite, J. (1999) 'Restorative Justice: Assessing Optimistic and Pessimistic Accounts', in M. Tonry (ed.), *Crime and Justice: A Review of the Research*, 23. Chicago: University of Chicago Press.

Braithwaite, J. (2003) 'Principles of Restorative Justice', in A. von Hirsch, J. R. Roberts and A. E. Bottoms (eds), *Restorative Justice and Criminal Justice*. Oxford: Hart.

Braithwaite, J. and Braithwaite, V. (2001) 'Revising the Theory of Reintegrative Shaming', in E. Ahmed, N. Harris, J. Braithwaite and V. Braithwaite (eds), *Shame Management Through Reintegration*. Cambridge: Cambridge University Press.

Bryman, A. (2001) *Social Research Methods*. Oxford: Oxford University Press.

Bryman, A. and Cramer, D. (2001) *Quantitative Data Analysis with SPSS Release 10 for Windows*. Hove, East Sussex: Routledge.

Cann, J., Falshaw, L., Nugent, F. and Friendship, C. (2003) *Understanding What Works: Accredited Cognitive Skills Programmes for Adult Men and Young Offenders*, Home Office Research Finding 226. London: Home Office.

Carter, P. (2003) *Managing Offenders, Changing Lives: A New Approach, Report of the Correctional Services Review*. London: Strategy Unit.

Chapman, B., Mirrlees-Black, C. and Brown, C. (2002) *Improving Public Attitudes to the Criminal Justice System: The Impact of Information*, Home Office Research Study No. 245. London: Home Office.

Christie (1982) *Limits to Pain*. Oxford: Martin Robinson.

Cullen, F. T., Fisher, B. S. and Applegate, B. K. (2000) 'Public Opinion about Punishment and Corrections', in M. Tonry (ed.), *Crime and Justice: A Review of Research*, 27, 1–79.

Cullen, F. T., Pealer, J. A., Fisher, B. S., Applegate, B. K. and Santana, S. A. (2002) 'Public Support for Correctional Rehabilitation in America: Change or Consistency?', in J. V. Roberts and M. Hough (eds), *Changing Attitudes to Punishment: Public Opinion, Crime and Justice*. Cullompton: Willan Publishing.

Daly, K. (2002) 'Restorative Justice: The Real Story', *Punishment and Society*, 4, 55–79.

Dignan, J. (1999) 'The Crime and Disorder Act and the Prospects for Restorative Justice', *Criminal Law Review*, 48–60.

Dignan, J. (2003) 'Towards a Systematic Model of Restorative Justice: Reflections on the Concept, Its Context and the Need for Clear Constraints', in A. von

Hirsch, J. R. Roberts, and A. E. Bottoms (eds), *Restorative Justice and Criminal Justice*. Oxford: Hart.

Doble, J. (2002) 'Attitudes to Punishment in the US – Punitive and Liberal Opinion', in J. V. Roberts and M. Hough (eds), *Changing Attitudes to Punishment: Public Opinion, Crime and Justice*. Cullompton: Willan Publishing.

Duff, R. A. (1996) 'Penal Communications: Recent Works in the Philosophy of Punishment', in M. Tonry and N. Morris (eds), *Crime and Justice: A Review of the Research*, 21. London: University of Chicago Press.

Duff, R. A. (1999) 'Punishment, Communication and Community', in M. Matravers (ed.), *Punishment and Political Theory*. Oxford: Hart.

Duff, R. A. (2001) *Punishment, Communication and Community*. Oxford: Oxford University Press.

Duff, R. A. (2003) 'Restoration and Retribution', in A. von Hirsch, J. R. Roberts, and A. E. Bottoms (eds), *Restorative Justice and Criminal Justice*. Oxford: Hart.

Falshaw, L., Friendship, C., Travers, R. and Nugent, F. (2003) *Searching for 'What Works': An Evaluation of Cognitive Skills Programmes*, Research Finding 206. London: Home Office.

Farrall, S. (2002) *Rethinking What Works with Offenders: Probation, Social Context and Desistance from Crime*. Cullompton: Willan Publishing.

Freiberg, A. (2001) 'Affective versus Effective Justice: Instrumentalism and Emotionalism in Criminal Justice', *Punishment and Society*, 3, 265–78.

Friendship, C., Blud, L., Erikson, M. and Travers, R. (2002) *An Evaluation of Cognitive Behavioural Treatment for Prisoners*, Research Finding 161. London: Home Office.

Garland, D. (1985) *Punishment and Welfare*. Aldershot: Gower.

Garland, D. (2001) *The Culture of Control: Crime and Social Order in Contemporary Society*. Oxford: Oxford University Press.

Gilligan, C. (1982) *In a Different Voice: Psychological Theory and Women's Development*. London: Harvard University Press.

Harris, N. (2001) 'Ethical Identity, Shame Management and Criminal Justice', in E. Ahmed, N. Harris, J. Braithwaite and V. Braithwaite (eds), *Shame Management Through Reintegration*. Cambridge: Cambridge University Press.

Hart, H. L. A. (1968) *Punishment and Responsibility*. Oxford: Oxford University Press.

Hedderman, C. and Hearden, I. (2001) *Setting New Standards for Enforcement – The Third ACOP Audit*. London: South Bank University and Association of Chief Officers of Probation.

Hedderman, C., Ellis, T. and Sugg, D. (1999) *Increasing Confidence in Community Sentences: the Results of Two Demonstration Projects*, Home Office Research Study No. 194. London: Home Office.

Her Majesty's Inspectorate of Probation (HMIP) (2003a) *2002/3 Annual Report*. London: Home Office.

Her Majesty's Inspectorate of Probation (HMIP) (2003b) *Valuing the Victim: An Inspection into the National Victim Contact Arrangements*. London: Home Office.

Holdaway, S., Davidson, N., Dignan, J. Hammersley, R., Hine, J. and Marsh, P. (2001) *New Strategies to Address Youth Offending: The National Evaluation of the Pilot Youth Offending Teams*, RDS Occasional Paper 69. London: Home Office.

Home Office (1988) *Punishment, Custody and the Community*, Cm. 424. London: HMSO.

Home Office (1990) *Crime, Justice and Protecting the Public*, Cm. 965. London: HMSO.

Home Office (1995) *Strengthening Punishment in the Community*, Cm. 2780. London: HMSO.

Home Office (1996) *Protecting the Public*, Cm. 3190. London: HMSO.

Home Office (2000) *National Standards for the Supervision of Offenders in the Community*. London: Home Office.

Home Office (2001) *Making Punishments Work*. London: HMSO.

Home Office (2002a) *Probation Statistics for England and Wales 2001*. London: Home Office.

Home Office (2002b) *Criminal Statistics for England and Wales 2001*. London: TSO.

Home Office and Lord Chancellor's Department (2002) *Justice for All*, Cm. 5563. London: TSO.

Home Office (2003) *Probation Statistics for England and Wales 2002*. London: Home Office.

Hough, M. (2003) 'Modernization and Public Opinion: Some Criminal Justice Paradoxes', *Contemporary Politics*, 9(2), 143–55.

Hough, M. and Moxon, D. (1985) 'Dealing with Offenders: Popular Opinion and the Views of Victims', *Howard Journal*, 24, 160–75.

Hough, M. and Park, A. (2002) 'How Malleable are Attitudes to Crime and Punishment? Findings from a British Deliberative Poll', in J. V. Roberts and M. Hough (eds), *Changing Attitudes to Punishment: Public Opinion, Crime and Justice*. Cullompton: Willan Publishing.

Hough, M. and Roberts, J. V. (1998) *Attitudes to Punishment: Findings from the British Crime Survey*, Home Office Research Study No. 179. London: Home Office.

Hough, M. and Roberts, J. V. (2002) 'Public Knowledge and Public Opinion of Sentencing', in N. Hutton and C. Tata (eds), *Sentencing and Society: International Perspectives*. Farnborough: Ashgate.

Hough, M., Jacobson J. and Millie, A. (2003) *The Decision to Imprison: Sentencing and the Prison Population*. London: Prison Reform Trust.

Hough, M., Clancy, A., McSweeney, T. and Turnbull, P. (2003) *The Impact of Drug Treatment and Testing Orders on Offending: Two-Year Reconviction Results*, Research Finding No. 184. London: Home Office.

Hudson, B. (1995) 'Beyond Proportionate Punishment: Difficult Cases and the 1991 Criminal Justice Act', *Crime Law and Social Change*, 22, 59–78.

Hudson, B. (1998) 'Mitigation for Socially Deprived Offenders', in A. von Hirsch and A. Ashworth (eds) (1998) *Principled Sentencing: Readings on Theory and Policy*, 2nd edn. Oxford: Hart.

Indermaur, D. and Hough, M. (2002) 'Strategies for Changing Public Attitudes Towards Punishment', in J. V. Roberts and M. Hough (eds), *Changing Attitudes to Punishment: Public Opinion, Crime and Justice*. Cullompton: Willan Publishing.

Johnson, C. and Rex, S. A. (2002) 'Community Service: Rediscovering Reintegration', in D. Ward and J. Scott (eds), *Probation – Working for Justice*, 2nd edn. Oxford: Oxford University Press.

Joint Prison/Probation Services Accreditation Panel (2002) *Annual Report 2001/2*, available at: *http://www.homeoffice.gov.uk/cpd/probu.htm*.

Kalmthout, A. (2002) 'From Community Service to Community Sanctions. Comparative Perspectives', in H. Albrecht and A. Kalmthout (eds), *Community Sanctions and Measures in Europe and North America*. Freiberg: Edition Inscrim.

Kury, H. and Ferdinand, T. (1999) 'Public Opinion and Punitivity', *International Journal of Law and Psychiatry*, 22, 373–92.

Lacey, N. (1988) *State Punishment: Political Principles and Community Values*. London: Routledge.

Lipton, D., Pearson, F. S., Cleland, C. M. and Yee, D. (2002) 'The Effectiveness of Cognitive Behavioural Treatment Methods on Recidivism', in J. McGuire (ed.), *Offender Rehabilitation and Treatment: Effective Programmes and Policies to Reduce Re-Offending*. Chichester: John Wiley & Sons.

Lloyd, C., Mair, G. and Hough, M. (1995) *Explaining Reconviction Rates: A Critical Analysis*, Home Office Research Study No. 136. London: Home Office.

Lucas, J. R. (1980) *On Justice*. Oxford: Oxford University Press.

McIvor, G. (1992) *Sentenced to Serve*. Aldershot: Avebury.

McIvor, G. (1998) 'Pro-Social Modelling and Legitimacy: Lessons from a Study of Community Service', in S. A. Rex and A. Matravers (eds), *Pro-Social Modelling and Legitimacy: The Clarke Hall Day Conference*. Cambridge: Institute of Criminology.

McKitterick, N. and Rex, S. A. (2003) 'Sentence Management: A New Role for the Judiciary?', in M. Tonry (ed.), *Confronting Crime – Crime Control Policy Under New Labour*. Cullompton: Willan Publishing.

Maguire, M. (1982) *Burglary in a Dwelling: The Offence, the Offender and the Victim*. London: Heineman.

Marshall, T. F. (1996) 'The Evolution of Restorative Justice in Britain', *European Journal on Criminal Policy and Research*, 4, 21–43.

Maruna, S. (2001) *Making Good: How Ex-convicts Reform and Rebuild Their Lives*. Washington, DC: American Psychological Association.

Maruna, S. and King, A. (2004) 'Public Opinion and Community Penalties', in A. Bottoms, S. Rex and G. Robinson (eds), *Alternatives to Prison*. Cullompton: Willan Publishing.

Matravers, M. (2000) *Justice and Punishment: The Rationale of Coercion*. Oxford: Oxford University Press.

Mattinson, J. and Mirrlees-Black, C. (2000) *Attitudes to Crime and Criminal Justice: Findings from the 1998 British Crime Survey*, Home Office Research Study No. 200. London: Home Office.

May, C. (1999) *Explaining Reconviction Following a Community Sentence: The Role of Social Factors*, Home Office Research Study No. 192. London: Home Office.

Mayhew, P. and van Kesteren, J. (2002) 'Cross-national Attitudes to Punishment', in J. V. Roberts and M. Hough (eds), *Changing Attitudes to Punishment: Public Opinion, Crime and Justice*. Cullompton: Willan Publishing.

Morgan, R. (2002) 'Privileging Public Attitudes to Sentencing?', in J. V. Roberts and M. Hough (eds), *Changing Attitudes to Punishment: Public Opinion, Crime and Justice*. Cullompton: Willan Publishing.

Morgan, R. (2003) 'Correctional Services: Not Waving but Drowning', *Prison Service Journal*, 145, 6–8.

Morris, A. and Gelsthorpe, L. (2000) 'Something Old, Something Borrowed, Something Blue, but Something New? A Comment on the Prospects for Restorative Justice under the Crime and Disorder Act 1998', *Criminal Law Review*, 18–30.

Morris, A. and Maxwell, G. (2003) 'Restorative Justice in New Zealand', in A. von Hirsch, J. R. Roberts, and A. E. Bottoms (eds), *Restorative Justice and Criminal Justice*. Oxford: Hart.

Morris, N. (1974) *The Future of Imprisonment*. Chicago: University of Chicago Press.

Morris, N. (1998) 'Desert as a Limiting Principle', in A. von Hirsch and A. Ashworth (eds), *Principled Sentencing: Readings on Theory and Policy*, 2nd edn. Oxford: Hart.

Morris, N. and Tonry, M. (1990) *Between Prison and Probation*. Oxford: Oxford University Press.

National Probation Directorate (2001) *Consultation on Sentencing Reform: National Probation Service Response*, Probation Circular 145/2001. London: Home Office.

National Probation Service (2001) *A New Choreography: Strategic Framework 2001–2004*. London: Home Office and National Probation Service for England and Wales.

Nellis, M. (2001) 'Community Penalties in Historical Perspective', in A. Bottoms, L. Gelsthorpe and S. Rex (eds), *Community Penalties: Change and Challenges*. Cullompton: Willan Publishing.

Pease, K. (1985) 'Community Service Orders', in M. Tonry and N. Morris (eds), *Crime and Justice: A Review of the Research*, 10. London: University of Chicago Press.

Philpotts, G. J. O. and Lancucki, L. B. (1979) *Previous Convictions, Sentence and Reconviction: Statistical Study of a Sample of 5,000 Offenders*, Home Office Research Study 53. London: HMSO.

Rawls, J. (1999) *A Theory of Justice, Revised Edition*. Oxford: Oxford University Press.

Raynor, P. (1997) 'Some Observations on Rehabilitation and Justice', *Howard Journal of Criminal Justice*, 36, 248–62.

Raynor, P. (2001) 'Community Penalties and Social Integration: "Community" as Solution and as Problem', in A. Bottoms, L. Gelsthorpe and S. Rex (eds), *Community Penalties: Change and Challenges*. Cullompton: Willan.

Raynor, P. (2002) 'Community Penalties: Probation, Punishment and "What Works"', in M. Maguire, R. Morgan and R. Reiner (eds), *The Oxford Handbook of Criminology*, 3rd edn. Oxford: Oxford University Press.

Raynor, P. (2004) 'Rehabilitative and Reintegrative Approaches', in A. Bottoms, S. Rex and G. Robinson (eds), *Alternatives to Prison*. Cullompton: Willan Publishing.

Raynor, P. and Vanstone, M. (1994) 'Probation Practice, Effectiveness, and the Non-Treatment Paradigm, *British Journal of Social Work*, 24, 387–404.

Raynor, P. and Vanstone, M. (1997) *Straight Thinking on Probation (STOP): The Mid Glamorgan Experiment*, Probation Studies Unit Report No. 4. Oxford: University of Oxford Centre for Criminological Research.

Rex, S. A. (1997) *Perceptions of Probation in a Context of 'Just Deserts'*. PhD thesis, Institute of Criminology, University of Cambridge.

Rex, S. A. (1998) 'Applying Desert Principles to Community Sentences: Lessons from Two Criminal Justice Acts', *Criminal Law Review*, 381–91.

Rex, S. A. (1999) 'Desistance from Offending: Experiences of Probation', *Howard Journal*, 38, 366–83.

Rex, S. A. (2001) 'Beyond Cognitive-Behaviouralism? Reflections on the Effectiveness Literature', in A. Bottoms, L. Gelsthorpe and S. A. Rex (eds), *Community Penalties: Change and Challenges*. Cullompton: Willan Publishing.

Rex, S. A. (2002) 'Re-Inventing Community Penalties: The Role of Communication', in S. A. Rex and M. Tonry (eds), *Reform and Punishment: The Future of Sentencing*. Cullompton: Willan Publishing.

Rex, S. A. and Gelsthorpe, L. R. (2004) 'Using Community Service to Encourage Inclusive Citizenship', in R. Burnett and C. Roberts (eds), *Evidence-Based Practice in Probation and Youth Justice*. Cullompton: Willan Publishing.

Rex, S. A. and von Hirsch, A. (1998) 'Community Orders and the Assessment of Punishment Severity', *Federal Sentencing Reporter*, 10, 278.

Rex, S. A., Gelsthorpe, L. G., Roberts, C. and Jordan, P. (2004) *Crime Reduction Programme: An Evaluation of CS Pathfinder Projects: Final Report 2002*, RDS Occasional Paper No. 87. London: Home Office.

Rex, S. A., Lieb, R., Bottoms, A. E. and Wilson, L. (2003) *Accrediting Offender Programmes: A Process-based Evaluation of the Joint Prison/Probation Services Accreditation Panel*, Home Office Research Study No. 273. London: Home Office.

Richards, T. J. and Richards, L. (1998) 'Using Computers in Qualitative Analysis', in N. K. Denzin and Y. S. Lincoln (eds), *Collecting and Interpreting Qualitative Materials*. London: Sage.

Roberts, J .V. (2002a) 'Alchemy in Sentencing: An Analysis of Reform Proposals in England and Wales', *Punishment and Society*, 4(4), 425–442.

Roberts, J .V. (2002b) 'Public Opinion and the Nature of Community Penalties: International Findings', in J. V. Roberts and M. Hough (eds), *Changing Attitudes to Punishment: Public Opinion, Crime and Justice*. Cullompton: Willan Publishing.

Roberts, J. V. and Stalans, L. J. (1997) *Public Opinion, Crime and Criminal Justice*. Oxford: Westview Press.

Roberts, J. V., Stalans, L., Indermaur, D. and Hough, M. (2003) *Penal Populism and Public Opinion. Findings from Five Countries*. New York: Oxford Univerity Press.

Robinson, P. H. and Darley, J. M. (1995) *Justice, Liability and Blame: Community Views and the Criminal Law*. Oxford: Westview Press.

Russell, N. and Morgan, R. (2001) *Research Report 1. Sentencing of Domestic Burglary*. Sentencing Advisory Panel, available at: *www.sentencing-advisory-panel.gov.uk*.

Sanders, T. and Roberts, J. V. (2000) 'Public Attitudes towards Conditional Sentencing: Results of a National Survey', *Canadian Journal of Behavioural Science*, 32, 199–207.

Schiff, M. F. (1998) 'Gauging the Intensity of Criminal Sanctions: Developing the Criminal Justice Severity Scale', *Criminal Justice Review*, 22, 175–206.

Searle, W., Knaggs, T. and Simonsen, K. (2003) *Talking About Sentences and Crime: The Views of People on Periodic Detention*. New Zealand Ministry of Justice, available at: *http://www.justice.govt.nz/pubs/reports/2003*.

Shapland, J. (2003) 'Restorative Justice and Criminal Justice: Just Responses to Crime?', in A. von Hirsch, J. R. Roberts and A. E. Bottoms (eds), *Restorative Justice and Criminal Justice*. Oxford: Hart.

Shaw, S. (1982) *The People's Justice: A Major Poll of Public Attitudes on Crime and Punishment*. London: Prison Reform Trust.

Sherman, L. W. (1993) 'Defiance, Deterrence and Irrelevance: A Theory of the Criminal Sanction', *Journal of Research in Crime and Delinquency*, 30, 445–73.

Sherman, L. W., Strang, H. and Woods, D. J. (2000) *Recidivism Patterns in the Canberra Reintegrative Shaming Experiment (RISE)*. Canberra: Centre for Restorative Justice, Australian National University; available at: *http://www.aic.gov.au/rjustice/rise/recidivism/in dex.html*.

Stalans, L. J. (2002) 'Measuring Attitudes to Sentencing', in J. V. Roberts and M. Hough (eds), *Changing Attitudes to Punishment: Public Opinion, Crime and Justice*. Cullompton: Willan Publishing.

Straw, J. (2001) 'Next Steps in Criminal Justice Reform', speech to the Social Market Foundation, 31 January (unpublished).

Toch (2000) 'Altruistic Activity as Correctional Treatment', *International Journal of Offender Therapy and Comparative Criminology*, 44, 270–8.

Tonry, M. (1998a) 'Intermediate Sanctions', in M. Tonry (ed.), *The Handbook of Crime and Punishment*. Oxford: Oxford University Press.

Tonry, M. (1998b) 'Parsimony and Desert in Sentencing', in A. von Hirsch and A. Ashworth (eds), *Principled Sentencing: Readings on Theory and Policy*, 2nd edn. Oxford: Hart.

Tonry, M. (1998c) 'Intermediate Sanctions in Sentencing Guidelines', in M. Tonry (ed.), *Crime and Justice: A Review of Research*, 23. London: University of Chicago Press.

Trotter, C. (1993) *The Supervision of Offenders: What Works*. Sydney: Victorian Office of Corrections.

Trotter, C. (1996) 'The Impact of Different Supervision Practices in Community Corrections: Causes for Optimism', *Australian and New Zealand Journal of Criminology*, 29, 29–46.

Trotter, C. (1999) *Working with Involuntary Clients: A Guide to Practice*. London: Sage.

Turnbull, P. J., McSweeney, T., Webster, R., Edmunds, M. and Hough, M. (2000) *Drug Treatment and Testing Orders: Final Evaluation Report*, Home Office Research Study No. 212. London: Home Office.

Tyler, T. R. (1990) *Why People Obey the Law*. New Haven, CT: Yale University Press.

Tyler, T. R. and Boeckmann, R. (1997) 'Three Strikes and You Are Out, but Why? The Psychology of Public Support for Punishing Rule Breakers', *Law and Society Review*, 31, 237–65.

von Hirsch, A. (1976) *Doing Justice: The Choice of Punishments*. New York: Hill & Wang.

von Hirsch, A. (1985) *Past or Future Crimes*. Manchester: Manchester University Press.

von Hirsch, A. (1993) *Censure and Sanctions*. Oxford: Clarendon Press.

von Hirsch, A. (1999) 'Punishment, Penance and the State', in M. Matravers (ed.), *Punishment and Political Theory*. Oxford: Hart Publishing.

von Hirsch, A. (2002a) 'Proportionate Punishment and Social Deprivation', in P. Asp, C. F. Herlitz and L. Holmqvist (eds), *Flores Juris et Legum: Festkrift till Nils Jareborg*, Uppsala: Iustus Forlag.

von Hirsch, A. (2002b) 'Record-enhanced Sentencing in England and Wales: Reflections on the Halliday Report's Treatment of Prior Convictions', in S. A. Rex and M. Tonry (eds), *Reform and Punishment: The Future of Sentencing*. Cullompton: Willan Publishing.

von Hirsch, A. and Ashworth, A. (eds) (1998) *Principled Sentencing: Readings on Theory and Policy*, 2nd edn. Oxford: Hart.

von Hirsch, A. and Jareborg, N. (1991) 'Gauging Criminal Harm: A Living Standards Analysis', *Oxford Journal of Legal Studies*, 11, 1–38.

von Hirsch, A., Ashworth, A. and Shearing, C. (2003) 'Specifying Aims and Limits for Restorative Justice: A "Making Amends" Model?', in A. von Hirsch, J. R. Roberts, and A. E. Bottoms (eds), *Restorative Justice and Criminal Justice*. Oxford: Hart.

von Hirsch, A., Bottoms, A. E., Burney, E. and Wikstrom, P. O. (1999) *Criminal Deterrence and Sentence Severity: An Analysis of Recent Research*. Oxford: Hart.

Walgrave, L. (2002) 'Restorative Justice and the Law: Socio-ethical and Juridical Foundations for a Systemic Approach', in L. Walgrave (ed.), *Restorative Justice and the Law*. Cullompton: Willan Publishing.

Walgrave, L. (2003) 'Imposing Restoration Rather than Inflicting Pain', in A. von Hirsch, J. R. Roberts, and A. E. Bottoms (eds), *Restorative Justice and Criminal Justice*. Oxford: Hart.

Walker, N. (1991) *Why Punish?* Oxford: Oxford University Press.

Walker, N. (1992) 'Legislating the Transcendental: von Hirsch's Proportionality', *Cambridge Law Journal*, 51, 530–7.

Walker, N. (1999) *Aggravation, Mitigation and Mercy in Criminal Justice*. London: Blackstone.

Wasik, M. and von Hirsch, A. (1988) 'Non-custodial Penalties and the Principles of Desert' *Criminal Law Review*, 555–71.

Woolf, Lord Justice (2001) 'The Woolf Report: A Decade of Change?', address to the Prison Reform Trust, 31 January (unpublished).

Worrall, A. (1997) *Punishment in the Community: The Future of Criminal Justice*. London: Longman.

Young, R. and Hoyle, C. (2003) 'New, Improved Police-Led Restorative Justice', in A. von Hirsch, J. R. Roberts and A. E. Bottoms (eds), *Restorative Justice and Criminal Justice*. Oxford: Hart.

Zehr, H. (1990) *Changing Lenses: A New Focus For Crime and Justice*. Scottdale PA: Herald Press.

Index

aims of sentencing 80, 106–7
  see also punishment; sentencing, as
    communication
  crime prevention 85–9, 137–8
  evaluation of disposals 89–94, 146–7
  instrumental 88–9
  male/female rating 89
  moralising aims 81–5, 135–7
alternatives to custody 8–9
amends
  as instrumental messages 97–100
  reinforcement 100–3
Ashworth, A. 21

Bottoms, A.E. 60, 62, 81
  communicative penalties 15–16, 18,
    56–7, 135, 139
  instrumental compliance 130
  theory v research 50, 133–4
boundaries, as normative message 95–7
Braithwaite, John 21, 23–4, 55, 161
  enforcement pyramid 24–5
British Crime Surveys (BCS) 32

Carter, P. 141
censure
  and consequentialism 155
  dialectically defensible 156
  as normative message 95–7
change of behaviour, offenders'
    preparedness 116–23
combination orders 8–9
  customised 163
communicative penalties 16–18, 27–8,
    154–8, 164
  application 26
  censure and consequentialism 155

as community penalties 19–20, 160–1,
    163–4
  courtroom practice 158–60
  and denunciation 156–7
  deterrence, appropriateness 157
  dialectically defensible censure 156
  future orientation focus 157
  importance of content 156
  obstacles 158–9
  opportunities 159–61
  proportionality as constraint 155–6
  and repentance 156–7
  research concerns 26–7
  and victim 161–2
community penalties
  as communication 19–20, 143–7, 151–2
  communicative framework 147–51
  as communicative penalties 19–20,
    160–1, 163–4
  customised 12–15
  new forms 162–4
  penal messages 103–5
  proportionality, and crime prevention
    theory 59–62
  purposes 90–4
  recent history 8–12
  and reparation 145–6
  research concerns 26–7, 133–5
  and restoration 161–2
community service *see* community
    penalties
compensation, as offenders' response
    116–23
consequentialism
  and censure 155
  proportionality, and crime prevention
    theory 55

v retribution 15–16, 64–7
constraint, and proportionality 155–6
contractual 'non-treatment' paradigm
    62
Correctional Services Accreditation
    Panel (CSAP) 11, 143–4, 145,
    149–51
courtroom practice 158–60
crime prevention
    see also proportionality, and crime
        prevention theory
    aim of sentencing 85–9, 137–8
    and retribution 140–3
Criminal Justice Act 1967 8
Criminal Justice Act 1991 8–9, 12, 19, 55,
    61, 75
    s 6 57–9
Criminal Justice Act 2003 12–15, 33, 57,
    159–60
Criminal Justice and Court Services Act
    2000 9
cross-national studies, public opinion
    35–7
CS Pathfinder projects 11, 145–6, 150–1,
    162
Cullen, F.T. 31, 37–8, 39–40
curfew orders 8–9
    penal messages 103–5
    purposes 90–4
    and sentencing purposes 90–4
    tagging, evaluation 146–7
custody
    evaluation 146–7
    new forms 162–4
    preoccupation 158–9
    purposes 90–4
custody plus/minus 12–15

denunciation 156–7
desert model 15–18
deterrence
    appropriateness 157
    offenders' response 116–23, 130
    special and general 85–6, 88–9
Dignan, J. 22, 25
disapproval 81t
    and sentencing disposals 90–4
drug abstinence orders 9
drug treatment and testing orders 9, 159
Duff, A. 1–2, 3, 27–8

communicative penal theory 16–18,
    26, 27, 41, 95, 125, 129–31, 144,
    155, 161
    and community penalties 19–20, 145–6
    offender and normative outlook 81, 95
    and probation 143
    proportionality, and crime prevention
        theory 55–7, 63, 75, 135, 137, 141
    restorative justice 21–3, 129–31, 138,
        148–9
    victim–offender mediation 162

education aims 86–9
encouragement 86–9
enforcement pyramid 24–5
Enhanced Community Punishment
    scheme 145, 151, 162
exclusion orders 9

Farrall, S. 139

Garland, D. 9
generic community orders 12–15

Halliday Report 12, 14–15, 33–4, 42, 62,
    63, 160
harm
    acceptance by offenders 110–16
    as normative message 95–7
Hough, M. 31, 36, 40–1
Hudson, B. 59
Human Rights Act 2000 159
hurt
    acceptance by offender 81t, 110–16
    as normative message 95–7

improvement aims
    as instrumental messages 97–100
    reinforcement 100–3
incapacitation 85–6, 88–9
    and sentencing disposals 90–4
instrumental messages 97–103
International Crime Victimisation
    Survey (ICVS) 35–7

Jareborg, Nils 60

Lacey, N. 77
lawful aims
    as instrumental messages 97–100

reinforcement 100–3
learning aims
  as instrumental messages 97–100
  as instrumental messages,
    reinforcement 100–3
leniency, and remorse 123–5
Lucas, J.R. 130

McIvor, G. 131
Magistrates' Association 43
Maguire, M. 32
Marshal, T.F. 21
Maruna, S. 40–1, 139, 160–1
Mayhew, P. 36
mediation, victim–offender 23, 162
Morgan, Rod 10, 40
Morris, Norval 56, 59

National Offender Management Service
  11
National Probation Service, Integrated
  Strategy 11
Nellis, M. 9
normative messages 94–7
normative questions, for stakeholders
  41–3

offender-related mitigation 73–5, 142
offenders' responses
  acceptance of punishment 110–16
  accepting harm 110–16
  accepting hurt 81t, 110–16
  change, and leniency 123–5
  compensation 116–23
  deterrence 116–23
  making up for wrong-doing 116–23
  payment of dues 116–23
  prepared to change 116–23
  putting right, and leniency 123–5
  remorse 11, 110–16, 130–1
    and leniency 123–5
  repentance 116–23, 130–1
  shame 110–16
  taking responsibility 110–16
  to instrumental messages 116–23
  to moral messages 110–16
  to penal message 125–9, 138–40
  to punishment 109–10, 129–32

Pathfinder projects 11, 145–6, 150–1, 162

payment of dues, as offenders' response
  116–23
penal-welfarism 8
persuasion 81t
Philpotts, G.J.O. 62
practitioners' groups, and public
  opinion 34–5
probation 20
  evaluation 146–7
  penal messages 103–5, 131–2
  persuasive power 143–5
  purposes 90–4
  and sentencing disposals 90–4, 146–7
proportionality, as constraint 155–6
proportionality, and crime prevention
  theory 55–7, 75–7
  accommodating prior record 62–3
  consequentialism 55
  and Duff 55–7, 63, 75, 135, 137, 141
  English case study 57–9
  hybrid models 57–8, 135
  in practice 59–62
  and von Hirsch 55–7, 58, 59–61, 63,
    75–7, 135, 141
proportionality, research findings 64
  see also stakeholders' views, research
  deciding amounts of punishment
    68–73
  offender-related mitigation 73–5
  prioritising punishment 64–7
prudential disincentive 129, 148
public opinion
  assessment 31–2
  authentic attitudes 39–40
  cross-national studies 35–7
  deliberative polls 32–5
  informed sample 32–5
  practitioners' groups see under
    stakeholders's views
  US research 37–8
  usefulness of research 38–41
public protectionism 9, 62
punishment
  see also aims of sentencing; sentencing,
    as communication
  acceptance by offenders 110–16
  conceptual confusion 7–8
  deciding amounts 68–73
  prioritising 64–7

Raynor, P. 60, 61–2, 68, 149
reform aims 86–9
rehabilitation 61–2
  aims 86–9, 91–2
reintegrative shaming 23–4
remorse 82–5
  acceptance by offenders 110–16
  and leniency 123–5
reparation 82–5
  and community penalties 145–6
reparative apology 130
repentance 156–7
responsibility, acceptance by offender
    110–16
restorative justice 20–4
  and community penalties 161–2
  replacement or reform 24–6
retribution
  and crime prevention 140–3
  exaction 82–5
  v consequentialism 15–16, 64–7
Rex, Sue 2, 58, 60, 62
Roberts, J.V. 36–7, 38, 40
Robinson, P.H. 35, 40, 41, 50, 77, 142
  community standards 134
rules
  as instrumental messages 97–100
  reinforcement 100–3

Sanders, T. 36, 148
Schiff, M.F. 60–1
Sentencing Advisory/Guidelines
    Panel/Council 32, 61, 163
sentencing, as communication 1–3,
    15–18, 94
  see also aims of sentencing;
      punishment
  communication failure 140
  instrumental messages 97–100
  normative messages 94–7
  offenders' response 125–9, 138–40
  reinforcement 100–3
  role of disposals 103–5, 146–7
shame, acceptance by offenders 110–16
shame-guilt feelings 23–4, 110–16
Shapland, J. 24
stakeholders' views 31, 51
  insights 2–4
  practitioners' groups, opinion 34–5
  research

see also proportionality, research
    findings
  design 41–3
  first-round interviews 43–5, 165–71
  follow-up interviews 48–50
  normative questions 41–3
  quantitive weight in questionnaires
    45–8
  significance 50–1
Stalans, L.J. 31, 50
Straw, Jack 10
supplementary prudential disincentive
    16–17

tagging (curfew)
  evaluation 146–7
  purposes 90–4
Thames Valley restorative cautioning
    project 22
threats
  as instrumental messages 97–100
  reinforcement 100–3
Tonry, M. 59, 61–2

United States, public opinion 37–8

victim
  and communicative penalties 161–2
  and offender 23, 81t
von Hirsch, Andrew 1–2, 3, 21, 27–8
  and community penalties 19–20, 161
  desert model 15–18, 154
  proportionality, and crime prevention
    theory 55–7, 58, 59–61, 63, 75–7,
    135, 141
  restorative justice 21, 25, 81, 94–5,
    129–30, 138, 148

Walgrave, L. 21, 161
Walker, N. 60, 74
Wasik, M. 58, 61, 63, 77
'What Works' principles 11–12
Woolf, Lord Justice 10–11, 111–12
Worrall, A. 10